Manon's World

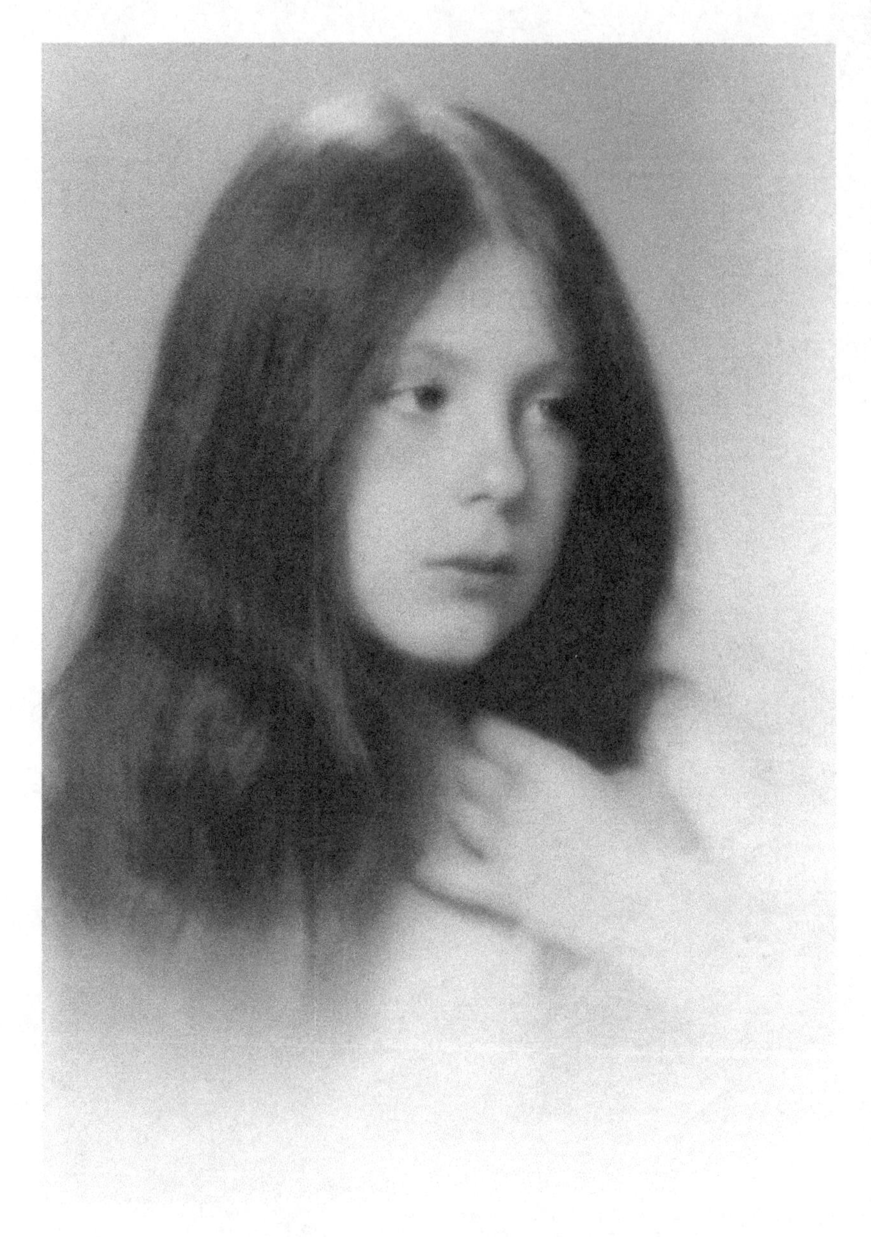

Portrait of Manon Gropius, *c.*1927, Studio Fayer, Vienna.
Walter Gropius Papers, Harvard University.

Manon's World

A Hauntology of a Daughter in the Triangle of Alma Mahler, Walter Gropius, and Franz Werfel

JAMES REIDEL

LONDON NEW YORK CALCUTTA

Seagull Books, 2021

First published Seagull Books, 2021

Unless indicated otherwise, all translations from the German are by the author.

ISBN 978 0 8574 2 749 6

British Library Cataloguing-in-Publication Data
A catalogue record for this book is available from the British Library

Typeset by Seagull Books, Calcutta, India
Printed and bound by WordsWorth India, New Delhi, India

CONTENTS

vii
Manonology

xiv
Acknowledgments

1
SHE IS

58
GIRLHOOD

113
THE GAZELLE

172
IN SICKNESS

291
Bibliography

295
Index of Names

Manonology

a creature over whom much fuss was made
—Ernst Krenek[1]

While still in exile in France in 1940, just weeks before he took his life after crossing into Spain, the philosopher Walter Benjamin finalized his famous essay on the concept of history in which he meditates on Paul Klee's painting *Angelus Novus* (1920) as this "angel of history," seemingly moving away, fixedly contemplating something, staring sidelong, wings spread.[2] This angel was both a comfort and warning to Benjamin, who could have added another specimen to this order of angels. I found her in Alban Berg's Violin Concerto (1935) and the composer, like the philosopher, surely contemplated his image, a photograph of a young girl who stares sidelong in the same direction as Klee's new angel, another new angel suggesting both hope and horror for a new age.

Manon Gropius was born during the First World War and died four years before the Second. Most of her life was spent in the aura-

1 Ernst Krenek, *In Atem der Zeit:* Erinnerungen *an Die Moderne* [In a Breath of Time: Memories of the Modern Age] (Hamburg: Hoffmann und Campe Verlag, 1998), p. 342.

2 See Walter Benjamin, "These on the Philosophy of History," in *Illuminations* (Hannah Arendt ed. and Harry Zohn trans.) (New York: Schocken, 1968), pp. 253–64. Klee's depiction of the angel was executed just before he received an invitation from Walter Gropius to teach at the Bauhaus. Benjamin purchased the work in 1921.

shadow of her celebrated mother, the object of desire in fin-de-siècle Vienna, the so-called muse and widow of geniuses, Alma Mahler Gropius Werfel. Manon haunts this aura and those caught in it, her mother, her father Walter Gropius, her stepfather Franz Werfel, and the next ring of stellar individuals and the ring after, who all circled Manon's mother at some point in their lives. Manon disturbs those orbits like some unseen celestial body. She is also a peripheral figure (*Randfigur*) whose existence is dependent on others who, nevertheless, are influenced by her. This disturbance-influence is, in part, what this cultural history, microhistory, and biography is about.

I liken it to hauntology, Jacques Derrida's curious neologism that, like Benjamin's angel, is from that rich source of appropriated ideas—the Marxian way of looking at history. It confuses *haunt-* and *ont-*, where the idea of a person or thing exists more between being and nonbeing, between life and death, this tension between absence and presence, entity and nonentity. This "paradoxical state" influences conduct, behavior. Here the meaning of hauntology is extended to *being* the unknown child of well-known parents. And her spectral state exists during her life, her recovery from illness, and her death. And in thinking and writing about her during the interwar period into which her existence almost neatly fits, Manon seems a revenant, a ghost from birth in the way Anne Frank is.

While it might seem as though the comparison is farfetched and nuanced. In the end it bears out—victims of where Nietzsche's philosophy strayed into being cheerful, being superhuman, and so on. And Manon is a kind of saint as well, an emblem child. She is that child the American writer Max Phillips imagines in his Alma-inspired novel, *The Artist's Wife* (2003). "[F]or years I'd carried round a little reverie of her, as tiny and clear as a picture in a locket," a fictional Alma meditates, and in a way not far removed from what she called her "idea" of Manon. "I'd seen Manon flying over endless rows of youths in uniform," her character muses. "Their cheeks show like lead as they looked up. She held a sword before them, to drive them back or maybe to urge them forward, and she kicked slowly along the way a swimmer does, her legs bare, or maybe she was naked, but there was nothing unseemly about it, because she was beautiful and graceful as, I thought, Truth. That's the way I always liked to think of her, beautiful and pure and above everybody—it gave me a better opinion of the world. And now her legs were hopeless dead stalks and she moved her arms like a crab."[3]

Oliver Hilmes, in his biography of Alma, *Witwe im Wahn* (Widow in Delusion, 2004), also believes that Alma had this "fixed idea about the purpose, the mission of her dead daughter."[4] And for Alma, Manon would be no one else's idea—especially in regard to her father, Walter Gropius, for Alma virtually forbade Manon any real contact with her father. Indeed, for the time he actually saw Manon—end to end, it could be measured in weeks—Gropius could only imagine her existence from afar—another kind of liminality-hauntology. He is like that man in the *Kindertotenlieder* of Gustav Mahler, Alma's first husband, who looks up, interrupted as he works, and thinks he sees his revenant daughter—but it is his wife putting out a candle.

Gropius, despite having to depend on desk photographs to see his daughter's image (including the same portrait referenced by Berg) is also the father of a daughter who haunts him. The difference is that Manon lives and he must conduct his fatherhood long distance, through long and often searching letters—many unanswered and some intercepted and left unread by Manon—and the occasional telephone call. Although Manon barely lived into adulthood, her father did not wait to write her almost always as an adult free of her overly possessive mother, and the daughter was well informed of her father's mission, his ideas, ideals, his work, and the Bauhaus.

---

3 Max Phillips, *The Artist's Wife* (New York: Holt, 2001), p. 219.

4 Oliver Hilmes, *Witwe im Wahn: Das Leben der Alma Mahler-Werfel* [Widow in Delusion: The Life of Alma Mahler-Werfel] (Berlin: Siedler, 2004), p. 274. Translations from the German are my own unless indicated.

Falling between the mother and father is Manon's stepfather, Franz Werfel, who conducts a true, literary quest. Although Manon did not live to become the theatre actor she wanted to be, she became first a presence and then an actor, and a ghost in his novels even before her death. She is a model for characters in every one of Werfel's books, beginning with Werfel's novel of the Armenian genocide, *The Forty Days of Musa Dagh* (1933). Werfel sees her as a doomed child, a saint, a bride, *his* ancient Egyptian lover, and even a Jewess—an affront to Alma who prized Manon as her "Aryan daughter" until polio ruined her child's legs and beauty. This is the *creature* whom Elias Canetti witnessed in his memoirs, for which he won his Nobel Prize in literature in 1981. Two chapters from his incredible book about the last years of interwar Vienna, *The Play of the Eyes* (1990), depict a young woman surrounded and wasted by an awful mother. His Manon resembles a fairy-tale creature, like Sleeping Beauty, Snow White, and Cinderella, with her beauty and otherworldliness, part-girl, part-gazelle, this shape-shifter. While Canetti—who was no romantic—certainly exaggerated her, he is at least right in seeing Manon as misunderstood and misprised by the grownups around her. And some did see Manon as "awful" in her own right, as her mother's "bad seed." The composer Ernst Krenek found her to be disturbing, a seemingly knowing child-spy who would haunt him for years because he knew, writing about her in his memoirs, that he might be quite mistaken to write ill of her.

Others, too, saw in contrast a girl with an aura of something more to her, of possibility and potential, more so than just genes, of having special traits and talents, and a greater empathy. Of course, her parents, Alma and Gropius—and Werfel too—saw her as such a special person, as did the people around them, including Alban and Helene Berg and members of the Bauhaus, such as Xanti Schawinsky. Of course, every generation has this conceit for the one that comes of it. Mine promised "indigo," "crystal," and "star" children for a time, until we settled on more sobering labels, such as ADHD and Asperger's. This promise *cum* disappointment, this confusion between the two, perhaps, is why I, for a lack of a better word, *adopted* Manon as a subject and out of curiosity, for I had just published a biography of a poet and the germ of that book was a single poem, a contradiction in verse titled "For My Daughter," which ends "I have no daughter. I desire none."

I found Manon similarly rejected or rather "orphaned" as I began to wade into translating Franz Werfel's poetry and fiction from the German. This necessitated composing a working, mental biography that eventually arrived on the life of Manon Gropius. In one of his novels, an ambitious false start that devolved into *The Song of Bernadette* (1942), Werfel promised Manon's spirit that he would write the "truth" and in the way a bardic poet promises a muse, for Manon becomes as much a muse to him as her famous mother was to Werfel and her other men. I followed the trail of words left by Werfel's promise for the truth, most of it fiction, ending with the posthumously published *Star of the Unborn* (1946). There his character, F.W., has his last encounter with her character, and sees the lifeline surface in her palm where none was. There was something occultic about that scene. Werfel had *emancipated* his obsession. Then it became mine.

So, what is the truth to—about Manon? Whatever it is, it becomes worthy of a book-length study given that two of the authors mentioned here wanted to rescue her from their greatest perils. For Werfel it is death. For Canetti it is her mother. I could say both, and that makes this an orphic text blended with other genres, part biography, part modern European and cultural history (from a macro- and micro point of view), essay, the translation arts, comparative literature and religion, architecture, musicology, and, even prose poetry. That said, Manon makes for a modest and quiet production that is nicely disproportionate to years spent on thin and scattered sources, notes, letters, diary entries, memoirs, and photographs. I have even included what is apocryphal about Manon, for I see in the made-up stories the art laid at her feet. And there is this aural Manon, too, found in listening to her presence in Berg's Violin Concerto. And, lastly, I have tried to interpolate a medical history of polio at a time and place where medicine reached a dead end in Manon's case. The vaccine that "cured" polio was brand new when I was born, but there were still children in leg braces and wheelchairs all around me then. (I still remember a vivid dream of picking up a classmate, a girl, who could not walk and her smile for me.)

Returning to the beginning, that Manon is this angel of history and hauntology—that paradox of being and not being—is the ultimate challenge and motivation. It exists even where her trail is at its coldest. I felt that on one early April day at her father's house, the Gropius House in Lincoln, Massachusetts. There I like to think that I saw Manon in her "paradoxical state." I even photographed this thereness and not, for what else could the image show? I took the photograph with me to Wellfleet on the Cape the next day, when I met Gropius' adopted daughter and niece, Ati Johansen Gropius.

We had corresponded over a decade (though we never met) and I wanted to show her I really intended to write such an impossible book that seemed quixotic. In part, she came to know her "older sister" better from our letters—many of them her father's letters she had never seen—for Gropius kept no visible reminders around him (or his second daughter) to remind him of his lost child, not even the photographs he treasured. He never spoke of her after her funeral, which he could not attend. When he could return to Germany and Austria in the postwar years, he never visited the grave he had designed for her. As deeply as he had to love his first daughter from that distance in life, almost to the point where Manon virtually existed only in her father's imagination, so Gropius deeply mourned her with a silence that was trusted by others who knew him to be the measure of that love, from a place inside of him where one could not drop a stone and listen.

Ati and I had tea. I had laid out my first manuscript on the table in front of the sofa, this really being for show-and-tell, for I still had a long way to go and she had no time to read something so rough. I also wanted to show her the photograph I had taken at the Gropius House. I thought it might testify as well to my commitment, this despite the uncanny, occult, and even sentimental character of an image seemingly in defiance of the architecture's rationality and my own objectivity. I listened for an opportunity to bring it up. But none came as I heard Ati repeat part of the title of my book with what I took to be an indifferent, almost dismissive, perhaps even incredulous voice—"architect's daughter"? Had I transgressed? Had I made too much of it in such a way that my precious photograph would make it worse? So I said nothing about the image of the spiral staircase at the Gropius House, which her father had designed for Ati, in a way that evinces his rapport for another daughter, to come and go as she pleased from her bedroom on the second story. Had I done so, I think Ati would have only seen an optical illusion from some dust mote floating on the lens, not what I let myself see, outside of my own rational box, this slender figure of light unmistakably standing at the top of those steps.

Acknowledgments

The research and writing of this book began in 2005, an endeavor that wove gradually around other books and other responsibilities (much like my 2003 biography of the poet Weldon Kees, which took almost as much time). Thus, with the publication of *Manon's World*, I feel like the subject of the book and I are walking away from a glacial journey, from the suspended animation of reading biographies, articles about polio and twentieth-century music, faded copies of correspondence (often in indecipherable hands), writing letters of inquiry, writing drafts and revising drafts, going out on limbs of speculation, examining and identifying the faces in photographs, even shadows and reflections, all of it out of pocket because no one had ever undertaken such a book, and doing justice to all the work—and the generous contributions of those who helped me. All my expressions of gratitude, for this reason, feel enormously belated! And I should feel this way for some of those people are now dead.

The first person I wish to thank is the late Rosemary Moravec, Alban Berg scholar and librarian of the Österreichische Nationalbibliothek (ÖNB), Austria's equivalent to the Library of Congress, for all her help, advice, and encouragement. In addition, I would like to thank her colleagues at the ÖNB, namely, its head, Andreas Fingernagel, and Rosemary's successors, Katrin Jilek and the late Brigitte Mersich.

Of equal importance to Rosemary, especially during my first years of work, is the archivist Violet Lutz, whose estimable assistance with the Mahler-Werfel Collection at the University of Pennsylvania Rare Book & Manuscript Library cannot be understated. Furthermore, I would like to thank Nancy Shawcross of the same institution, the former Curator of Manuscripts.

Friends and colleagues, too, provided much help in my work. First among them is Heinz Wohlers, whose patience and willingness to help me transcribe the voluminous correspondence needed for my research and for accurate quotation can only be described as priceless. Chris Lewis of the University Library of American University, provided me with much material and even shared his home with me when I came to Washington, D.C., to conduct research. He also read and edited my manuscript from the point of view of the general reader, for whom all this scholarship and significance for a girl and those around her from a time and place quite remote from us had to be carefully distilled and made intelligible. To this list I should also add Bernard Geoghegan for his willingness to be an intermediary for me in Berlin.

I wish to thank fellow biographers who were willing to correspond with me about issues going beyond what they put on paper, among them Oliver Hilmes, Alma Mahler-Werfel's biographer; Peter Stephan Jungk, the biographer of Franz Werfel; Sven Hanuschek, Elias Canetti's biographer; and, especially, Fiona McCarthy—the author of the first biography of Walter Gropius in English—and Mary Dearborn and Lori Rubinfeld who both provided me with peer reviews. To this list, too, I should also add the late Erich Rietenauer, who was kind enough to correspond with me and to meet with Heinz Wohlers on my behalf before the publication of his memoir, which is as much about Manon Gropius as it is about her mother Alma. (A telling moment that evinces his true love is in the Austrian television documentary about him, when Rietenauer regards Manon's death mask in the ÖNB.) Rietenauer had originally been enlisted by Manon's nurse, Ida Gebauer, to write a tell-all about the Mahler-Werfel household, a text that he, as the self-styled "last living witness," could only approximate. I wish I had found others coming to this story so late. But I did benefit from the vivid memories of Kay Loewi-Robertson, who, as an adolescent, saw Manon and Alma in Venice. Lastly, I would like to thank Hannes Kammerstätter for sharing his work on the Lieser family.

Manuscripts, letters, and like materials for research and reproduction in this book were provided by several individuals and institutions, including the Kislak Center for Special Collections of the University of Pennsylvania; the Österreichische Nationalbibliothek; the Bauhaus-Archiv; the Archives of American Art; the Special Collections of the Charles E. Young Research Library, University of California, Los Angeles; and the Nachlass Elias Canetti of the Zentralbibliothek Zurich. For permission to quote from Julius Tandler's letters held by the ÖNB, I am grateful to his grandson, William Tandler.

Photographs were, of course, a primary source and without the assistance of certain individuals, I would not have been made aware of such images or had access to them. First among them is the actor Paulus Manker, the producer of the play *Alma*, who shared many of the images from his collection. Rosemary Moravec and Violet Lutz should also be thanked again for their help in this regard. Of special mention, too, is Sabine Hartmann and Wencke Clausnitzer-Paschold of the Bauhaus-Archiv in Berlin.

The gentle and mindful cooperation, enthusiasm, and blessings of Manon Gropius' heirs have been important assets to my work and seeing it through to completion. Firstly, I would like to thank Marina Mahler for the use of the family photographs. Additionally, I would also like to thank the late Ati Gropius Johansen for permission to quote from her father's letters. I would also like to thank her daughter Erika Pfammatter for her ideas for small but key revisions on interpreting her grandfather's conduct.

ACKNOWLEDGMENTS

No book such as this one is a reality without a kind and patient publisher and staff. Thus, I would like to thank the team at Seagull Books for making *Manon's World* for this world and the next. Too, I would also like to thank my dear wife, M. Lori Reidel for her patience and willingness to endure my fascination in this other woman.

SHE IS

When your mother dear comes through the door
With the candle's glow, it is to me as ever,
You coming with her, darting from behind,
Into the room as before!
O you too brief flicker of joy
Of your father's cell, alas, snuffed out.
—verses from Gustav Mahler's *Kindertotenlieder*

Paternus Interruptus

As a spiritual as well as physical event, Manon Gropius' conception took six years for her mother, Alma Maria Mahler, the wife of the composer and conductor Gustav Mahler, an Olympian in the music world of the early 1900s. He had been the director of Vienna's *Hofoper*, the Court Opera, appointed by the Hapsburg emperor, Franz Josef I of Austria-Hungary, who ignored centuries of prejudice and appointed the first man of Jewish heritage to such a high position. Mahler was also, by 1910, the guest conductor of New York's Metropolitan Opera and Philharmonic orchestras. He had completed his Symphony no. 9 and was now on the verge of surpassing Beethoven with his Symphony no. 10, an achievement not only considered disrespectful by some in the music world, but hubristic in the extreme, prideful, and courting what many saw as a curse. To Mahler, however, Alma had been his greatest personal triumph since their marriage in 1902, when he was forty-two and she twenty-three.

Like him, she was a musician—a pianist—and a composer of art songs. Her pedigree did not come from Austria's nobility, but from artists in a country where artists had become a nobility unto themselves, for Alma was the daughter of the nineteenth-century Austrian Impressionist painter Emil Jakob Schindler and an operetta singer, Anna Bergen. Alma had been educated to be an emancipated young woman, with a library of German philosophy, including a complete set of set of Friedrich Nietzsche's works given to her by the director of the Burgtheater, Max Burckhard, one of the first of many older men who fell in love with her in a way that was both paternal and erotic. And coming of age during the Austrian Secession, Alma attracted the attention of two of its chief painters, the first being Gustav Klimt, who became one of her earliest suitors.

Klimt did not need to paint her for Mahler to see Alma as a glittering trophy in the cultured society of Vienna. That she proudly considered herself an "Aryan" and belonging to a no-less chosen race did not matter to Mahler, a Roman Catholic convert but still Jewish to Alma. He found her sexuality intoxicating, whereas she found him at times physically repulsive. However, as an assimilated Jew and one of the most important men in music at the turn of the century, Mahler represented a trophy to Alma. "The analytic mind, social democracy, liberalism, all this 'enlightenment' has come into the world due to the Jews," she would later tell a Jewish friend and suitor. "But without me you would never become human"—and thus Alma virtually stated her personal mission, which she first undertook with her marriage to Gustav Mahler, according to her biographer Oliver Hilmes, "to liberate [Jews] from their Jewishness."[5] To Mahler, such magnanimous expressions only reinforced his image of Alma as a muse, for to be worthy of her was his personal mission. It authenticated him as a German and artist.

---

5 Alma Mahler to Joseph Fraenkel, quoted in Hilmes, *Witwe im Wahn*, p. 150.

Mahler is important to the *spiritual* genealogy of Manon Gropius because he is the father of the void she would eventually fill. In July 1907, Gustav and Alma's firstborn, the five-year-old Maria (b. 1902), came down with scarlet fever. She had contracted the dreaded disease from her two-year-old sister, Anna (b. 1905). The older girl, called "Putzi"—meaning "Precious"—by her father, died after an emergency tracheotomy on a kitchen table, an operation Alma witnessed because the village doctor had made her hold her choking daughter still as he cut a hole in her throat and windpipe. Mahler saw the tragedy as punishment for composing the *Kindertotenlieder*—"Songs on the Death of Children." Soon after, Mahler was diagnosed with a weak heart. His fear of an early death caused him to redouble the time he spent on his composing and conducting. Thus, he could not help but neglect his grieving wife, whose increasing bouts of depression and withdrawal over the next three years took a toll on their marriage, for she could not enjoy sex with Mahler and often sent him away when he came to her.

In the spring of 1910, Alma's doctors advised her to take a "rest-cure." Mahler readily agreed. With the many rehearsals needed for the enormous choruses needed for his Symphony no. 8, the "Symphony of a Thousand," he needed Alma in a good place, where he need not worry about her. He also knew that the third anniversary of Putzi's death loomed. On June 1, Mahler escorted Alma, their surviving daughter, Anna—whose large blue eyes earned her the pet name of "Gucki," idiom for opera glasses—and the child's English nanny Maud Turner to Tobelbad, a small spa town in a forested valley ringed by the peaks and massifs of Lower Austria's Rax Alps. Its thermal spring is discussed in various nineteenth-century Baedekers. It is often referred to as a *Wildbad*, German for a water spa situated in a remote and natural setting. Thus, visitors find a "way to get back to nature." As far back as the fifteenth century, men and women bathed naked together here. Indeed, a visit to Tobelbad was considered good for both male impotence and female frigidity, the latter being why Mahler put such faith in the now modern spa.

Tobelbad's director, the neuro- and homeopath Ernst von Düring, formerly of the famous Sanatorium Lahmann in Dresden, had devised a grueling yet rewarding regimen to help patients, among them the Austrian imperial family and the poet Rainer Maria Rilke, to overcome the vicissitudes of modern life. He prescribed a spartan diet of lettuce and buttermilk, cold morning outdoor calisthenics, and radioactive thermal baths in the hot springs, which made Alma faint on her second day. Tobelbad had a cure for virtually every ailment, from migraines and neurasthenia to hay fever and constipation. For women, the thermal waters made an excellent douche that, allegedly, restored their sex to its proper sensitivities and elasticity. Seeing the facilities to his liking, Mahler left Alma in Dr. von Düring's care and returned to Vienna with the promise that he could visit Alma if she needed him and as his schedule allowed.

The good doctor also prescribed an appropriate form of dress intended to improve circulation and be as close as possible to going about naked in order to achieve balance and cure one of vertigo. Thus Alma went barefoot and wore a long coarse white linen gown that made her and the other guests of the sanatorium look like the inmates of an insane asylum or some religious order. She abhorred being deprived of her wardrobe, which at the age of thirty-one accentuated her lingering hourglass figure. Too, she thought that she would be bored to death left alone until she apprehended the admiring glances of a tall younger man with piercing dark eyes, dark hair, and a perfectly trimmed moustache at one of the therapeutic waltzes.

Walter Gropius, an architect from Berlin, had also recently arrived at Tobelbad to recuperate from the stress of running his new architectural practice. Dr. von Düring introduced him to Alma, which then allowed Gropius to do the gallant thing and ask her for the next, and therapeutic, dance. Then they took a moonlit walk, where Alma learned that Gropius was four years younger, that he had studied with one of her father's friends, and that they were distantly related on her mother's side. The next day they slept together.

The attention Alma now gave to the young architect allowed for little time to write Mahler anything but terse notes. So much was she infatuated with her new lover that she forgot to write Mahler a letter acknowledging his fiftieth birthday, an incredible omission given its significance. After a month of treatment, Mahler visited his wife and found her little changed. Without apprehending the real situation, he wrote his sister Justine Rosé, "the news from Tobelbad flows meagerly [and] the fun didn't do the little one [i.e. Alma] any good."[6] But what happened in Tobelbad did not stay in Tobelbad. Soon after Alma left in the middle of July to rejoin Mahler in the Tyrolean town of Toblach, where Mahler summered and worked, Gropius sent her passionate letters and she responded in kind. Gropius also wrote Mahler, asking the "Herr Direktor," as though he were Alma's father, for her hand in marriage. Taken aback by his wife's incredible infidelity and the boldness of her lover, Mahler confronted his rival in his summer cottage and heard him out. Then he sat down with his wife in another room and asked her to choose between him and the young architect. Realizing Mahler's stature as an artist—and the certainty of his income—she chose to remain with him for now. For his part, Mahler took the blame for his wife's infidelity. He even sought out Sigmund Freud on a visit to the Dutch resort of Leyden. There Freud conducted a rather informal and brief psychoanalysis of the estranged couple and told Mahler that Alma served an Oedipal need of his, a *Maria*—Holy Mary—*komplex.*

Alma's mother, Anna Moll, played her part in facilitating Manon's conception. She had taken Gropius' side in the affair. She believed that

---

6 Gustav Mahler to Justine Rosé, July 15, 1910 [letter 315], in Stephen McClachie (ed.), *The Mahler Family Letters* (New York: Oxford University Press, 2006), p. 398.

a woman should be allowed to seek sexual gratification and companionship outside of marriage if the husband failed to do his part. And the husband in question should also accept this. Thus Anna Moll's first husband, Emil Schindler, tactfully accepted Alma's half-sister Grete as his own child, even though Grete was the daughter of his wife's lover, the painter Julius Victor Berger. Schindler had also looked the other way when his wife had another affair with his protégé, Carl Moll, who went on to marry Alma's mother soon after her father's death. In this rather decorous, chivalrous way, such complex and contentious familial relations were smoothed over for the parents, lovers—and their children until they understood them, this being especially true for Alma.

Despite the mother's and daughter's progressive practice of free love, they were still Victorian in their sensibilities and virtually polyandrous in a tribal way, too. To conceive a child was still considered one of the ultimate expression of a woman's love for a man—risking her body for his kin. "I want a child—and I want to conceive it and care for it," Alma wrote Gropius, "until the day comes when we, without remorse, safe and sound—sink smiling into each other's arms forever."[7] To Alma (and her mother), Gropius was seen as an antidote to having married a "Jew." To Alma he had sprung from the pages of her beloved Nietzsche, from the operas of Wagner, whose music to her was still superior. Gropius was Aryan and that complemented her. Since Alma—like many creative people of her time—identified with the Theosophist movement, she would have regarded Gropius as a member of the "Root Race" to use Helen Blavatsky's term for the Aryan race, of which Jews were only a degenerate branch. Gropius, whom Alma saw as the personification of the young knight Walther von Stolzing from Wagner's opera *Die Meistersinger von Nürnberg*, would provide Alma

---

7 Alma Mahler to Walter Gropius, September 19, 1910, quoted in Reginald Isaacs, *Walter Gropius: Der Mensch und sein Werk* [Walter Gropius: The Man and His Work] (Berlin: Gebr. Mann Verlag, 1984), VOL. 1, p. 103.

with a child to replace the one lost, and not only a hybrid in her mind, but a pure Aryan child. So, with "*Phantasie und Energie*," according to Oliver Hilmes, Alma arranged to meet a "Walter Groh" aboard trains whenever she could part from Mahler.[8] Throughout the late summer and early autumn of 1910, however, her ovulation and railroad timetables refused to properly align so that she would be impregnated before her husband's next engagement in New York.

Just before the mid-September premiere of the Symphony no. 8, Mahler came down with a nagging sore throat. He still suffered what he believed was a minor case of tonsillitis in late October, when he, Alma, Gucki, and Miss Maud sailed for America and his second season as the conductor of the New York Philharmonic. Rather than worry over his health and the music he intended to conduct, Mahler doted on his daughter but especially on Alma. He kissed Alma's hand again and again, in that charming way of the Viennese gallant. He even went to her closet and kissed her shoes, indeed, everything that symbolized her. Charmed, Alma likewise responded like a real wife and shared everything with him—save for Gropius' letters, which arrived at the front desk of their hotel via general delivery. Mahler even indulged Alma's enthusiasm for Theosophy by attending "Theosophical teas" with a mysterious young American lady, who taught the couple occult rites, practices, and the ability to apprehend the unseen vibrations of all phenomena. She lent Alma books by C. W. Leadbeater and Annie Besant, such as *Man Visible and Invisible* (1903), about clairvoyance and the ability to see the souls of the dead, and surely *Thought-Forms* (1905). The latter book inspired Alma and Mahler together with their little daughter to shut their eyes so as to see the psychological colors in their minds, like the examples shown in the book's plates, colors for religious feeling, fear, intellect, malice, and the like. There was even a chapter to intrigue Mahler, about the colors and shapes emitted by

8 See Hilmes, *Witwe im Wahn*, pp. 113–4.

classical music, inexplicably depicted on chromos of Worcester Cathedral and with Wagner achieving an enormous purple mountain—the color of spiritualty.

Mahler tried to live like a man half his age. He took time from his busy concert schedule to take side trips with Alma, including one to see Niagara Falls during that fall and winter of 1911, which had been particularly snowy. Then he returned to the Philharmonic and toured East Coast cities and sometimes ventured inland. For Christmas, Mahler spent lavishly on a tree and presents, including a diamond solitaire for Alma worth $1,000 (about $28,000 adjusted for inflation). He even took Gucki for a walk in Central Park, where Alma watched father and daughter tossing snow at each other from her window at the Savoy Hotel. Not long after he complained of his sore throat as he continued to conduct concerts into January and February. Despite a fever that should have bedridden him, he insisted on conducting his last concert on February 21 at Carnegie Hall. Then, at last, he sought treatment from his personal physician in New York, Dr. Joseph Fraenkel. A throat culture confirmed that Mahler had a strep infection. But this did not stop him from rehearsing with the singer who would perform one of Alma's songs.

In March, a heart specialist was consulted as Mahler's condition worsened. He diagnosed a far graver disease, one common given Mahler's heart problems. The sore throat had resulted in bacterial endocarditis, an infection of the heart valves that was virtually a death sentence before antibiotics. Despite the excellent care he had thus far received in New York, Mahler decided to sail with his family for France, so that he could seek treatment in Paris from the famous French bacteriologists Élie Metchnikoff of the Pasteur Institute and André Chantemesse. The latter, upon seeing the many luxuriant and fatal strands of streptococci in Mahler's blood under a microscope, made Alma look to show how much they resembled "seaweed." Undaunted, Dr. Chantemesse prescribed a serum therapy and had Mahler transferred to a private clinic in Neuilly.

When he failed to improve, Alma wired the hematologist Franz Chvostek, who came at once and had Mahler transported to the Löw Sanatorium in Vienna. While he tried to encourage Mahler, he told Alma on the side that if her husband pulled through, she would have to care for an "ancient child" who would spend the rest of his life in a wheelchair. That did not happen. Mahler died on May 18, 1911, the same day as Gropius' twenty-eighth birthday. The fateful coincidence came as a shock to Alma.

In the week leading up to the funeral, Alma fell sick from a lung infection she had contracted at the hospital caring for her dying husband. The traumatic experience of listening to his death rattles, which reprised the last hours of their dead daughter Maria, had also worn her down. But these were not the only reasons why Alma was not among the 500 mourners who saw her husband buried in Vienna's Grinzing Friedhof. After seeing her father buried, she had promised herself never to attend another funeral.

When Gropius sent his condolences at the end of May, probing Alma's mood and need for him, his letters were met by a woman who had virtually remarried her husband's memory. She had to behave now as a society widow, a role that she found suited her, for it not only made her a wealthy woman but an independent one, too. The architect, too, saw his own life change over the past half year. The death of his father in February made him head of the family and after seeing Mahler's Symphony no. 7 performed in Berlin, the experience released "many streams of empathy in [his] breast" for Mahler. "What became clear about Gustav and you and—me—face to face," Gropius wrote Alma, was that "you are a pure angel"—a being Gropius now wanted for his muse.[9] He had achieved much since he had met Alma, including the

9 Walter Gropius to Alma Mahler, January 23, 1911, quoted in Isaacs, *Walter Gropius*, VOL. 1, p. 110.

Fagus-Werk, a modern factory complex unlike any other in Europe at the time. He attributed much of his newfound recognition to her. However, despite his entreaties from Berlin and his family's summer seaside residence at Timmensdorf on the Baltic, Alma did not ask him to come to Vienna until August. Even though they spoke intimately and made love then as before, Gropius could see that Alma's loyalty to "G."—which stood for Gustav—was an impasse and that Alma had cooled toward him.

On a sheet of hotel stationary Gropius wrote a long letter expressing his dismay of being faithful to her, of playing the role of Tristan to her Isolde, of being celibate such that his hair stood on end, of not being a consolation to her. She wrote him an apologetic letter for her behavior in which she also suggested that she could be pregnant by him and would need to do something if that were the case—that is, whether to abort since having a child so soon after Mahler's death would be frowned on by Viennese society. As their relationship faded further, Gropius began to feel guilt and to question his maturity for having pursued Alma and destroying the marriage of a fellow artist, a "strange, distant Titan." He saw himself as more a sham, a troublemaker. Gropius' mother, Manon Scharnweber Gropius and his sister, Manon Gropius Burchard, were also made uncomfortable by Alma, whereas Alma saw them, and his family in general, as social inferiors. Gradually the letters that Gropius and Alma exchanged became increasingly platonic and both moved on with their lives.

Manon's conception underwent yet another delay.

For the next four years, Alma Mahler hardly spent her time as a lonely widow. Her residence became one of Vienna's leading salons, especially among Mahler's heirs, such as Arnold Schoenberg and Alban Berg. She had a number of admirers and suitors. For a time, she enjoyed the company of the composer Franz Schreker and was escorted by Mahler's doctor from New York, Joseph Fraenkel. They, in turn, gave way to the biologist Paul Kammerer—a man whose devotion to Mahler's music led to an attempt at suicide, putting a pistol to his forehead at Mahler's grave. However, this urge gave way to his equally unsuccessful and suicidal obsession with Alma. Although he could never woo her, he did convince her to be his laboratory assistant—given her own interest in how traits were transferred to offspring—at the new Institute for Experimental Biology of Vienna in the Prater. An advocate of the Lamarckian theory of inheritance, Kammerer rivaled Charles Darwin and sought to disprove the eugenic theories of Social Darwinists by proving that environment dictated the organism, not genes.

Eventually, Alma became bored with helping Kammerer perform his dubiously scientific experiments herself, such as transplanting the eyes of lizards into blind amphibians—and with Kammerer himself who ultimately was accused of being a fraud in 1926 and shot himself over this shame rather than for his love of Mahler and Alma.

Alma also enjoyed the company of a woman after Mahler's death and her leave from Gropius. Henriette Amalie Lieser, called Lilly, was married to the textile manufacturer Justus Lieser—who, with his brother Adolf, had founded the first hemp-fiber factory in Austria and amassed private art collections that included many works by Klimt and other Secessionists. Though Alma had been acquainted with Lilly in the past, it was not until after Mahler's death that Lilly befriended Alma. However, as a lesbian, Lilly Lieser wanted something more from Alma, going as far as to trick Alma into disrobing her on a bed. But Alma claimed that she found nothing for her "erotic health" in the rich Jewish woman and never reciprocated. Lilly had to continue as Alma's duenna and the foil of Alma's next serious lover—the painter Oskar Kokoschka.

In April 1912, Alma met Kokoschka ostensibly for the purpose of his painting her portrait. Her stepfather Carl Moll had made the arrangements and vouched for Kokoschka's talent as a rising young member of the Austrian Secession. His informal training and innate, even brutal gift for capturing anxiety and serenity of his subjects in the same agitated line and brushstroke had made him a popular portrait artist among Vienna's elite—this despite Archduke Franz Ferdinand's judgment, after visiting a gallery hung with Kokoschkas, that the so-called *enfant terrible* painted like "pig shit."

At their first meeting, a dinner party hosted by Moll, Kokoschka, like Gropius, and like many others before, fell instantly in love with Alma's generous figure, blond hair, and her way of carefully following everything he said with this fascinated look in her eyes—more due to her mild deafness in one ear—this despite her being older than him. Rather than enjoy an after-dinner cigar with Moll, Kokoschka accompanied Alma to the music room, where he intended to do a preliminary sketch. Although his intense expression made her uncomfortable, she began to appraise his coarse but handsome "proletarian" features. As he worked in charcoal, she noticed his extraordinarily long fingers, which ended in fingernails pared so closely that they appeared to be still bleeding. To relieve the silence, she excused herself, sat at the piano, and played the *Liebestod* from Wagner's *Tristan and Isolde*. The choice proved electric. At some point into the piece, she felt a presence behind her, felt it breathing upon her. The music forced Kokoschka to put down his sketchbook, come up from behind her and do what he had been thinking of ever since he arrived, and appraised Alma in her black, befitting mourning dress. When she stood up in surprise, he embraced her. She did not resist. Then he left abruptly into an unusually snowy April night.

After the anniversary of Mahler's death in May, Alma and Kokoschka "were inseparable" as Alma wrote in her memoir. "Never before had I tasted so much tension, so much hell, so much paradise."[10] For months

10 Alma Mahler-Werfel, *And the Bridge Is Love* (New York: Harcourt, Brace, 1958), p. 74.

she virtually became Kokoschka's only model and subject. The portrait he ultimately painted from his first drawings—the so-called red painting—depicted Alma as a Renaissance princess, with the inscrutable smile of the Leonardo's Mona Lisa and the loose ringlets of Veneto's Lucrezia Borgia—his gift Alma prominently hung in the sitting room of her new apartment at Elisabethstrasse 22 in Vienna's First District.

Even Gropius, when he attended a Berlin art exhibition in February 1913, became aware of Kokoschka's place in Alma's life. The architect easily recognized her, wearing a satin red peignoir he well knew, in a large double portrait that included Kokoschka. Intensely jealous and horrified by Kokoschka's style, Gropius walked out and ceased writing Alma altogether. What he did not know was that Kokoschka was hardly secure in his love for Alma Mahler. His many portraits of her, including the famous *Windbraut—Bride of the Wind—* canvas and his series of exquisite, painted ostrich-skin fans, were as much testimonies of his losing Alma as possessing her. In so many of them, he depicted himself as a tortured figure and much of this was due to his need for her to bear him a love child. When he did at last make Alma pregnant, it came on the day of the arrival of Mahler's finished plaster death mask, which so haunted her that she got an abortion. (So that he could have something over which to mourn his lost child, Kokoschka begged the doctor for Alma's bloody cotton.)

Gropius' architectural firm flourished throughout 1913. Although a poor draftsman, he had vision and knew how to lead and impart his ideas to the other members of his practice in designing modern factories, stores, homes—and their entries for the first Werkbund Exhibition in Cologne in the spring of 1914. These included an entire model factory complex, with its main building featuring many details never before seen in industrial application, including an overarching glass clerestory that ran the length of the main work floor—everything designed to harmonize the humanity of the workers with the efficiency of their machines. Gropius' other exhibits included furnished rooms, automobile designs, and interiors, and a new design for a railway sleeping compartment, which surely owed some of its improvements to those assignations with Alma in the Pullman cars of the Orient Express and like luxury trains.

News of the coming exposition in Cologne appeared in the newspapers as well as the enormous success of one "young architect [. . .] a certain young Walter Gropius" as Alma learned from Vienna's other great *Salonistin*, the cultural journalist Berta Zuckerkandl. She was well connected to many departments of Viennese life, including its medical establishment as the wife of the great anatomist Emil Zuckerkandl. Karl Kraus, Vienna's leading literary and social critic, called her "Aunt Klara" for the way she nurtured and promoted her favorites throughout Europe—implicit too was Berta's skill as a matchmaker, for she had arranged the dinner party that brought Mahler and Alma together.

Berta's praise of Gropius provided a new impetus to the conciliatory—and unanswered—letters Alma had written Gropius. In May 1914, she congratulated him on his triumph in Cologne and invited him to her nearly finished summer villa, "Haus Mahler," near the town of Breitenstein am Semmering in Lower Austria. Gropius, however, did not join Alma for her first summer idyll there. He still believed she was seeing Kokoschka, even though she had distanced herself from the painter.

Kokoschka could only imagine Alma that summer. He gave her a sixth painted fan in which he depicted her wearing a peasant dirndl, tending crops and livestock while dancers perform in a circle under an oak. In the center of the fan, is Kokoschka depicted as St. George on horseback, whose lance falls protectively or, perhaps, procreatively across her belly and loins while Alma carries a small likeness of Kokoschka, the child he still wanted from her. The point of the lance impales one of four apocalyptic beasts with the bodies of lions and human heads that resembled the older men Kokoschka saw as rivals for Alma's attentions. The tableau continues, marking how the summer of 1914 ended with Austrian and Russian soldiers fighting and dying. On June 28, 1914, that archduke who had disparaged Kokoschka's work was assassinated along with his wife in Sarajevo, the capital of Austria-Hungary's restive province of Bosnia-Herzegovina. This event gave the empire a premise to declare war on its Balkan rival, the Kingdom of Serbia—which called on its ally, the Russian Empire, to declare war on Austria-Hungary. Soon other treaties had to be similarly honored when the German Empire and Ottoman Empire came to the aid of Austria-Hungary, which, in turn, forced France and Great Britain (and later Italy) to side with Russia. Thus ended the status quo and peace of the Belle Époque.

"On Semmering"—as Alma called her summers in Breitenstein—the world war did not rise to the downfall of the West as it even seemed then, but rather as a "theatrical distraction from personal tedium and dullness" as she put it.[11] Unable to attract Gropius to her side or to rid herself of Kokoschka, she contemplated taking her daughter Anna and sailing to India to study Sanskrit at Annie Besant's Theosophy school in Benares. However, when Alma returned to Vienna and witnessed soldiers praying for their safekeeping in the city's cathedral, the Stephansdom, she felt the same sense of patriotism and certain victory that so many Austrians did with Germany at their side—and men like Walter Gropius.

As a reservist and excellent horseman, Gropius entered the war as a sergeant major in the 9th Wandsbeck Hussar Reserve Regiment, a reconnaissance cavalry unit kitted with tall bearskin hats that looked little different from the time of Waterloo. During the first weeks of August, he participated in the German invasion of northern France,

---

11 Hilmes, *Witwe im Wahn*, p. 148.

which nearly took Paris. Being on the cutting edge of the offensive, Gropius fought pitched battles and captured numerous French prisoners, for which he was awarded an Iron Cross in late September and promoted to lieutenant. Newspaper accounts of Gropius' heroism soon made their way to Alma. When she learned that his regiment was resting at Strasbourg in early September, she wrote him a praiseful letter. She offered to travel to Berlin as soon as the Germans marched into Paris. And as she waited for the city to surrender and Gropius to respond, Alma at one point retired to her newly decorated and red-painted music room, her "red salon," to play stirring passages from *Die Meistersinger* on her piano.

The "Miracle on the Marne," however, that great Allied counter-offensive, frustrated Alma's gift of herself to Gropius—and he still did not answer her letters. Nevertheless, she still obsessed over him as an artist-warrior and the bearer of precious and Theosophical Aryan seed. While celebrating *Silvester*—New Year's Eve—at Haus Mahler, she wrote him yet another letter. "I want you to return from battle *sound* [. . .]. Just now I went to my north balcony—there is moonlight—the mountains lie silent and great—not a sound—a whisper.— [. . .] tomorrow guests are coming [. . .].—so I am not so alone tomorrow—so alone. Will the time come when I can bring you here—here where you measured out the ground with *your steps*? I press your hands, Alma."[12]

This letter achieved the desired effect and its sincerity would be assisted by fate. The very next day, New Year's Day 1915, Walter Gropius miraculously survived a mortar grenade that exploded right in front of him. Suffering from nervous insomnia in the days that followed, Gropius was ordered to rest in a Berlin military hospital. There he found Alma's letter of December 31. Although not a religious man and not a believer in guardian angels, Gropius could hardly have

---

12 Alma Mahler to Walter Gropius, December 31, 1914, quoted in Isaacs, *Walter* Gropius, VOL. 1, p. 140.

missed the providential tenor of Alma's words—and because of her he was no stranger to Theosophy and the concept of *karma.* He wrote Alma back in mid-January. Then, against the advice of his mother, he agreed to see his former lover, who traveled to Berlin with Lilly Lieser in late February.

Hearing Gropius out on his mother and sister and Kokoschka, Alma assumed the role of the one who had been in the wrong for all this time, and "with the ignominious intent, I bowed to this son of the muses."[13] She endured days of "tearful" questions and answers. "At last he fell in love with me again," she wrote, "at Borchardt's restaurant, with wine and the atmosphere to stimulate the emotions, and the farewell mood doing its share, for in an hour he had to catch a train to Hannover, to see his mother. I went to the station with him, and there, overwhelmed by his ardor, Gropius simply pulled me up into the moving train."[14] In her diary, she hardly disguised that they did more than talk in their compartment. "Without a nightgown, without the least comforts and conveniences, I pretty much became physically the plunder of this man. I must admit it was not unpleasant."[15]

The next day Gropius and Alma returned to Berlin. She noticed how he had assumed the bearing of a man already married to her. Back at her hotel room, Alma fended off Lilly for the last time, perhaps, and contemplated her success with Gropius. In her diary, however, she noted that her "solitary existence" still suffered in long dashes the fact that she still had "—no child—" with Gropius.[16]

---

13 Alma Mahler-Werfel, "Tagebuch der Alma Maria [hereafter "Diary of Alma Maria"] (1902–1944)," 1915, p. 62, MWP.

14 Mahler-Werfel, *And the Bridge Is Love*, pp. 85–6

15 Mahler-Werfel, "Diary of Alma Maria," pp. 62–3, MWP.

16 Mahler-Werfel, "Diary of Alma Maria," pp. 62–3, MWP.

Conception and Birth

On the first Sunday in May 1915, Alma reminded Gropius of their first encounter at Tobelbad. Although it was hardly the right day—they had met in June—to her the day was the day of their *Hochzeit*—that German word for the high point in a couple's life, their marriage. Nevertheless, the couple had corresponded over setting a time and place for a real marriage. Alma desperately wanted another child, and what we now call the "biological clock" was a factor, for she would turn thirty-six in August. She had also set aside—or repressed—her social superiority, humbling herself so that Gropius would have an easier time of persuading his mother to give her blessing to "Maria," as Gropius had come to prefer calling Alma by her middle name. The impasse for the elder Manon Gropius was that Alma to her was still capable of infidelity. Her son knew this risk, too; but he wrote from the Western Front and begged his mother to appreciate with him Alma's loyalty to her own freedom. "You are an artist and a very modern person," mother wrote son, "and your requirements are very different from mine." Despite having what she called an "old-fashioned heart," she promised to see his choice in a wife from his point of view.[17]

With his next furlough, in late May and early June, Gropius and Alma met in Berlin, not only to win over the elder Manon, but to make Alma pregnant and marriage a point of honor for a German officer. Writing Gropius on June's full-moon night—the twenty-seventh—Alma told him she had had her period, but such an urgency and his mother's feelings were no longer contingent for marriage. Alma proposed meeting Gropius in Strasbourg to marry him in secret and live as his wife "incognito" there, as it was against military regulations. Eventually, the couple met in Berlin on August 18, 1915, at Registrar's Office III on Parochialstrasse. Beside the magistrate, the only attendees

---

17 Manon S. Gropius to Walter Gropius, April 24, 1915, quoted in Isaacs, *Walter Gropius*, VOL. 1, p. 141.

to the civil ceremony were the two needed witnesses Gropius found on the street—a stonemason and an infantryman. Then the newlyweds spent the rest of the day together. But a significant part of that day was hardly romantic. Since Gropius would soon return to the front, he and Alma visited a military supply store shortly after their wedding. As Gropius took his time examining and trying on pair after pair of riding boots, Alma, sickened by the smell of oiled Russia leather, rushed outside to get air. Fortunately, she found a bookseller and purchased a little journal, in which she had read a poem by a poet unfamiliar to her, Franz Werfel, one of the so-called Expressionists. The poem, "Der Erkennende" (The Enlightened), left her spellbound in the August heat, for it touched on what she felt, especially having to get away from Gropius, albeit temporarily. "And the word that prevails is: Alone!" the third stanza began, "When we are burning together helpless. / I know one thing: mine is never and nothing. / My sole possession: being thus enlightened." Thankfully, however, Gropius finally finished in the shop and a night of lovemaking ensued in a hotel room and continued once more aboard the train to Frankfurt am Main, where the newlyweds parted. Sated, Alma continued on to Vienna, writing in her diary that "Golden days lie behind me"—and hoping that Gropius' child had been planted inside her at last. [18]

For Alma's birthday on August 31, her new husband sent her an onyx necklace, a Gropius family heirloom, which she dangled before her envious friends, including a baroness. Although she called Gropius by her new, girlish pet name for him, "Mutzi," the German equivalent of "kitty cat," and thanked him for the necklace, she began to reassume her identity as the widow of Gustav Mahler, in part to boost her new husband's career. For much of 1915, he had been courted by representatives of the Grand Duchy of Saxe-Weimar to head the Grand-Ducal

---

18 Mahler-Werfel, "Diary of Alma Maria," 1915, p. 80, MWP.

School of Arts and Crafts at Weimar, which had been closed due to the war. Gropius considered the offer, for he envisioned a new institution that combined the trades with fine arts into one mission. Alma encouraged Gropius in this venture. Given her reputation and experience in the musical and cultural life of Germany and Austria, she understood its political nature, its officialdom, and how to get her way. Alma made this clear during a dispute with Gropius, his mother, and the matter of *who is who*. "[T]he doors of the whole world, which are open to the name Mahler, will fly shut to the entirely unknown name, Gropius," she wrote thinking of her mother-in-law, who also saw herself as a proud widow, and Gropius, who was still only on this verge with so many unknowns now given the war. "If she perhaps ever thinks about that, *what* I gave up. Because I want a husband at my side [. . .] I know what you are and what you are to me, but for the world you are an unwritten page.—She should listen to a symphony for once, then she will—*perhaps* understand more—although I put little faith in her judgment. *I* stand above all [. . .] the time will come to tell her while 10000-wise privy councilors stroll about—there was just *one* Gustav Mahler and there is just one—Alma—too."[19]

As Christmas approached, Alma looked forward to her husband's next long furlough. Being canny about her ovulations, which came toward the end of the month, the time would be opportune for the making of a child. For Alma, however, this involved more than just the animal operation of sex. On this, Gropius read an extraordinary admission from a woman who made love with the eye of a missionary, eugenicist, and artist-mother schooled too in acquired characteristics vis-à-vis Paul Kammerer. "[T]he umbilical cord is something I find horrible," she wrote when her mother-in-law had crossed her in Gropius' last letter. "I only respect spiritual relations [. . .]. We are not

19 Alma Mahler to Walter Gropius, undated [September 1915], quoted in Isaacs, *Walter Gropius*, VOL. 1, pp. 156–7.

fabrications of our parental stock, from somewhere something new is added, something that nobody knows about—the entelechy. Every individuum is new and unique and I would prefer to think that a soul floating in the universe looks for a container, called a body, then to have to think of my origin in an ugly, dirty belly. The emphasis on the word 'mother' in your mother's letter is disgusting to me."[20] And what did Gropius make of the obscure word *entelechy*—which Alma would have known or assumed he understood as she did—a vital force that directs an organism toward perfection. The term goes back to Aristotle and is refined by many others over centuries and called other things, such as the "will to live" (Schopenhauer), the "will to power" (Nietzsche), and "élan vital" (Bergson) by Alma's day. It was more than simple "animal magnetism" and "life force"—to Kammerer it was "formative energy" and it drove evolution.

To release this formative potency, Gropius had to be suitably aroused and Alma did not wait for him to arrive in Vienna. In one of her undated letters from early December, she described how she would conduct their first reunion since August. "I will sink to the ground before you, remain on my knees, begging you to stick that sacred member with your hands inside my mouth and I will employ every finesse, every refinement that I have learned for you so as to give you a furious [unreadable]," she promised. "Then, when you become wild, you will carefully tear me apart on the bed that is so wide, as we are long together—flowers are in the room and candles burn and I lie there inside and torture myself while you make me wait, always make me wait."[21]

The waiting came to an end during the last week of 1915. Walter Gropius spent his Christmas leave with Alma in Vienna. Back in the Vosges, he wrote his mother about the warmth and intimacy, the love

---

20 Alma Mahler to Walter Gropius, undated [September 1915], BHA.

21 Alma Mahler to Walter Gropius, undated [November or December 1915], quoted in Hilmes, *Witwe im Wahn*, p. 167.

and joy he had experienced with Alma. He gave her a pretty picture, indicating that he had, indeed, encountered Alma in the above manner. If all went well, and using Naegele's Rule, a due date could be calculated in thirty-eight weeks in September, under the sign of Virgo. "I hope that I am BLESSED," she wrote in her diary on New Year's Day 1916.[22] Yet crossed out in its transcript is a dream she recorded, in which she was a little girl and her father still alive. He told her that the emperor was coming and asked her what he should tell his highness when he asked for her name. "You tell him my name is Pereat Schindler," she said in the dream.[23] *Pereat* came from the well-known Latin motto of Franz Josef's father, Ferdinand I—"Let there be justice, though the world perish." Alma took the dream to mean that her name was *Perish* and a curse to others. It reinforced her conceit that Mahler, her daughter Maria, her father, and others had died from their contact with her.

When Alma missed her period at the end of January, she informed her mother-in-law who quickly congratulated her and invited Alma to Berlin—but Alma, with her "*souverän*" tone as Gropius described it, refused the offer. Alma during the winter and spring of 1916 preferred the diversions of Vienna, her salon, and a new male admirer. Her relationship with the Austrian writer and jurist Albert von Trentini was chaste but still passionate, such that during this time the idea of Gropius "faded" in and out of her. On Semmering, where Alma spent much of the spring and summer, she wrote letters that could be tender and angry from page to page. When he asked her to oversee a Portland cement veranda that he had designed for Haus Mahler, Alma took umbrage at being asked about enough steel rebar or whether the porch had been expanded to the dining room window. "This is written by an 'architect'—or one who would like to pass himself off as one to his

22 Mahler-Werfel, "Diary of Alma Maria," New Year's, 1916, p. 86, MWP.
23 Mahler-Werfel, "Diary of Alma Maria," New Year's, 1916, p. 86, MWP.

pregnant wife—during a war," she wrote in a tantrum, "whose house is 1000 m high. I would be quite mad assuming such an undertaking *now* [. . .]. Open doors—a parade—dirt—strange men in the house—great expense—but above *all*—a danger of becoming over-exhausted. [. . .] As dear as your letters were—this has *really* shocked me and I have to think you lack in respect. *Considerateness* is something that I expect of you. Otherwise I could have just as well married a German poet, a *sheep in the clouds* that is."[24]

In a matter of days, or even hours, Alma's regard for and her tone with Gropius changed when her thoughts turned to the child she carried. "This GLORIOUS time of pregnancy," she wrote as she neared the end of the second trimester. "But I simply long for delivery; it will give me some new revelation. It must again bring a new, incredible, enormous moment of ecstasy into my life. And the pain—that which ONLY women experience, must disappear as well. It can be this and not otherwise. Everything can be seen as joy. I am becoming a world clairvoyant."[25]

By early September Alma had returned to her apartment in Vienna for her confinement. Soon Gropius arrived on a two-week furlough to await his child's birth. The expectant mother, however, did not go into labor, and the father returned to the front. Alma wrote in her diary how much she had wanted to put a baby in Gropius' arms, while he, from the battlefield, poignantly wrote his mother that this "child shows no wish to appear in this world gone mad."[26]

Two weeks later, in October, Alma wondered if something had gone wrong, for the child that was now nearly a month late. She could

---

24 Alma Mahler to Walter Gropius, undated [spring 1916], quoted in Isaacs, *Walter Gropius*, VOL. 1, pp. 160–1.

25 Mahler-Werfel, "Diary of Alma Maria," June 11, 1916, p. 87, MWP.

26 Walter Gropius to Manon S. Gropius, October 5, 1916, quoted in Isaacs, *Walter Gropius*, VOL. 1, p. 168.

feel it kicking and feared that the fetus would run out of room, forcing her to get a caesarian, which, before sulfa drugs, risked death due to sepsis. Her attending physician—Dr. Wilhelm Knöpfelmacher of the Vienna Academy of Medicine—tried to allay her fears, for it was not unusual for a pregnancy to last forty weeks. He had served as the pediatrician for Alma's first two children and was an expert on an incredible range of childhood diseases, from hydrocephalus to poliomyelitis (about which he had published original research on how the virus spread in monkeys). Despite his assurances, however, Alma took a sharp object, probed herself vaginally, and either cut or punctured herself to make it look like she had hemorrhaged and so "prod [the doctor] into a surgical delivery," meaning his return with a nurse to assist, mechanical dilators, and forceps to pull the fetus from the womb.

Alma described the child's birth on October 5 as difficult and painful, taking hours until she delivered a dark-haired child whose hair had time to grow unusually long in the womb. Its presence intensified her maternal feelings to the point of being, perhaps, mildly erotic, especially when she breastfed the infant girl for the first time. "[H]er whole asthenic personality," Alma remembered as she regarded Manon Gropius for the first time, "her hesitancy, her exaggerated quiet, were already present at her birth." Indeed, she felt herself "falling in love."[27]

Gropius received a telegram from Alma that he had a daughter. As soon as he got a two-day leave in mid-October, he returned to Vienna overnight, riding in the cab of a locomotive pulling a freight train. What happened next was likely based on a real fear of contagion given the rampant epidemics and venereal disease of wartime. It may have been postpartum depression, too. In any event, it set a strange and ironic precedent for what Gropius would suffer later. After dashing from the railroad station, after being led by the maid to the nursery, he found Alma warding him away from the swaddling table on which the

27 Mahler-Werfel, *And the Bridge is Love*, p. 220.

infant girl lay. Alma made him leave the room. "When I saw him, grimy, unshaven, his uniform and face blackened with railroad soot," Alma wrote later, "I felt as though I were seeing a murderer. Only after long pleading did I allow him to glance at his child from a distance."[28] All Gropius could see was that the baby had his dark brown hair and green eyes.

In deference to Gropius, Alma had converted to his Lutheran faith. Thus, their child was baptized in Vienna's Evangelical Church on Christmas Day 1916. She was christened Alma Manon Anna Justine Caroline Gropius. Breaking conventional German naming patterns—and indicative of her mother's sense of eminence—her first name honored Alma. The child's second name—which became her "call name" (*Rufname*)—honored both Gropius' mother and sister and, perhaps, Alma's dead daughter since Manon is a French diminutive of Maria. Her other names included her maternal grandmother's, her half-sister's, and even Mahler's favorite sister. In time, however, Manon ceased to go by her given name, but rather by the name Alma took from Gropius, "Mutzi," for Manon's feline qualities, such as her slender form and green eyes, and for *Mutwille*, meaning mischievous or wanton. (In regard to her father, Alma likely meant the latter.)

Only the parents, godparents, and Alma's family attended the ceremony. "Pastor von Zimmerman gave a dull, empty baptism speech, but that never lessened the serenity for us," Gropius wrote his mother in Berlin. "The room was trimmed very beautifully. An abundance of white lilies, just candlelight from a chandelier, and a Christmas tree. Alma looked lovely in white and the little one behaved herself with such knowingness, as though she already understood that something going on with her was important and interesting."[29]

28 Mahler-Werfel, *And the Bridge is Love*, p. 89.
29 Walter Gropius to Manon S. Gropius [January 1917], quoted in Isaacs, *Walter Gropius*, VOL. 1, p. 171.

To reward Alma for giving birth to such a beautiful child, Gropius gave her a painting, Edvard Munch's *Summer Night on the Strand* (1902). Its current owner, Carl Reininghaus, a wealthy Austrian art collector, had known Alma since girlhood and was a frequent guest of her salon. Knowing Alma's love for this painting, he graciously sold it at a price Gropius could easily afford. Two servants carried the seascape to her apartment with a note that at last the "right reason" for her to have it had come. As darkly beautiful as its swirling blues and yellows were—Alma loved it for the way it teased one's inherent death wish—the painting's ambivalent motif of a setting sun and turbulent waters could hardly darken Gropius' joyous vision of his new daughter.

From Vienna and from the field, he contemplated her beauty, what he had at last been allowed to hold in his arms. "This child is our sun," he told his mother. "She is *pretty as a picture*, having these large, ever-changing intelligent eyes that already peer into the world aware, these little hands with long, slim aristocratic fingers and long, pillow-soft limbs, hair a hand's length, dark brown. You are quite right, she is my spitting image, only the eyes are Schindlerish."[30] In March 1917, after seeing Manon again, he continued with his impressions. "I am already in love with her. At first I did not recognize her again, she is so changed after 3 months of not being together. She lies right next to me in the carriage and sings endless songs to herself like a twittering little bird. We think she has a cheerful disposition and filled with vitality. While she's picture pretty, it's so funny how much she still looks like me."[31]

---

30 Walter Gropius to Manon S. Gropius [December 1916], quoted in Isaacs, *Walter Gropius*, VOL. 1, pp. 170–1.

31 Walter Gropius to Manon S. Gropius, March 26, 1917, quoted in Isaacs, *Walter Gropius*, VOL. 1, pp. 171–2.

Infancy and Onkel Werfel

Manon Gropius in photographs from the summer of 1917 already looked like a child who would be walking and talking soon, especially with her luxuriant dark hair. Like her father, her mother was also enchanted by her daughter and in a sensual and metaphysical way given one of her diary entries from that time. "No one has any idea how I love this creature," she wrote. "To be direct, I am carnally [*sinnlich*] falling in love with her. I would like to kiss her hands and feet all day, for I would hardly dare kiss her on her little mouth. A child is the ultimate purpose of existence [*Dasein*]. And again and again the Beginning."[32] Among the photographs, Alma had her daughters Manon and Anna—who already had breasts—pose naked at Haus Mahler. The series of *Jugendstil*-like images, which were also taken the following summer, include two older, unidentified teenage girls—possibly the daughters of Lilly Lieser, whose summer villa was nearby. The poses are mildly erotic and suggest the Symbolist allegories of Gustav Klimt and like painters—indeed, Alma's father had taken such pictures of her and her sister Grete. The older girls could be Graces and Manon a new, fourth one. All wear wreaths of alpine flowers on their heads. Today's objections—abuse, pedophilia, and so on—were unknown to Vienna's cultural elite. (The writer Peter Altenberg decorated his hotel room with images he collected of naked, nubile girls.) And Alma would hardly be seen as a sociopathic mother, for letting children go naked served a healthful, hygienic purpose in the mountains of Lower Austria. Doctors recommended *Luft-*, *Licht-*, or *Heliotherapie*—that is, being naked in air, light, and sun, and performing normal activities. Such a regimen maintained health and one's natural resistance to such urban diseases as tuberculosis, polio, and those neurasthenic ailments that so often affected girls and young women of this period.

32 Mahler-Werfel, "Diary of Alma Maria," 1916–1917, p. 102, MWP.

That said, Alma's salon in 1917 included an erotologist, Franz Blei, a translator of Claudel and the editor of private magazines, such as *The Opals*, *Hyperion,* and *Amethyst*, in which he had published the work of Aubrey Beardsley. Interspersed with the sexually charged content were poems and stories by newcomers such as Robert Walser and Franz Kafka. And with his reputation, Blei lorded over his own corner of Vienna's most important literary gathering place, the Café Central, the so-called *Schachhochschule*—Chess School—for its many tables and players, in the Herrengasse. There—often in the company of his lovely lesbian daughter, the actress Sibylla—Blei befriended Robert Musil, Hermann Broch, and other talented young writers. A gifted and monopolistic conversationalist, with an encyclopedic memory for important names and learned concepts, he made a perfect guest for Alma—and Gropius, too. When he was on furlough, he found he could hardly get a word in edgewise and compared people's fascination in Blei to lead poisoning, playing on the German word for lead—*Blei.*

During a stay at Haus Mahler in August or September 1917—around the time when Alma had made photographs of her nude children—Blei tried to flatter Alma with various "declarations of love," which to her lacked any feeling. He was out of his element in the mountains and away from the cafe life of Vienna. However, in the course of their talk, the thought occurred to him that the poet Franz Werfel was back from the front. Like Blei, Werfel now worked as a propagandist for the Military Press Bureau in Vienna (which also employed Rainer Maria Rilke and Stefan Zweig, among many others). Alma was not only intrigued by the news of Werfel. It meant something to her personally, and she performed for Blei the song she had composed from Werfel's poem, the one she had found in Berlin two years before. Naturally, Alma agreed to Blei's offer to bring Werfel to her apartment when it could be arranged upon her return to Vienna.

In mid-November, Franz Blei and Franz Werfel met at Elisabethstrasse 22 for tea. Alma herself had just returned from offering her condolences to the German ambassador's wife, whose little boy had died from a phenol enema (a solution of diluted carbolic acid) that, if not diluted properly, burns through the intestines in a matter of hours. Alma, having lost her firstborn to a similar botched procedure—that is, an *iatrogenic artifact*—knew all too well how much the mother of the boy had suffered and had little desire for conversation or for meeting someone new with her own grief stirred up.

While Blei's long black coat reminded Alma of Pater Filucius, an amusing but disreputable Jesuit cartoon character, Werfel was hardly impressive to her. He was younger, short, bald, pudgy, and obviously Jewish. His war record was hardly heroic. As a corporal in the Austro-Hungarian army, he had served as a telephone operator for an artillery regiment on the Eastern Front. He saw little direct action and used much of his time to write poetry. Transferred to the Italian front, Werfel suffered two broken legs after falling from a funicular. The accident soon proved beneficial for his writing and his love life, too, for he had fallen in love with a nurse, Gertrud Spirk. How much of this backstory Alma already knew came from Blei and, at least, the newspapers and their feuilletons, for Werfel already had two collections of poetry, *Der Weltfeund* (The World Friend, 1911) and *Wir Sind* (We Are, 1913). These had been bestsellers for his publisher, Kurt Wolff, and few discussions of German poetry could hardly exclude his rising reputation. He already knew many writers throughout Central Europe. Werfel was from Prague, where he had been a close friend of Max Brod and Franz Kafka. He maintained friendships with Karl Kraus, Martin Buber, Else Lasker-Schüler, and many other prominent German—and mostly Jewish—writers. When he met Alma, he had translated Euripedes' *The Trojan Women* (1917) for the Viennese stage and recently conducted a series of literary matinees at the New Vienna Theater with Blei and his daughter.

Werfel did very little work for the Military Press Bureau. He tended to sleep late in his room at the Hotel Graben, down the hall from Peter Altenberg and his gallery of prepubescent girls and child prostitutes. The latter's company Werfel enjoyed too when not at the Café Central, where he might have felt more at home than in Alma's salon. But Werfel, from a wealthy family of assimilated Jews—his father manufactured gloves—had gravitated toward a brand of socialism called neo-Catholicism, had formally endorsed what he called the "Christian mission," and seemed to his Jewish friends to be on the point of conversion. Werfel also had grown disaffected with his dissolute cafe existence. He was ripe for a major life change and his meeting Alma Mahler Gropius allowed for it.

The tea and the evening that followed proved unusually successful. At first, Werfel expounded on the virtues of social democracy and communism for the Russian Revolution had occurred the week before. Alma saw this as the idealistic rubbish that so many younger men proclaimed. Gradually, however, Werfel, who was eleven years her junior, found his stride with the hostess, becoming ever "more eminent, open, and clear."[33] Others showed up and witnessed his performance, including the art historians Hans Tietze and his wife Erica Tietze-Conrat, and the young Swiss painter Johannes Itten. Blei looked surprisingly "threadbare beside Werfel" and left Alma's apartment early as Werfel moved away from politics to his more natural subjects, humanitarianism and Christianity. "How can I be happy," he asked rhetorically, "when somewhere a creature suffers?" To Alma, this sounded as pleasantly deluded and endearing as Gustav Mahler did. That Werfel, like Mahler, was estranged from his origins appealed to Alma too. And when Werfel gave a dramatic reading in her red salon from Arnold Schoenberg's *Jacob's Ladder*, she had all the confirmation she needed.

---

33 This and other quotations in this passage are from Mahler-Werfel, "Diary of Alma Maria," 1916–1917, pp. 98–9, MWP.

Werfel looked up from reciting the oratorio and cried out, "Now I know the entire conflict of this person. He is a Jew! The one who suffers, a Jew suffering in *himself*."

Over the next weeks Alma overlooked Werfel's comically short stature, his fingers yellowed from chain smoking, and his bad teeth stained brown from drinking so much coffee. The only thing of physical beauty about him was a "Goethean forehead," which pardoned his being a "bow-legged, fat Jew with thick lips and liquid slit-eyes." She invited Werfel to come and see her alone, too, and on one of these occasions he was given a rare privilege, that of meeting another man's offspring before making love to his wife behind his back. This ritual seemed important to Alma, almost like a test that Werfel seemed to have passed with just a few nice words anyone could have said, to make up for the test he could only dismally fail, that of being Aryan.

"When I first saw her, she was hardly a year old," he wrote years later in Manon's necrology, recalling when Alma led him into the nursery. "She already had that long dark, wonderfully full hair by then. She could not yet talk. But when you asked her, 'How do dogs bark?' she would go 'baff-baff,' and likewise, when you asked about a pony, 'trrrab-trrrab.' I said to her mother, as we stood over her baby bed's bars, 'You have a beautiful child there' . . . Manon watched me with her calm eyes, in which there already was this observant shimmer."[34]

Like Corporal Werfel, Lieutenant Gropius no longer served in the front lines. He headed a German army canine unit in which he and his assistants taught carrier pigeons, dogs, and their handlers how to convey messages from one trench to another. By the autumn of 1917, Gropius'

34 Franz Werfel, "Manon," in *Erzählungen aus zwei Welten* [Tales from Two Worlds], VOL. 3 (Frankfurt am Main: S. Fischer, 1954), p. 392. First published in English translation in *The Commonweal*, 1941 (May): 31–4. All quotes from this document are translated from the German original unless otherwise noted.

reputation as a canine instructor earned him a temporary assignment with the Austro-Hungarian army in Italy. Alma, however, rather than feel relieved that her husband would now be out of harm's way, felt humiliated and likely forced Gropius to assume other duties. "Since I know that I don't have to be writing the address for the superintendent of a dog school," she wrote, "I can write once more. Also, I did not marry a person named Kohn. And I beg you—if you have to touch some *dirty* animal anywhere, I would rather you not write me if you don't have the opportunity to wash yourself thorough beforehand. It fills me with *horror* that *you* are so close to such animals."[35] Her anti-Semitic taunt is all the more incredible given that some of her antipathy for Gropius resulted from his Christmas furlough and how his presence had interrupted the pleasure she had in Werfel's company. "On my KNEES I thank *my* God," she wrote in her diary. "ONLY THIS SUSTAINS ME. ONLY this!"[36]

In mid-December, at a dinner party given in honor of his return to Vienna, Gropius was introduced to Alma's new friend, Franz Werfel. At first this young poet from Prague hardly seemed a threat. To Gropius he was just another ornament in his wife's salon, and one more entertaining than Blei. Werfel had a beautiful tenor voice and sang selections from Charpentier's comic opera *Louise*, Wagner's *Die Meistersinger*, and arias from his favorite Verdi operas as Alma accompanied him on piano. And though she found Werfel's exhibitionism sometimes annoying, Gropius, despite being her Aryan hero with an Iron Cross and trim mustache, looked and sounded tedious to her, like a man who should not be opening his mouth. Alma felt "ashamed" to be his and living in a state of "spiritual adultery" with Werfel.[37]

---

35 Alma Mahler to Walter Gropius, undated [January 1918], quoted in Isaacs, *Walter Gropius*, VOL. 1, p. 175.
36 Mahler-Werfel, "Diary of Alma Maria," 1916–1917, p. 99, MWP.
37 Ibid., "Der Urlaub des Walter Gropius" [The Furlough of Walter Gropius], "Diary of Alma Maria", p. 107, MWP.

Amazingly, as Christmas approached, the family of Walter Gropius posed for a photograph. He wore his uniform, Alma had on a long string of pearls, and Manon had been dressed in a white pinafore. The girl looks on wide-eyed, presumably at the studio photographer coaxing her to smile. She grasps her mother's pearls. Alma, in profile, looks at her daughter while above them, leaning over protectively, is the father. *Gropius is the only one smiling*. Whether it was forced is unknown. Alma's affections, however, were. In bed, she felt degraded by her husband, who, still unaware of Werfel's inroads, continued to see Oskar Kokoschka as a rival and made Alma sell her paintings by the artist, including her favorite portrait, to the German industrialist Karl Ernst Osthaus. Gropius only let her keep Kokoschka's painted fans, his allegorical history of his tortuous affair with Alma. Even so, Gropius burned one in a fireplace to appease his jealousy.

When Gropius' leave came to an end on December 29, Alma rejoiced as she heard his steps receding in the stairwell. Later in the day, he returned home, for all trains had been cancelled due to a snowstorm, and found something far colder in his wife. She had been looking forward to attending a rehearsal of Mahler's Symphony no. 8, where she hoped to see Werfel. Now Gropius made what seemed to him a reasonable request, to attend the concert with her. But Alma snapped at him, telling him she had no ticket. When Gropius insisted, he was forced to walk alongside Alma's carriage through the deep snow, begging her for permission to go, which she denied him.

Later, upon her return, she found Gropius outside her apartment waiting in the snow. The next day, when he at last boarded a train for France, he wired Alma a plea from the telegraph office at the border—"Shatter the ice in your face!"—his paraphrase of the closing verse of a poem Werfel had recited in their presence.

In early February 1918 Alma realized she was pregnant by either Gropius or Werfel, and in keeping with the pretense of being a married woman, she informed Gropius' mother that she would be a grandmother again in September. Since Alma could not get pregnant twice, she and Werfel now slept together regularly. She let herself be seen in his company, like a couple, and took an active interest in bettering Werfel's career and transitioning him from cafe to high society, for she found his lifestyle of hotel rooms and companions—from dubious intellectuals to working-class prostitutes—objectionable. Enjoying her attentions, Werfel complied as much as he backslid, and he at least avoided the embarrassment of a breach of promise by confessing his infidelity to Fraulein Spirk.

Gropius had long ago prepared himself for his wife to exercise her freedom, but he hardly suspected it would be with Werfel. Gropius also had to worry about surviving the war. In late March, freed of the Russian front by the Treaty of Brest-Litovsk, the German army launched the largest military offensive in human history to deliver a massive blow to the Allies in France. Nearly six weeks later, in mid-May, Gropius' involvement in what turned out to be another stalemate ended on the Soissons–Reims line. A French heavy artillery shell crashed through the roof of the town hall in which his regiment was headquartered and he was buried alive as the first floor collapsed into the basement. Covered in plaster dust, pinned under oak beams and broken masonry, with dead bodies rotting around him in the spring heat, Gropius was not dug out until a passing patrol heard his pistol shots. After a month of treatment in a field hospital, he was sent to Vienna to be nearer to his family, then on to a spa near Breitenstein to convalesce.

During this time Werfel remained in the background. Gropius enjoyed what had long been denied him—a semblance of family life. Alma came to see him in the hospital. Like a changed woman, she comforted him. Alma also encouraged him and offered advice on how to staff the school he would establish at Weimar as soon as he was discharged from the army, which seemed soon given the Allies' counter-offensive and rumors that Germany would sue for peace. Alma also brought Manon with her (albeit carried by the nurse, Miss Maud). The sight of his daughter, while it gave him pleasure, also reminded him of how powerless he was, in the face of the defeatism, the collapsing economy and food shortages, and the toll this took on his self-esteem. Visiting Haus Mahler, he was struck by the irony of its name and the sight of his daughter playing there. "[M]y pride can no longer suffer it," he wrote his mother, "that my child will be raised on money that another man made"—meaning that the dead Mahler was more Manon's breadwinner than her own father.[38] Gropius also had to consider fatherhood again, for his wife was five months pregnant.

Alma, as she did when she carried Manon, preferred to stay at Haus Mahler in the spring and summer. She only came into the city to see her mother, shop for what little food there was, and to see Gropius, who had been transferred to a military hospital in Grinzing. On Semmering, Alma could live somewhat comfortably. She sent Anna into the nearby forests to hunt mushrooms, including large and tasty chanterelles. These she handed over to the cook, Agnes Hvizd, who made ersatz sausage from the mushrooms with powdered birch bark. This was then fried in margarine and served with polenta. Alma also procured potatoes from local farmers or traded the chanterelles for tinned meat. Given the photographs from this time, Manon looks happy and healthy, playing with her Steiff bear on the sundeck at Haus Mahler and seemingly untouched by the vicissitudes of the war. "Alma and I [are] perpetually, mutually jealous of her," Gropius wrote his mother in July. "Every instinct now awakens in her. She is wild and innately alive [*urlebendig*]. She seems filled with gifts, and Alma's

38 Walter Gropius to Manon S. Gropius, June 22, 1918, quoted in Isaacs, *Walter Gropius*, VOL. 1, p. 179.

upbringing [of her] is admirable. I know this child is being fussed over wonderfully well."[39]

Franz Werfel, meanwhile, had remained in contact with his lover, waiting for when he could safely be invited to Haus Mahler. He now lived in a large, spacious apartment on Boltzmanngasse in Vienna, with a view of a park, the Spanish Hospital, and its chapel. He had been sharing it with the editorial offices of Franz Blei's neo-Catholic magazine, *Summa*. Although he did not lack for prostitutes—Vienna was now teeming with streetwalkers, a trade swelling with war widows and those who had lost a fiancé, euphemistically called "friendless women"—Werfel had tried to "save" himself for Alma and took the morning train to Breitenstein on Saturday, July 27. Although Blei had told Werfel that it would be amoral of him to have intercourse with a pregnant woman, Werfel disregarded the warning. He had written a verse play inspired by Alma as a mother goddess and her gravid condition not only made that real, it had become highly inspiring if not erotic for his feelings of potency as an artist and man. Even the early newspapers pointed the way that day, with German tanks rolling unopposed across No Man's Land, each decorated with skulls-and-crossbones, and firing their erection-like cannons.

Werfel arrived at Haus Mahler around noon. Alma still had guests—Emmy Redlich, the wife of the Austrian sugar refiner, Fritz Redlich, and their teenage daughter. Werfel would have to be careful not to show any obvious or unseemly affection, even though Alma had the cheek to give him the guest bedroom next to hers. Their plan was to tire Frau Redlich such that she would go to bed early. Thus, despite being seven months' pregnant, Alma, Werfel, and her guests made the strenuous hike up the Kreuzberg, whose summit offered panoramic views. Then, after supper, Alma and Anna played the entire second

39 Walter Gropius to Manon S. Gropius, July 17, 1918, quoted in Isaacs, *Walter Gropius*, VOL. 1, p. 181.

movement of Mahler's Symphony no. 8 on the harmonium. Instead of wearing Frau Redlich down, however, the music inspired her and she spent nearly two hours talking to Alma. Eventually, the women retired for the night, and Haus Mahler grew quiet, and Werfel stole into Alma's room. What happened there is generally known from the "secret diary" that Werfel kept and Alma's diary.[40] Instead of being gentle with her, Werfel behaved like an incubus ("I did not spare her") through the night, while the rain poured and a strange bird sang ominously.

Later, on the morning of July 28, Werfel woke to Maud Turner knocking on his door and whispering that Alma was bleeding. He needed to fetch a doctor. So began Werfel's "evil day." It became a signature event in his life that initially resembled a postmodern black comedy yet worthy of the silent movies: Werfel running through wet alpine meadows; Werfel bringing a coughing tubercular doctor; Alma hemorrhaging in her bed; a teenage Anna Mahler having the presence of mind to call her stepfather for help; a wounded Gropius sporting his Iron Cross First Class and escorting a gynecologist from Vienna; Werfel watching them unseen as he waited for a train going in the opposite direction; Alma adamantly refusing to be operated on by the famous gynecologist because his blood-stained hands looked like those of a meat cutter; and back to Werfel, again, carousing in the Café Central and promising God he would swear off cigarettes and whores if Alma lived.

When Alma had at last been stabilized, Gropius drove her to the train station. She lay in the back of a wagon and, before departing, bid Maud to bring Manon in order to say good-bye. As a cold, mistral-like

---

40 The narrative here is drawn from Chapter 6, "The Diary of Franz Werfel" in Mahler-Werfel, *And the Bridge Is Love,* pp. 102–22; *Mein Leben* (Frankfurt am Main: Fischer, 1963), pp. 93–117; and "Diary of Alma Maria," undated supplement to 1918, "Der Sommer der all diesen Ereignissen vorangegangen Jahr war der böseste [The summer of all these events of foregoing year was the worst]." MWP.

wind blew from the mountains, Alma wanted to say, "Put something warm on her." What stopped her was the possibility that she might die. "Who would say it tomorrow," she remembered thinking, "and the day after tomorrow, and perhaps forever?" This feeling of mortality was all the more reinforced by the horrific nature of the first train to Vienna and the railway car in which she found was the only one in which she could lie down in privacy with the doctor and her husband—a *Leichenwagen*, a corpse car, used to transport the war dead. After her confinement in the Löw Sanatorium, her doctors performed several operations with the objective of preventing the fetus from being born dead or two months premature. The procedures, however, failed and on August 4, Alma gave birth to a baby boy, tiny but still viable.

On the rainy evening of August 8, Helene Berg, the wife of Alban Berg, arrived in Breitenstein. Though reputed to be the illegitimate child of Emperor Franz Josef, Helene served as a kind of lady-in-waiting for Alma to ensure the latter's favor, for Mahler's widow had inherited his protégés among Vienna's young composers. Thus Alma knew she could wire the younger woman from the hospital and have her stay with her daughters at Haus Mahler and assist Miss Maud.

Helene found Manon asleep, looking very much like the sketches Anna made of her sister. Anna herself was now sick from running errands in the cold and rain during her mother's crisis. After settling into her room, Helene woke Manon. Since she could not have children herself, she had attached herself to the little girl and kept a photograph of her hanging over her bed, which she kissed at night. Helene was quickly charmed by how the girl recognized her and how she came to her so trustingly to patter away with what words she knew. She lifted Manon onto her lap and wrote her husband a letter—its text interrupted several times by the lines and circles she let the two-year-old draw with a pencil.

Helene took advantage of having Manon to herself at Haus Mahler, especially after Miss Maud had gone to the city to help with the new baby. Helene took the two girls for walks. At one point they visited the Lieser villa, where one of the daughters let them in to see the artwork, the music room—and to use the telephone so that Alma could talk to her daughters from her hospital room in Vienna. In the days that followed, Helene wrote her husband again, giving the longest documentation of Manon's existence thus far, a pastiche of the woes and pleasures of babyhood. "This child is delectable," Helene began. "In the morning she comes to thump on my door and scream with a rather uncannily loud voice, 'Aunt Lene.' She is terribly affectionate: Yesterday afternoon she woke with an incredible yell! 'My pretty ball, give!' Apparently she had been dreaming about it. In the evening she wet her panties. Maud disappeared with her. Suddenly [Anna and I] heard a heart-rending scream. Then it didn't stop—I went to have a look. She is sitting on the pottie, with tears streaming. Maud is seething with rage. She had spanked her, her popo is all red. At first the child could only weep over and over again Auntie! Auntie! She pressed her little head against me and sobbed. I whimpered along for it hurt me just as much. This child doesn't cry like any other, wicked, or spiteful. There is this touching expression of profound pain—that is irresistible. When she could speak at last in trembling voice, 'Auntie—peepee—popo—booboo—Maudy, be good!' and 'Make nice-nice to it!' I took her with me. But she is so sad—such that she doesn't want to play. I sing for her (normally she sings along with me) but she says, 'no—no—no' and remains quiet and serious until she goes to bed. Supper! Noodles with tinned meat and peas."[41]

---

41 Helene Berg to Alban Berg, August 10, 1918, in Martina Steiger, "*Immer wieder werden mich thätige Geister verlocken*": *Alma Mahler-Werfels Briefe an Alban Berg und seine Frau* ["Again and again am I tempted by dynamic intellects": Alma Mahler-Werfel's Letters to Alban Berg and his Wife] (Vienna: Seifert, 2008), p. 325.

Broken Home

The day Manon turned two, October 5, 1918, the German Reich, Austria-Hungary, and Turkey requested Woodrow Wilson, president of the United States—the land of "Barnum & Bailey" as her father once heard a German general joke—to negotiate a general ceasefire. If the shortages of flour, sugar, butter, and eggs had made buying a birthday cake from Demel's or one of Vienna's other famous patisseries impossible, Alma would have been resourceful in serving something sweet on Manon's special day. And among the celebrants would have been her yet unnamed, unbaptized baby brother, known only as "Bubi" and, perhaps, his real father, the man she was encouraged to call "Onkel Franzl"—that is, "Little Franz," Alma's pet name for the man who virtually lived under the same roof now.

Gropius could not be with his daughter on her second birthday. He had been recalled to active duty—and he knew the truth about his wife's adultery. The revelation came in late August when he surprised Alma in the middle of a telephone conversation and heard her hurriedly ring off with the familiar German *you* (*du*). When she confessed that it was Werfel, Gropius now understood why the other man had taken such an inordinate interest in her health and that of the baby boy. Jealous and insulted that Alma could love Werfel, whom even she saw as a dissolute cafe poet and an apostate Jew, Gropius attempted to confront Werfel and consulted a lawyer. When he was transferred to the military hospital at Franzensbad—ironically and literally "Franz's bath"—Gropius felt his anger cool. He immersed himself in Werfel's poems and his *Trojan Women*. Knowing that Werfel had the advantage of being in Vienna, Gropius wrote a conciliatory letter in September. "I the one *absent* greet you the one *present*," he began. "With affection and, healed of hate, I hover over you. I absorb your spirit inside me. I read your works and am ever closer to you. In this way, anger will lose its every power over us. Three times death has passed over me, in battle, with the birth, and in the terrible moment of knowing. You have a part in all of it. Your soul's tenons [*Seelenzinken*] are inseparably gripped in mine." And Gropius proposed that he and Werfel devote themselves to the woman who had transfigured their lives. "We *have found* our Messiah," he wrote. All that mattered was that this "divine woman" and their child lived—"All else pales in comparison."[42]

Alma, however, was not so generous in spirit to her husband. After he had been given another medical leave in October, he reopened his architectural practice in Berlin and headed to Vienna—in the midst of the Spanish influenza epidemic—with the intention of reuniting with his family. Alma, however, made him move out of her apartment and she refused to let him take Manon back to Weimar, where Gropius would soon take up his position as the director of his new school—what became the Bauhaus. She refused to listen to Gropius about Werfel's bad character and accepted his flirtation with revolution and the communist Red Guard, his being Jewish, and his perverse living conditions at his Boltzmanngasse apartment, a "furnished lie" (*Möbellüge*) that "screamed of vices," dominated by a big square sofa with a mattress to facilitate the "sexual escapades" (*Lustereien*) of Blei and his consorts.[43] That Werfel was such a lax person made him all the more a challenge to Alma—and once Gropius returned to Germany empty-handed, she could further groom Werfel as her "REAL" husband and the father of her son, given his obvious resemblance to Werfel. And along with this prize, Alma had Manon.

---

42 Walter Gropius to Franz Werfel, September 10, 1918, MWP. Gropius uses some wordplay in this letter to impart some lingering resentment. The word *Seelenzinken* is both poetic and explosively allusive, even anti-Semitic. The root word *Zinke* can mean a large nose. The verb *zinken* means to mark cards and to load dice, thus a play on Werfel's name, for the German word for dice is the rhyme *Würfel.*

43 Mahler-Werfel, "Diary of Alma Maria," [undated entries], 1918, p. 113–4, MWP.

After New Year's Day 1919, it could no longer be denied that the premature birth of Alma's son had left the infant convulsive. The child's head was growing faster than his body, so much so that the painter Johannes Itten volunteered a name in keeping with his Mazdaznan faith, that syncretic fusion of Zoroastrian ideas and a yogic-like regimen of breathing exercises, vegetarian diet, and body culture. In his black docent's cassock, with his thin "Egyptian mouth" according to Alma, Itten looked down at the child and, inspired by the infant's skull, christened the little boy "Tao"—which means *head* as it does *truth* and *path*. Such symbolism was hardly enough to console Alma, who threatened to end her life over the child in Itten's presence. "Your extraordinary life calls for an extraordinary ending," he told her. "Not suicide, though."[44] Nevertheless, Alma wanted such a way out, to even rejoin Mahler in the afterlife. "It would solve everything," she wrote, "leave Anna free and at ease, Manon to comfort Gropius, Werfel unburdened."[45]

Alma, however, soon returned to managing Werfel's life and career. So that he would not contract the Spanish flu, she sent him to Haus Mahler in early February. A valiant attempt was made to treat their son that winter, too. He received several cranial punctures to insert a metal shunt for draining the fluid that pressed on his brain, a delicate operation likely performed by Dr. Knöpfelmacher (who contributed to the early literature and treatment of hydrocephalus). On March 9, Alma and Werfel christened the little boy, Martin Johannes *Gropius*, for Alma was still married and Gropius was legally the baby's father.

Two days later Gropius came to see Alma to convince her to honor a promise she had made to bring to bring Manon to Germany in April and live with him as his wife in Weimar. Not only did he want a semblance of family life, the director of the Bauhaus also wanted

44 Quoted in Mahler-Werfel, *And the Bridge Is Love*, p. 130.

45 Mahler-Werfel, "Diary of Alma Maria," February 2, 1919, p. 136, MWP.

Alma's help and advice. Gropius also saw Alma as necessary for assembling a faculty. He wanted her confidante Johannes Itten to teach art and a unique, holistic introductory course (*Vorkurs*). Arnold Schoenberg and Alma's piano teacher, Hans Pfitzner, were seen as possible music teachers at the Bauhaus.

Alma had no desire to "vegetate" in Weimar or risk losing Manon to Gropius there, and so spent much of late March and April inventing one pretext after another to delay coming to Germany. Her letters and telegraphs to Gropius were full of questions (and accusations) about passports, how to ship her trunks and furniture, how she and her children would live in Weimar. Her trump card for remaining in Vienna was the world revolution she saw coming, given the recent declaration of a soviet republic in Hungary and the street-fighting in Germany between the Freikorps and Spartacists, right- and left-wing paramilitaries, respectively. When Gropius begged Alma for some kind of resolution, her bizarre response seemed more to uncoil than demand anything. Gropius was to give her Manon after Weimar and let her leave from the nearest transoceanic seaport. "There I would set sail on a steamship going around the world, turning my back on the coming barbarism [*Unkultur*]," she wrote in her diary, "cruising for years, now and then going ashore in distant, quiet parts of the globe, resting a while, then go on, and so, perhaps, find happiness and live a rich cultured existence, a world to trust, while stupid, sterile humanity gets into each other's matted hair."[46] Alma, too, entertained yet another fantasy, one even stranger, that of giving Oskar Kokoschka, now living and working in Dresden, her furniture, paintings, music, and other belongings. Her better memories and regrets for having parted ways with the painter had become a pleasant distraction from her problems with Gropius and Werfel. For his part, Kokoschka had moved on from

46 Mahler-Werfel, "Diary of Alma Maria," April 21, 1919, p. 143, MWP.

her, or so it seemed. He had a life-size and anatomically correct doll made, ostensibly to serve as a static model he could sketch and paint but also use as a "Dutch wife." Gossip, some of it fed by Kokoschka himself, had it that the doll, which he christened "Silent Woman," resembled Alma. On this point, Kokoschka was never satisfied with the doll's unshapely appearance. Eventually, he gave it a party and beheaded it.

So began Manon's life of living out of a suitcase, while being little more than her mother's chattel herself, when Alma left for Germany and the Bauhaus. Meanwhile, Manon's little brother remained in the Leopoldstadter hospital. So that Alma could depart with a clear conscience, she inquired with Dr. Knöpfelmacher about her infant son's prognosis in late April. Implicit in the guarded tenor of a note he sent, after a private consultation with her at her apartment, was the option of euthanizing Martin Johannes should it be necessary. "Dear madam, seldom have I been at a loss for words, but I must tell you that your poor child is beyond hope," he wrote. "Sadly, it cannot be saved, and I have not forgotten my promise. Just don't you, dear lady, suffer on top of everything else!"[47]

Two weeks later Alma and Manon boarded a train that would take them to Berlin first. The seamless express from one empire to the next no longer existed. "The emergence of the new Czech state astride the Vienna–Berlin route," Alma wrote, "added to the annoyances and delays, the vicissitudes and discomforts of the journey."[48] She also endured the strain of having to carry Manon all the way by herself, for Maud Turner had left her employ (with the war over, English servants now had that option).

Soon after the Gropius family's reunion came word of Martin Johannes's death on May 15. "If only I had died instead," Gropius said grimly, for he had been attached to the little boy even though he likely

47 Wilhelm Knöpfelmacher to Alma Mahler, April 25, 1919, MWP.
48 Mahler-Werfel, *And the Bridge Is Love*, p. 133.

knew it was not his child.[49] There is no evidence that the infant was given a funeral or even buried. One of the nightmares Alma records in her diary for 1919, however, suggests how the body was disposed of and the desire to undo it. She dreamed that she had fallen into a stream of sewage and filthy water into which she led her little boy with his head covered with streaming blond hair while her feet trailed bandages. In a later dream, she saw Martin Johannes in an open coffin surrounded by flowers with snow falling on his exposed face.[50] In any event, Manon was her father's only child once more.

Manon also remained a lonely child at Weimar. Her mother, at one point, stole away to Berlin to find Kokoschka. And though she stayed with her father for a month between May and June, Gropius spent most of his time establishing the Bauhaus—the House of Construction—which would not only teach theory but incorporate shops to produce the designs of its instructors and students. Thus, the heir to his *Geist*, his spirit and intellect, would only be further imprinted by Alma's dated Viennese tastes and prejudices. Indeed, Alma had no interest in her husband's work, in his "charts and graphs and calculations" that left her baffled and impatient.[51] However, at official occasions and receptions, she made a grand impression on Bauhaus "masters," such as the Swiss artist Paul Klee, whose virtuosity on the violin appealed to Alma.

Despite his responsibilities to the Bauhaus, Gropius did try once more to win Manon from Alma. He assumed that Alma wanted a divorce in order to marry Werfel. And her need to be free of having to care for Manon herself and the lack of a permanent nurse were also reasons for a tactful, rational conversation about custody. But when Gropius broached the subject, Alma's histrionics caused her to faint. Unable to revive her, a desperate Gropius called a doctor who lived in

49 Quoted in Mahler-Werfel, *And the Bridge Is Love*, p. 133.
50 Mahler-Werfel, "Diary of Alma Maria," 1919, pp. 145, 152, MWP.
51 Mahler-Werfel, *And the Bridge Is Love*, p. 134.

the same apartment building (where the couple's marital problems were much overheard and discussed by the residents). The doctor took her side. "'Do you want to kill her?' he asked Gropius earnestly. 'She can't stand much more.'"[52] So Gropius stood down once more and Alma left Weimar with Manon at the end of June.

Though Alma said she was going to Franzensbad to recover from the nervous exhaustion she had endured for the past four weeks, she returned to Werfel and spent the early summer with him at Haus Mahler. While he worked, Alma enjoyed her daughter's presence and steeled her resolve not to let the little girl become a bargaining chip for her estranged husband. "Only Mutzi, this sweet child, only she is my fear for without this elfkin I could not live," she confided in her diary in July, as the heated arguments of Weimar were continued in letters and telegrams between her and Gropius.[53] "You say: 'Give me our child!'" she wrote, quoting him. "You have no idea what that means for me. You could just as well then put a loaded revolver beside me!"[54] Gropius knew that Alma had no need of obtaining a pistol from him, for she long carried one in her purse. One thing that surely could have limited what he could do was the vision of Alma shooting Manon and then herself. The "elegant gentleman in spats," Alma wrote disdainfully, as though Gropius were some cardboard display in a tailor shop. She used the word *fad*—stiff, stuffy, boring—to describe him. She bridled again and again at how his name and legal rights lay on her "like a roll of barbwire." "I AM not Gropius and can never be called Gropius. My name is MAHLER for all eternity.[55]

As Alma walked across the lawn of Haus Mahler in one of her long, flowing, and colorful Kolomon Moser gowns, Manon protested

52 Mahler-Werfel, *And the Bridge Is Love*, pp. 134–5.

53 Mahler-Werfel, "Diary of Alma Maria," July 3, 1919, p. 146, MWP.

54 Alma Mahler to Walter Gropius, undated [*c.*summer 1919], BHA.

55 Mahler-Werfel, "Diary of Alma Maria," July 3, 1919, p. 146, MWP.

certain damage that to her such eminence would make, "Mommy, you bother the grass!"[56] On the same day Alma recorded this precocious remark, Gropius wrote a long letter to Alma asking her for a "DIVORCE" in capital letters and sending a legal document for her to sign. He begged her to stop using the "white magic" of her words on his heart. "I no longer believe in a universe of words [*Wortewelt*]. I live in a new world where each word, each thought is only great and true when it is fully realized," he continued, building toward what he saw as Werfel's influence. "Your splendid nature is being subverted by this Jewish intellect. [. . .] and our sweet child is the one who bears the fate of our coming apart in perpetuo. [. . .] I see many tears yet—for us, for our child who I cannot let go, who you cannot let go, this indivisible crystal from us both whose destiny is so dark."[57]

Despite Gropius' lapse into anti-Semitism, Werfel tried to intercede and offer friendship, while Alma provided a chaff of sweet-nothings. "She is so sweet. She is getting taller and prettier day by day. Her hair is growing into infinity," Alma wrote Manon's father. "She already takes long faraway walks—speaks correctly and with extraordinary grammar. I will enjoy it when you see her again—but when will you want to see her!"[58] In an undated letter further reporting news of Manon's accelerated development ("she can already do every new thing imaginable") and beauty, Alma surely caused Gropius further dismay. She casually name-drops her latest celebrated visitor at Haus Mahler, the chief stage designer at the Vienna Opera, Alfred Roller, and proudly admits to stripping the little girl "naked for him."[59] (Given the photographic

---

56 Mahler-Werfel, "Diary of Alma Maria," July 12, 1919, p. 146, MWP.

57 Walter Gropius to Alma Mahler, July 12, 1919, quoted in Isaacs, *Walter Gropius*, VOL. 1, pp. 223–5.

58 Walter Gropius to Alma Mahler, August 20, 1919, quoted in Isaacs, *Walter Gropius*, VOL 1, p. 228.

59 Alma Mahler to Walter Gropius, undated, quoted in Hilmes, *Witwe im Wahn*, p. 258.

evidence, Alma often exposed Manon for her guests to admire, such that it became quite natural to encounter the girl nude during the warm weather. The photographic evidence, if not the practice, would end before puberty.)

The only thing that sounded remotely real from Alma was her conciliatory offer to live part of the year with Gropius as his wife and bring Manon. She enlisted Johannes Itten to speak for her in Weimar and promised Gropius that she and Manon would arrive in September. Looking forward to their visit, Gropius wrote his new lover, Lily Hildebrandt, that he longed to see his "little moppet," for she had recently had her tonsils removed because of "three horrific episodes of tonsillitis."[60]

In reality, Anna Mahler had suffered an ear infection that spread to her throat despite the tubes inserted to drain off the infection. Either Gropius had misunderstood or been misled that the sick child had been his. In any event, Alma had her pretext to put off Weimar for months.

Sister Ida

In February 1920, Gropius rented a suite at the famous Hotel Elephant, a seventeenth-century building on the south side of Weimar's main market square. Long a guesthouse favored by artists, it had been the temporary residence of not only the *Bauhauskunstlers*—the masters and other teaching artists—but of the great national poet Goethe and the playwright Schiller, and composers such as Bach, Liszt, and Wagner. Thomas Mann used the hotel for the setting of his novel *Lotte in Weimar*. In 2009, the hotel opened the rooms that Gropius, Alma, and Manon occupied as the "Gropius-Suite," refurbished in the period's

---

60 Walter Gropius to Lily Hildebrandt, [*c.*September 1919], quoted in Isaacs, *Walter Gropius,* VOL 1, p. 229.

Art Deco décor. For a time, gilt commemorative statues were erected on the main balcony of Walter Gropius and Alma Mahler—with their backs to each other as though in an argument—but no statue of Manon Gropius, which could have been posed in between.

Undoubtedly Manon played with her dolls and cast-metal toys as not only her parents fought over her, but Germany approached a state of civil war. "Now I finally see what this marriage of everything that is evil has done to me," Alma wrote in March, once more seeing Gropius as a philistine, "a new, self-righteous burgher [*Spießbürger*], the kind I would despise anywhere. And now that I have this sweet child by him, it's even worse. What to do! [. . .] I have now seen the beast in this man hideously in full bloom." Having Alma in person at last provided her estranged husband with a rare opening. His arguments over custody of Manon, however, were likely meticulously rational rather than as grotesque as Alma made them out to be. "Gropius, with this angry, hateful face, wants the child fifty-fifty, wants me fifty-fifty," she continued in her diary, a bourgeois arrangement she would counter by becoming for Gropius an "anarchist" spouse, letting him see his daughter in exchange for letting "everything go on out of wedlock."[61]

Meanwhile, a nationwide strike had been called on March 13 by German communist and socialist parties to protest the right-wing Kapp Putsch in Berlin and its Freikorps units determined to remove the new federal government based in Weimar. Alma's sympathies ran more with the Freikorps, identified by the hand-painted swastikas on their helmets, than with the "proletarian" demonstrators. She looked down both literally and figuratively on the red flags of the workers, the white flags of the surrendering putschists, the civilians running for cover, the storming of the city hall and saw the insurrection as a "school play," an "operetta." During the ensuing week, telephone, electricity, and water services became disrupted. Sewers backed up. When the

61 Mahler-Werfel, , "Diary of Alma Maria," March 5, 1920, pp. 160–1, MWP.

street fighting lulled, there were long funeral processions of the dead in plain wooden coffins with great banners inscribed with "Long live Rosa Luxemburg, Long live Karl Liebknecht." The many dead, however, went unburied and bodies rotted in the streets or piled up against the cemetery walls. Stench blanketed the city, forcing Alma to waste her expensive perfume as she splashed it about in lieu of proper disinfectant.

Gropius moved his family into his new, unfinished apartment as the civil war came to an end in late March—and Alma noted all that was wrong with Weimar and the Bauhaus milieu as an unsuitable place for her daughter. Illustrative of this were Alma's impressions of the home and wife of Johannes Itten.

Alma had long taken an interest in the Swiss painter's life. She had urged him to care for his student Emmy Anbelang, who had tried to starve herself to death in grief over the death of her lover, Gustav Klimt, who had died of Spanish influenza in early 1918. Alma suggested that Itten give the young woman Veronal and take her to one of the Semmering clinics to recover. When he fell in love with Emmy, Alma convinced him to rename her Maria to help her cast off her old identity and obsession with Klimt. Alma was overjoyed to hear that the new couple would marry in the new year, but Emmy, too, died of Spanish flu in December 1919—a tragic coincidence that Alma saw as "symbolic logic." This *logic* had also played out for Itten, for he had fallen in love with and married Emmy Anbelang's younger sister Hilde, who exemplified the *Bauhausgeist* or spirit of the school's early days.

Hilde styled herself after an African fertility sculpture, which Alma noticed when she visited the Itten apartment in Weimar. This "ebony Madonna," with her much smaller consort smothered in her breasts, evinced to Alma how much Itten himself had been eclipsed by his own mate—and Hilde's belly revealed she was obviously pregnant. What also surprised Alma about Frau Itten was her way of childrearing *in utero.* When Alma arrived, she found Hilde still sitting on the high chair where she had just undergone an hour-long session of "suggestive education" with her fetus with the aid of another woman—a "*Hexe*" or witch—who made the expectant mother stare into a crystal ball to relax and then respond for the child as questions to it were posed. Manon would, especially as she got older, need to be protected from the peculiars and peculiarities found at the Bauhaus, ranging from "communists" and "radical Jews" to fluid morals and neo-pagan beliefs (anticipating what is called New Age now), and such events at the Bauhaus canteen as "Nietzsche Night"—festivities Alma missed.[62]

On April 2, Good Friday, Alma and Manon arrived in Berlin to spend Easter there with Werfel. He had worried about them for weeks given the dangers of the Kapp Putsch. With both safely and happily adjacent—"*Tür an Tür*"—in the same hotel, Werfel once more enjoyed what was now his family. After a dramatic read-through of Werfel's new play *Spiegelmensch* (Mirror Man, 1920) hosted by Max Reinhardt, the leading director-producer in German-language theatre, and an evening performance of his latest production, Hugo von Hofmannsthal's adaptation of Calderón's *Dame Kobold*, Werfel, Alma, and Manon left for Dresden on Easter Monday. Not only did Alma want to visit her sister-in-law, Emma Mahler Rosé, but was to conduct a special interview with a former army nurse whose procurement had been arranged by Vienna's new Social Democratic health minister, Dr. Julius Tandler.

Though Agnes Ida Gebauer had long served in Vienna, her accent revealed her to be a native of Saxony. From a peasant family, she moved to Dresden as a teenager and trained to be a *Seuchenschwester*—

62 "Nietzsche Night" was intended to win the financial support of Nietzsche's sister and editor, Elisabeth Förster-Nietzsche, which she could afford to do, having already sponsored an Aryan German colony in Paraguay.

"epidemic sister"—the title still given to lay nurses in Europe. When the Great War broke out, Sister Ida was transferred to the medical corps of Germany's ally, Austria-Hungary and sent to Galicia on the Eastern Front. There, in 1916, she contracted typhus and it took almost a year for Sister Ida to recover enough to be allowed to return to her vocation. Through Dr. Tandler, she found a position at Leopoldstädter Children's Hospital, where he soon appointed her to care for a baby whom she assumed to be the secret love child of aristocratic parents. The parents, however, were Alma and Werfel—both friends of the doctor—and the baby was Martin Johannes.

The baby's appearance startled the nurse. He had a puny body with bright red skin. He could not cry. After several weeks, Ida could see that the child's head was growing at an alarming rate. He also resembled an old man. When she asked the chief physician about this "*Wunder*," he calmly told her that the baby was a classic case of *progeria*—premature aging. When Martin Johannes died, he allegedly had the wrinkles and folds of seventy-year-old as well as a snow-white beard.

Ten months later, sometime in March, Dr. Tandler presented Sister Ida with a new opportunity to care for another child. Not only would she make more money than she could in the children's hospital, she would also get room and board and other perquisites given the wealth and status of her prospective new employer, who, to Sister Ida's surprise, was the mother of the strange-looking baby the nurse had cared for during his last months. According to Alma's own account, Werfel, too, had a hand in procuring Sister Ida and in bringing the nurse to Dresden in early April, perhaps owing to his friendship with Julius Tandler—or through an acquaintance with the nurse herself, for Werfel was no stranger to the field and military hospitals of the Galician Front. And he, like Gropius, could see that Manon desperately needed a full-time nanny given her mother's state of mind and her obvious need for existential freedom to be Mahler's widow, Gropius' estranged wife, and Werfel's girlfriend.

While still in Dresden, Alma met with Sister Ida in a hotel room. There the nurse was introduced to Alma's four-year-old daughter. Although Manon behaved shyly at first, it did not take Sister Ida long to win the child over, letting the little girl call her "Schulli," Ida's pet name, which she had been called since childhood and which was far easier for Manon to pronounce than *Oberschwester*, a title Alma enjoyed using especially when being sarcastic, for there could be no one over Alma.

Gropius was soon informed that Alma wished to hire the German nurse. As Alma's husband, he saw it as his duty to pay the woman's salary and to even assume the role as her real employer. But that role did not last long, for Sister Ida *understood* that she was in Alma's employ and loyal to her, even when she served in Gropius' household. That Manon trusted the nurse was important, but Alma's trust and a matter of expediency also factored in Sister Ida's employment. Thus, surprisingly and uncharacteristically given the rancor toward him in her diary, Alma let Gropius have his daughter for nearly a month, from early May to early June 1920. The Dutch conductor Willem Mengelberg had invited Alma and Anna Mahler to Amsterdam to be guests of honor at a Mahler festival marking the tenth anniversary of the composer's death. Thus, on May 5, at a railroad station on the German frontier, Alma handed Manon over to a waiting Gropius and Sister Ida, who had come from Dresden to formally begin her duties.

Despite having his daughter for four weeks, time for Gropius was a precious element and he managed it with a precision that rivaled the American managerial science of Taylorism that fascinated Central Europe before and after the world war. He had a new lover, Maria Benemann, a war widow for his physical needs and Lily Hildebrandt as a confidante in the way Alma had been. In addition to his personal life, the Bauhaus, and his architectural practice, Gropius spent a good part of the day simply writing letters by hand. For his voluminous correspondence, he surely used either a real—or mental—master copy for individual letters to family members, lovers, lawyers, government officials, faculty, and his colleagues in the field of architecture and "new building" around the world. Gropius, too, had to raise funds for the Bauhaus, go on lecture tours, and visit his Berlin office. He had to make himself available to his colleagues—as well as Bauhaus students. Gropius appeared at their various theme parties or the canteen, where he took his meals with them, meals which were often the Mazdaznan dishes that Alma shoved away for being nothing but uncooked mush smothered in garlic—fare that Gropius insisted was "the healthiest food there is."[63]

Maria Benemann accused Gropius of ignoring her at public Bauhaus functions. He defended himself, telling Manon that as the director he could not be connected to any one person. And one of these persons was his daughter. Gropius could give her little of what we euphemistically call "quality time" now—and then, in early June, there was no more time. "I am expecting my wife any day from Amsterdam," he lamented to Lily Hildebrandt. "Then she'll disappear again into the fog with my kid."[64]

Alma arrived in Weimar in early June to fetch Manon. "God loves me," she wrote with some sarcasm in her diary about her one conversation with Gropius. "You have gotten a new line in your face," he told her, "a terrifyingly immoral line." She was shocked to hear this and fascinated, too, for Gropius had seen what was true. She had fallen in love with Werfel again and with his "perversely crippled pictures and crippling addictions [. . .] Thanks Walter, thanks! Every one of my erotic experiences with this man can be summarized in one sentence: The more important the man, the sicker his sexuality."[65] What Gropius apprehended of this is unknown, but he surely wondered what it would mean for Manon's development.

---

63 Mahler-Werfel, *And the Bridge Is Love*, p. 143.

64 Walter Gropius to LH, undated [late May or early June, 1920], quoted in Isaacs, *Walter Gropius*, VOL. 1, p. 245.

65 Mahler-Werfel, "Diary of Alma Maria," June 4, 1920, p. 168, MWP.

After hearing Gropius out about future visitation with his daughter and a divorce, Alma took Manon and Sister Ida back to Vienna and on to Haus Mahler. Perhaps knowing that he would need the nurse's good will over the coming months, Gropius included an extra 200 German marks for her travel expenses couched in his gratitude and with the sincere hope that she would feel at home in Vienna. He also thanked Sister Ida for the love and care she had shown to Manon despite the "intense solitude" of Weimar, which hints at how little he saw his daughter.[66]

During the summer of 1920, lawyers in Berlin and Vienna prepared the legal proceedings necessary for the Gropius divorce. Who Manon would live with remained a sticking point, for Alma insisted on full custody, which included deciding when and *where* Gropius could see his daughter. For his part, Gropius could ill afford the distraction of his personal life as the Bauhaus weathered its first political crisis. State elections had replaced the Social Democrats with a conservative government that was hostile to Gropius' progressive views and the school's mission. This required delicate political maneuverings to prevent the Bauhaus from becoming subservient to local craftspeople rather than well-designed, mass-produced Bauhaus articles that Gropius wished to leverage into the market and society. Thus, after nearly two years of fighting over Manon, Gropius faced the reality of virtually giving her up entirely. To do this, his lawyer advised that Alma would need to file for divorce to have a legal advantage over her husband and the father of her child in German law. She would need to be the wronged woman and Gropius would have to stand as the defendant, to which he agreed.

The expedient solution was both tawdry and done all the time. Gropius would be caught—*in flagrante delicto*—in violation of his marital vows. In the early autumn, his lawyer arranged for Gropius to

66 Walter Gropius to Ida Gebauer, June, 14, 1920, ÖNB.

rent out a hotel room. A prostitute was hired to play the part of the "other woman." As Gropius and this woman waited in the room and performed what little theatre was needed—small talk, a postcoital cigarette, perhaps, without the preliminary—a detective and a few other hired witnesses would enter and discover the "lovers."

On October 9, Alma and Manon arrived in Weimar to complete the legal process in magistrate's office. Alma did not want go, and it seemed "pointless" to come all this way. "But Gropius," she wrote in her diary, "swore he needed me. Perhaps he does need me . . . "[67] Two days later the divorce was final and Alma and Manon returned to Vienna. For a time, Alma indulged in a postmortem. "Why had this marriage with Gropius not worked out?" she asked herself, weighing his virtues, his likeness to herself. "He was [. . .] of my blood—we even had some common relatives in Hamburg." She considered that "Lady Music" had not been his element, this despite how much he had esteemed and now understood Mahler and his music, not to mention the music of Werfel's poetry. That she had shown little interest in his architecture and the Bauhaus was true enough, and that she might have been the real philistine in their relationship was something she was incapable of grasping. So, too, that Gropius had been little more than a sperm donor. She did come close to admitting it was pure biology in her cleaned-up and redacted memoir. "But what homogeneity means—this I would have to see in my child from Walter Gropius," she wrote. "The miracle of sameness—which I would shun otherwise—was born in her. She was the most beautiful human being in every sense. She combined all our good qualities. I have never known such a divine capacity for love, such creative power to express and live it."[68] Alma contemplated whether it might have been better to have conceived Manon in free love, illegitimately. "My right to her would be indisputable. But her future would

67 Mahler-Werfel, "Diary of Alma Maria," October 9, 1920, p. 175, MWP.
68 Mahler-Werfel, *And the Bridge Is Love*, p. 135.

be clouded by a kind of Bohème despotism that would be bad for her and for myself. I am free, and I'll stay free. I will not deliver myself into the hands of any law, reactionary or radical-futuristic."[69]

If Manon suffered anything from the divorce, her mother did not record it. Nor do the few photographs from this time, in which the little girl appears wearing nothing but a barrette, and in the company of Schulli. She simply appears naked, free, and untouched by the distress around her, unlike those who were old enough to have "real lives," such as her half-sister Anna. The teenager had gone on a hunger strike in the weeks before the Gropius divorce because her secret had been found out, that she wished to marry a young man over ten years older, an aspiring conductor whose family also summered on Semmering. Alma saw the parallel here. She, too, had fallen in love with a much older man—Mahler—a musician and Anna's father. And Anna's desire to marry so young filled Alma with a sense of vicarious pleasure—and foreboding, given the summer-long negotiations with Gropius. Alma wondered if she might be cursed. "I'm a *jettatore*," she wrote, alluding to that figure from Neapolitan folklore, a melancholy jinx whose injurious gaze is directed at those who make him feel the most miserable: happy, innocent children. "I feel filled with terror by this clearest of insight," Alma continued, "that everyone touched by my aura is ruined by me."[70]

---

69 Mahler-Werfel, *And the Bridge Is Love*, p. 153.
70 Mahler-Werfel, "Diary of Alma Maria," July 27, 1920, p. 170, MWP.

GIRLHOOD

[T]he predisposition to develop [poliomyelitis] from tonsillectomy, which I have stated to be of the utmost importance, is the elimination from the system of a valuable protective substance the nature of which is yet unknown.

—Dr. Max Talmey[1]

A House on the San Tomà Canal

Franz Werfel welcomed the return of Manon and Alma from Weimar in October 1920 with a lavish dinner party at their Elisabethstrasse apartment. Although free to marry him, the traumatic experience of parting with Gropius and securing Manon's custody had turned Alma against the idea of matrimony. Since her reputation as Mahler's widow had survived her long affair with Kokoschka, she decided that Werfel would remain her companion. Nevertheless, Alma did consent to a kind of family honeymoon in Italy for her and Werfel in the late autumn, accompanied by Manon and Sister Ida.[2]

The end of the world war and the Spanish influenza epidemic saw the return of the lucrative German and Austrian tourist trade to Italy,

1 Max Talmey, "Predisposing Factors in Infantile Paralysis," *New York Medical Journal* 104(1)(1916): 202. Talmey (1869–1941) was the boyhood mentor of Albert Einstein.

2 This timeframe is supported by an undated letter from Werfel to Kurt Wolff found in the publisher's business correspondence for late 1920 that places Werfel and Alma at the Grand Hotel Luna in Venice.

if not the prewar creature comforts of the Gilded Age and the Belle Époque. The railroads evinced the wear and tear of being commandeered by the military for five long years. The railroad tracks were in poor condition. The windows in coaches were cracked or missing and let in the cold, wet winter air. Even the Pullman cars were filthy and still looked as though they had just been crowded with soldiers. Alma itched with the thought that she and her party would be infested with lice. The Italian trains ran abysmally slow. The so-called express to Rome lacked the all-important amenity of a dining car, which meant that Alma and her party had to bring bottles of soup and baskets of food. They did not reach their final destination until 4:00 A.M.

Fortunately, the composer Alfredo Casella, a friend to Alma and Gustav Mahler, had been wired of her party's arrival and met them at the train station. He had also made reservations for her, Werfel, the nurse, and the little girl at two different hotels, given the high demand for rooms. Surprising to Casella were Alma's sleeping arrangements. When the night porter informed her that only one room had been saved, "an elegant marital suite," Alma gave that room to Manon and Werfel. Ordering a thirty-year-old man to share a bed with a four-year-old girl was simply protecting her prized daughter and her new Goethe-in-waiting from Spanish influenza and other contagious diseases. Alma also knew of Werfel's past lack of sexual discipline. In her diary, Alma disapproved of his tendency to masturbate (to which he confessed) and she believed that he had ceased to consort with prostitutes, including adolescent ones, whom he seemed to esteem from afar in his latest book of poems, *Judgment Day* (1919):

> She herself was a budding already of breasts,
>   an emergence of lips . . .
> I still called—
> As though in mild pain,

Reluctantly,
She blew her precious girlhood toward me.[3]

Such effusions could be defended as Werfel's being true to matriarchy. In another, more Expressionistic poem from the same collection, he even invokes the "Almighty Mother," personified by the sun as this "midday death." Her rays fall on "benches in the park" swirling with children at play, so as to "reap" humanity, especially the girls in "under blond clouds," joyously aswelter and seemingly dying in "pretty, heliotropic skirts," as "bushels of fertility."In the poem, the poet asks to die, too, but out of shame:

Kill me,
That I of this shifty lie
And of this faul eavesdropping forget,
That I of this fiend
Within and before me forget![4]

If Alma knew these poems, their self-flagellatory nature would have pardoned them in her eyes. Thus, she—and Sister Ida, too—could presumably sleep soundly under the tables of the hotel dining room as did the other overflow guests, without a worry about the curious pairing of her daughter and poet in the same room upstairs.

After some days in Rome, the journey continued on to Naples. The unheated coaches and the cold rain and sleet left Manon with a bad cold, necessitating a longer stay at a smaller and cheaper hotel. Alma could not risk the child getting an infection.

---

3 Franz Werfel, "Der Ruf" [The Call], *Der Gerichtstag* [Judgment Day] (Leipzig: Kurt Wolff, 1919), p. 31.
4 Werfel, "Gewaltige Mutter" [Almighty Mother], *Der Gerichtstag,* p. 81.

There would be two outcomes from Manon's first journey to Italy as a matter of health and comfort: the imperative that she should have her tonsils removed in the very near future, and her mother's purchase of a house in the warmer climate of Venice. Alma acted on the first of these, for her firstborn's death still haunted her, and Anna Mahler's history of throat and ear infections were fresh memories. During one bout, before she had had her tonsils removed, Anna had suffered an episode of facial paralysis from the toxins in the pus. On the way from Breitenstein to see her pediatrician in Vienna, Anna's pitiful moaning and tears attracted the attention of a mysterious man in the Sudbahn as she and her mother stepped from the train. He asked if he could help and then looked at her and spoke some words that left Anna pain-free long enough to reach her doctor's office. Only later did Alma learn that he was a "famous hypnotist" (an assertion that suggests the stranger could have been Austrian clairvoyant Erik Jan Hanussen).

In May 1921, Manon had her tonsils excised, using a form of cauterization at Vienna's Luithlen Sanatorium, a new private clinic that featured two operating theaters under glass-domed towers illuminated only by natural light. Each recovery room was adjoined by an additional furnished apartment for family members staying with the patient. Having loved ones nearby was considered part of patient therapy. Nevertheless, having mother and nurse present surely helped only a little for a surgery that had to be terrifying even for the bravest child. The procedure used in the early 1920s required the surgeon to perform numerous incisions to remove the tonsillar tissue. Then a metal probe heated over an open flame until bright red, or an electrocautery which differed little from a soldering gun, was used to seal the incisions.

The procedure had to be performed with the patient fully awake, without chloroform or ether, since general anesthesia predisposed one to bleeding and risked asphyxia from choking on one's own blood. Recovery made swallowing difficult and painful—about which Werfel was apprised. "I desperately must have news as soon as possible, such as Mutzi is over the shock." he wrote Alma from Breitenstein. "I love that child enormously, she is close to me and holy!! It makes me feel terrible that there must be two days of pain."[5]

Gropius had expressed his own sympathies prematurely and likely remained in the dark about Manon's tonsillectomy. He also likely did not see her for all of 1921 despite his verbal agreement with Alma that she would bring their daughter to Weimar at least twice a year, a promise she probably did not honor. And when Werfel and Alma brought Manon with them to Germany in October, not long after she celebrated her fifth birthday, they did not go to Weimar. They stayed for a week in Leipzig for the premiere of Werfel's new "magical trilogy," *Spiegelmensch*.

Werfel himself prefaced the play with what it was about, that is, a pastiche of everything that interested—and frustrated—him until now: "Eucharistic and Thomistic/Yet a little bit Marxistic,/Theosophistic, Communistic,/Gothic-small-town-cathedral-mysticistic/Activistic, Arch-buddhistic,/Ultra-eastern Taositic,/A rescue from the era's sludgistic,/Seeing truth in the negro sculpturistic,/Throwing up barricades and talk,/Jauntily mixing God and the foxtrot . . ."[6] But, in synopsis, it was revenge—a "bomb" according to Kurt Wolff who published both men—for stinging remarks Karl Kraus had made in print about Werfel's over-the-top literary ambitions. In response, Werfel created a caricature of Kraus, sending up his literary self-aggrandizement and Jewish self-loathing, and without any real comedy at all, infused it with a meditation on assimilation, that is, the "mirroring." Thus, any *useful* synopsis of the play—say, "A Faust-like character, having sought the quietude of a monastery, becomes disaffected by the contemplative

5 Franz Werfel to Alma Mahler, undated [May 1921], FWP.

6 Franz Werfel, *Spiegelmensch* [Mirror Man] (Munich: Kurt Wolff, 1920), p. 130.

life," and so on hardly seems like something that would imprint itself like a fairy tale on a child's imagination.

Because Sister Ida was unavailable and because Alma did not want to leave her daughter alone or with a stranger at the hotel, Manon was brought to the dress rehearsal. Her mother expected the girl would tire and fall asleep across one of the divan-like loge seats. To her surprise—and Werfel's—Manon fixed her eyes on the stage and the bizarrely lit Expressionistic sets, which had been designed and painted by Alexander Baranowsky. The actors performed under the direction of the young Alwin Kronacher (who later directed the Bertolt Brecht's first plays). The title role was played by Ewald Schindler, with Lutz Altschul as Thamal and Margarete Anton as Ampheh. Harry Täuber, who had recently dressed Anita Berber for her performance of *Dances of Vice, Horror, and Ecstasy*, designed their flamboyant costumes. If this was Manon's introduction to the theater, it was a far cry from the Christmas ballets of *Hansel and Gretel* and *Puppenfee* (*The Doll Fairy*) of most Viennese children.

Manon did not get to see the play to its end. The larger playhouses during this era were difficult to heat and the furnace would not have been stoked for a rehearsal. Werfel and Alma could see the girl was shivering and turning pale as she doggedly watched the actors below and followed the dialogue because, as Werfel supposed, it concerned a dead child. Eventually, Alma bundled her daughter up and rushed her back to the hotel despite Manon's screams of protest, which echoed throughout the nearly empty theater. But in the days to come, and once back in Vienna, she found various articles of grownup clothes and reenacted her favorite scenes. Such make-believe must have obsessed the child, for Alma would sometimes bring guests into Manon's playroom to see her strut about in a long, trailing costume and declaiming lines. When the Wagnerian soprano Barbara Kemp asked Manon why she was all dressed up, the five-year-old replied in a serious and perturbed little voice, "'Can't you see I am Ampheh!'"[7]

Manon especially liked the graveyard scene in *Spiegelmensch*. With her hand outstretched, she intoned Thamal's question as deep as her little girl's voice allowed, "Where's my child?" Then she gave Ampheh's response, "You're standing at its grave." Werfel also saw her playing these parts and "insatiably" repeating these questions. "Why didn't you choose a funnier scene for yourself?" he asked her. "There are plenty of funny things going on in that play."

"I don't like funny," said Manon. "I just like the sad. Sad is much prettier."[8]

Alma and Manon did visit Weimar in March 1922, when her favorite Johannes Itten and students loyal to him were being purged from the Bauhaus. Mother and daughter did not stay long and nothing happened worth documenting. A few weeks later, back on Semmering, the cold Austrian winter-spring wore on, which finally convinced Alma to telephone her mother, Anna Moll, in Vienna and arranged for the pair, as well as Manon and Sister Ida, to travel to Venice in mid-April 1922, not only for Easter but to find a *palazzo*. And doing so would also please Werfel, given the realignment of his mental compass from Germany to Italy, for "that subjective experience of opposites," writes Peter Stephan Jungk, between the north and south, between Germany and Italy. Such had become "more and more the theme: his disdain for everything cool, abstract, his passion for emotion and ecstasy . . . an ideological conflict, one he also took rather personally when he compared his work with the ideas of Walter Gropius and the Bauhaus group."[9] This realignment took with it the architect's daughter.

7 Mahler-Werfel, *And the Bridge Is Love*, p. 160.

8 Werfel, "Manon," *Erzählungen aus zwei*, p. 393.

9 Peter Stephen Jungk, *Franz Werfel: A Life in Prague, Vienna, and* Hollywood

After days of crisscrossing Venice's little bridges and eyeing this and that house along the narrow streets, a real estate broker at last steered Alma to a blind alley in the Campo San Polo district, in a square next to the Gothic basilica of Santa Maria Gloriosi dei Friari—the site of Titian's tomb, where his painting of the Assumption adorns the nave—near the Grand Canal. The alley ended at San Tomà 2542, with the San Tomà canal on the other side, from which one could come and go by gondola or motorboat and so avoid the winding walk to the center of the city's social life: St. Mark's Square. The house's other amenities included a walled garden with a vine trellis and a large gate. In the center of the garden was a round stone planter bench. In the corner of the garden was a large, ornamental stone ball. The three-story building, which the city had deemed a historical structure, had enough rooms for some guests, as well as Alma, Werfel, Manon, and, with some additions, the Molls and their daughter Maria, Alma's half-sister and Manon's first cousin. Meanwhile, the agent pressed Alma to make a decision, using the time-tested ploy that buyers were "waiting in line." Exhausted from the walking and searching—and falling in love with the house and the garden on the spot, Alma agreed to his price and had papers drawn up for the purchase.

Also during this time, Alma encountered Oskar Kokoschka in St. Mark's Square, for he was exhibiting his work in Venice's renowned art exhibition, the Biennale. At the Caffé Florian, the former lovers testily reminisced. Kokoschka blamed her for the ill-treatment he had received at the hands of his officers during the war. He also made fun of Werfel's height and Alma's bustline. "You are going to really become flat-chested," he said, "having always to look down on such a little twerp [*Knirps*]."[10] Although there is no mention of Manon being present,

(Anselm Hollo trans.) (New York: Grove Weidenfeld, 1990), p. 147.

10 Mahler-Werfel, "Diary of Alma Maria," December 12, 1922, p. 183, MWP. In this analeptic passage, Alma sums up events from the spring of 1922.

Kokoschka must have met her, for he sent her a New Year's present later in the year—a conventional drawing of a kitten, like the animals he had drawn and bound in a book for Anna Mahler years before. In return, he only asked that Alma send him photographs of her daughters and herself.

During the train journey north, Alma began to confront the reality of paying for her extravagance. She would now have to maintain three homes with a limited income, the German hyperinflation, and the wartime restrictions still in place that made it difficult to make large withdrawals from Gustav Mahler's American investments. Despite having shown the house to an elated Werfel in May, Alma had second thoughts and tried to cancel the deal, but the seller, whom Alma called a "Venetian crook," refused. It was not until Werfel's father came through with 1,500 Czech crowns for his son that Alma felt she could go through with the purchase of what became "Casa Mahler," where she and Manon spent their Easter holidays for the next twelve years.

During her sixth year, Manon Gropius acquired the general appearance she would have for the rest of her life—the long dark hair with a part that contrasted with her fair complexion and eyes described as green and blue. Her face and features remained recognizably her father's in a softer, feminine form. Her slender figure and height continued to give the impression that she was tall for her age, especially when she posed for photographs with her Onkel Werfel. Indeed, the photographs of Manon bear this out during the 1920s, and especially those taken in Venice. In them one can see this expression, this deportment that made her look older, too, even as a child of six, seven, or eight. The photographed child has this look of an elegant young woman in miniature, a Brooke Shields in the era of Baby Peggy and Bemelmans' Madeline. It makes one think that she is only pretending to be a child in the images of her squinting into the camera like a Little Rascals' character, chasing the ubiquitous pigeons of St. Mark's Square with her straw cloche ready to fly off, or holding a panini sandwich at the Caffè Florian.

Among the Venice snapshots is a studio photograph taken there. Manon, at seven or eight years old, is costumed as a late Renaissance- or Baroque-era lady in what could be a sumptuous carnival dress or the costume of a child supernumerary in a play or opera. What inspired this image? Who wanted it made? It would seem to be Werfel, who had published *Verdi: A Novel of the Opera* in 1924, with his new publisher, Paul Zsolnay. And coming off the great success of that book, Werfel hoped to translate into German Verdi's *La forza del destino*—The Force of Fate. Perhaps Manon is the heroine, Leonora, as she stands on a Turkish rug that covers a wooden stage on which she poses, with a backdrop of velvet curtains. Her wide, high-waisted skirt is as fulsome as the one worn by Velazquez's infanta. (All that is missing is the proper chapeau, for Manon is bareheaded.) Although only a silver gelatin print, the viewer can still apprehend the presence of the rich, red-dyed silk brocade for which Venice was once famous, the luster of the floral pattern's gold-and-pearl embroidery, or what would be a *documentary textile* in museum parlance. The photograph was likely taken in April or May 1924 at the studio of Giacomelli on the Ponte San Moisè. It would have been this image that Werfel referenced years later, when he attempted to beatify Manon as a Venetian child saint in his unfinished novel *Legends* discussed in the final part of this book.

As much as Alma enjoyed images of Manon in costume, she still took pleasure in having the girl go about naked. In the family photographs Alma had taken of Manon—wearing only a pair of strap shoes—in the garden of Casa Mahler, the child's white, ghostly body, stands in contrast to the fully clothed adults posed with her. Among them was her half-sister Anna, now too old to strip for her mother and in a second marriage—to Ernst Krenek, the composer of the jazz opera *Jonny spielt auf—Jonny Strikes Up* (1927).

Krenek was an outsider in the Mahler-Werfel family. To his mother-in-law, he was a "cannibal" who exemplified her older daughter's poor taste in men, especially when this marriage proved to be as short-lived as her first. Being an outsider, however, allowed Krenek to be an objective, even hostile witness to both Alma and Manon Gropius. To Krenek her mother was a faded Brünhilde—for like many younger men, his standard of beauty had radically changed since the war. And to Krenek, Alma was an alcoholic, addicted to sipping her favorite liqueur through the day. What made it worse was how she had trained Manon from an early age to fetch her bottles on command—"Quick, the Benedictine, Mommy's thirsty!"[11] Surely, too, Krenek saw Manon naked in the same garden and on Semmering, too. It would have been in keeping with how Alma was *hors du combat* in matters of love since she no longer saw anyone else in her bed but Werfel. The overt sexuality in Alma's household offended Krenek. She relished low gossip and her chief topic of conversation was bedroom habits of family, friends, and enemies. Her half-sister Maria Moll provided much of this entertainment at Casa Mahler. The young woman, plump and plain, made up for these handicaps by hiring young Italian men to make love to her for a nominal fee. She also offered their services to Anna, much to Krenek's chagrin.

He likened Alma's salon and family life to an "*Affenzirkus*"—a monkey circus—and found Manon particularly disturbing. She seemed to be a creature of her mother, always watching him and Anna, rather than special in the way others saw her. "Alban Berg liked her very much and dedicated his Violin Concerto to her memory," Krenek wrote in his memoir. "Unfortunately, I must admit that I generally did not like her

11 Quoted in Karen Monson, *Alma Mahler: Muse to Genius* (New York: HarperCollins, 1984), p. 240.

because to me she seemed guarded and sly and played the role of a stool pigeon and spy for her mother. May God forgive me if I err in this.[12]

In late May 1923, Walter Gropius gave a lecture titled "The Unity of Art, Technology, and Economy" at Hanover's Provincial Museum. As he spoke, he noticed two attentive young women in the front row. Hoping to meet the prettier one, he sought her out at the reception that followed but could not find her. Fortunately, his nephew Joachim Burchard knew both sisters, the younger Hertha and the one who caught his uncle's eye, a twenty-six-year-old bookstore clerk and university student named Ilse Frank. In June, Gropius was in Hanover again and a meeting was arranged so that he could meet Ilse. Soon after, he sent her love letters in which he not only professed his feelings but that he wanted to marry her as soon as possible. That she was engaged to be married to her cousin Hermann Frank mattered not to him. Gropius encouraged her to break off the summer wedding and quickly displaced him as her lover.

By July, Ilse was pregnant with Gropius' child. He made her get an abortion and accept that "procreation" and a "new generation" would not be in their future together, for he was *designing* their relationship to appear and function not unlike his buildings and the Bauhaus. Another precondition Gropius insisted on was dropping the *l* in her name and becoming Ise (pronounced *ee-zee*) when he brought her to Weimar to live in the late summer. Following a vacation to Italy, Gropius and Ise were married on October 16, 1923, with Paul Klee and Wassily Kandinsky serving as witnesses.

After five months of marriage, Gropius felt settled and secure, while Ise shone as the first lady of the Bauhaus in a way Alma had not. Ise had a progressive worldview and an empathy for the school's

12 Krenek, *In Atem der Zeit*, p. 342.

mission and could relate to the *Bauhäusler*, meaning the faculty and students of the Bauhaus, many of whom were communist and whose presence attracted the suspicion of the increasingly right-wing Weimar government. That she could speak English fluently also proved a godsend for Gropius.

Ise also became Gropius' advocate in pressing Alma to honor her promise of allowing Manon to visit him twice a year. However, she had to get over being intimidated by her husband's legendary first wife. When the opportunity arose for Ise to accompany Gropius to Vienna in the spring of 1924, she remained behind to recuperate in a Dresden clinic for a "stomach ailment"—which may have been a euphemism for a second abortion that left her sterile. "If I didn't have this desperate need to see Mutzi," Gropius wrote guiltily, "I would stay here despite your encouragement [to go to Vienna] so as not to draw you into some emotional dilemma. But in this life I am dedicated to her and I must take care of my obligation to her. You may not express any dark thoughts about her [. . .]. Thoughts have power. You will love her even if she is not your child. Love me in her."[13] In this, Gropius read his new wife wrong, for Ise very much wanted to be a stepmother to Manon. "I have never directed the pettiest thought against Mutzi," she wrote, willing to come to Vienna, "she looks just like you!! If I remember right, it's more likely I have these tender feelings for her without ever having met her."[14] She asked Gropius to pick out some clothes for her and a proper spring hat. But when he came to Dresden to fetch her, he found her passport had expired.

Gropius likely saw Manon on Easter Saturday, April 19. The mood at the Elisabethstrasse apartment was less than warm. Alma—whose

---

13 Walter Gropius to Ise Gropius, undated [mid-April 1924], quoted in Isaacs, *Walter Gropius*, VOL. 1, p. 325.

14 Ise Gropius to Walter Gropius, undated [mid-April 1924], quoted in Isaacs, *Walter Gropius*, VOL. 1, p. 325.

diary entry for that day screams with her disquiet ("ALWAYS SOMETHING ELSE!"[15])—did not give Gropius any time alone with his daughter for play and conversation, for he surely would tell Manon that he had a new wife and she a stepmother. Instead, Alma hovered nearby or removed herself no farther than the next room. A normal outing, such as a visit to the famous menagerie at the Schönbrunn Palace—which now had enlarged its reptile collection with specimens from North Africa—would have been out of the question even though Manon liked such animals (much to the surprise of her elders).

"All those emotions came alive again," Alma wrote of her conversation with Gropius. "The endless torments of those dead years were loud and lurid."[16] When he left, Alma languished the rest of the day in bed where she pined not for Werfel, but for Kokoschka.

Alma and Manon left for Venice and Casa Mahler after Gropius returned to Germany. Manon loved to travel and possessed her own play passports (*Reisepässe*) that Werfel made for her. As virtual satires of the Central Europe's new political landscape of rump states, the country of issue was the "Republic of Kreuzberg," after the mountain visible from Haus Mahler on Semmering. The official seal—drawn in Werfel's hand—was a crowned griffin. For added authenticity, the passport bore her mother's rubber address stamps for Haus Mahler and Elisabethstrasse addresses as well as the signature of "Minister Feodor Tertullian Brecka"—which suggested not only one of the newly minted civil servants in the countries carved from the old Hapsburg empire, but Werfel's mix of identities as a writer, Jew, outsider Catholic, former Red, and one constantly feeling his rootlessness. His "Personal Description" of Manon provides this amusing tally of characteristics:

15 Mahler-Werfel, "Diary of Alma Maria," April 19, 1924, p. 188, MWP.
16 Mahler-Werfel, "Diary of Alma Maria," April 19, 1924, p. 188, MWP.

Birth Year	October 1916
" Place	Vienna
" Country	still Austria at the time
Jurisdiction	Kreuzberg Republic
Character/Occupation	Nutritional Slave
Status (single/married)	pending further notice virginal
Facial Characteristics	
Eyes	Averted
Nose	still not entirely pronounced
Mouth	Charming
Distinguishing Feature	Oppositional, especially to the request to drink milk[17]

The photograph of Manon that Werfel pasted into the passport continued his theme of the little girl's independence as well as his sardonic commentary. Her back is to the camera and she is dressed in a white frock, long white knickers, and a white butterfly bow, striding away toward her father's Haus Mahler porch in the background. A further satirical touch was the way Werfel signed his work as "Police Superintendent Franz Werfel" and indicated that the "bearer of this passport is hereby permitted to travel abroad (into those states surrounding the Kreuzberg Republic)." The only prohibition was travel to Russia because of its certain dangers—Bolsheviks, bandits, civil war, and the like. But Werfel added, as the "Crown Governor of the King-dom of White Gardenias," special dispensations and extensions for travel into the Republic of Sludgeastica, C-Sharp, and Transbank-

17 Franz Werfel, "Reisepaß, Bescheinigung und Verpflichtungserklärung" [Passport, Attestation, and Declaration of Commitment], 1922, 1928, ÖNB. Werfel made three such passports in the early 1920s that reveal further details, such as eye color (green), face (oval), build (medium), and the police number 3570, which may have mystical connotations.

ruptia, including its capital, Paranoiapolis. Werfel also made her a passport for Venice, illustrated with the seal of the Winged Lion of St. Mark, as though to acknowledge her allegiance to that city.

Manon more often remained behind as much as her mother and Werfel traveled. She was left in Sister's Ida care in January 1925, when Alma and Werfel sailed to Egypt to attend a performance of Verdi's *Aïda* at the same Cairo opera house where it had premiered in 1871. If Alma had considered sending Manon to stay with her father during her long winter journey—for it included a side trip to Palestine—there is no record of it or any protest from Gropius. Given that the Bauhaus was in a state of turmoil after it had been closed, he may have been relieved not to have Manon during Bauhaus's move from Weimar to Dessau.

Alma and Werfel toured ancient Thebes, including the tombs in the Valley of Kings. There Werfel saw in the light of his electric torch long bands of hieroglyphs and brilliantly painted images from daily life in which he saw an image as familiar and everyday as Alma and Manon were to him—an aristocratic wife introducing her daughter to her friends. "The child is naked," Werfel recalled, "so that the ladies can admire her lovely body with suitable exclamations of delight."[18]

In late March, Alma and Werfel returned via Syracuse, where they were met by Anna Mahler—now separated from Ernst Krenek, living in Rome, and studying painting under de Chirico. The three toured Sicily where, purely by chance, they encountered Gropius and Ise in Taormina. Alma does not mention this first encounter with Gropius' new wife. Ise, however, found Alma cordial and charming after their initial shock of running into Alma in their hotel garden, this despite the fact that, according to Gropius, "she was not being quite herself."[19] Presumably,

---

18 Franz Werfel, "Of Man's True Happiness," in *Between Heaven and Earth* (New York: Philosophical Library, 1944), p. 16.

19 Ise Gropius to Manon S. Gropius, undated [c. March 1925], quoted in Isaacs, *Walter Gropius*, VOL. 1, p. 352.

Manon was discussed in a way that did not touch on any controversy, such that Alma felt comfortable enough to see Ise and Gropius off at the train station, where she brought along Werfel and Anna.

Soon after, Alma and Werfel traveled on to Venice to be reunited with Manon and her nurse. They remained together there until after the Easter holiday, when Werfel traveled on to Breitenstein in order to write without any "family" distractions before they arrived for the summer. And this pattern of Vienna–Venice–Semmering–Venice and back to Vienna again became Manon's transit for nearly the rest of her life save for those rare interruptions when she was allowed to visit her father in Germany.

On Semmering, Manon lived for the most part as an only and lonely child save for Sister Ida's companionship. She had her books and toys, a servant's child for the rare playmate, her pets, and the neighborhood of Haus Mahler. It was an idyllic, parklike setting like the one Werfel adapted for his novel *Embezzled Heaven* (1938), with "a spacious grove of fruit trees which concealed the greenhouses, kitchen gardens, and potato patches." There was also "a gradual descent down to the road, covered with dense clusters of fine old trees—elms, platans, chestnut, and copper beeches such as one has never seen rivaled for height and beauty. Some way from the house began the real, 'wild park,' which stretched up a slope of the mountain and merged above into an endless forest of larches."[20] From one roll of film taken of Manon in 1925 or 1926, in her ninth or tenth year, she is shown flying on a swing tied up in the branches of one of the trees Werfel describes. The images, when placed one after the other, suggest a filmstrip, which shows her legs pumping to make the swing—the *Schaukelbrett*—go higher.

In one of these images she is at rest, clutching the ropes of the swing. She looks into the camera, but she does not wear a smile. Her expression is at once serene, sad, even bored or perturbed at being made

---

20 Franz Werfel, *Embezzled Heaven* (New York: Viking, 1940), pp. 15–6.

to stop for this portrait. This is the girl outside of what her mother's biographer Oliver Hilmes calls Alma's "exalted life," in which the girl was a victim of her mother's disruptions such that she developed no apparent personality of her own save to be guarded and terribly shy. The swing portrait also documents Manon's dusty patent-leather Mary Janes, which have surely dragged on the ground to stop her flying for the camera, and the fallen state of her knee socks gathered around her ankles. It is a haunting image given what would come later, for her dangling legs in an innocent childhood photograph resemble the *polichinelle* state, a medical term, borrowed from the *commedia dell'arte*, to describe paralysis in polio patients and how the limbs are slack like those of a marionette at rest.

The Stepmother

In the summer of 1927, while Manon took to her swing, Alma began to contemplate a more formal education for her daughter, who, in her eleventh year, was at an age where children were tested and certified for gymnasium, that is, middle school. Thus, Manon took and passed her equivalency exam for *V. Classe*—"*Quinta*"—or fifth grade in early July in order to meet the rigorous standards set by the Ministry of Education. Given Manon's shyness, she undoubtedly felt anxious, for such tests were usually given at a public school, a strange environment where what had been learned from a governess and nursery maid now faced modern pedagogical reforms and state requirements, and where "meeting the demands of the examiners" included the ability to "to draw animals in motion, street crowds," or one's "impression of summer."[21]

---

21 Ernst Lothar, *Little Friend* (New York: Putnam, 1933), p. 6. Lothar was a pseudonym and often used when referring to his two daughters rather than by his surname Müller or in combination. (Agathe was buried as Lothar Müller.)

This description of these tests is drawn from Ernst Lothar's *Little Friend* (*Kleine Freundin*, 1931), one in a series of coming-of-age novels, based on his daughters Agathe and Hanni, and written when both were still alive. Agathe, who was only a year older, befriended Manon, and many of the same rites of passage for an Austrian girl that the latter's father portrayed in his novels would have also been experienced by her.

Manon earned a "*gute*" (the equivalent of a B) on her exam, a grade sufficient enough for the *Internat*—boarding school—that Alma found in Geneva, where the headmistress offered to take Manon on a trial enrollment in early September. How much say Gropius had in the matter is unknown, but he must have played some part in the decision, for he was in Geneva to meet Manon and Alma when they arrived. The next day, however, when Gropius went to the school to see his daughter, he found that she and her mother had already left for Venice. The explanation seemed plausible: since Manon had never before attended school with children her own age, she had a bad experience on her first day and begged her mother not to leave.

But Gropius had to entertain another explanation for the sudden departure: Alma's possessiveness with their daughter. Seeing Gropius in Geneva and perhaps learning that he had professional ties to the city (his friend and colleague, the Swiss architect Siegfried Giedon) meant that her father would have a new avenue of access to Manon in a neutral country. In addition to being able to see his daughter unchaperoned, he could attempt to revive his parental rights and take her back to Germany. And Alma, too, had made (or forced) her daughter into being more and more a friend and confidante as the girl verged on adolescence. In all likelihood, Alma realized how far away Geneva was from her. Whatever happened, it necessitated finding a combination boarding and day school in Vienna's First District, one that would be close enough to fetch Manon and bring her home or to take her out when Alma needed her company—a school Alma claimed to have attended herself in the 1890s.[22]

The Institut-Hanausek was located in a modern *Jugendstil* building at Weihburggasse 10–12. It had been founded by the Austrian educator Marie Hanausek in 1869 to offer girls a liberal lyceum education to prepare them for teaching and like careers—and the university. The school prided itself on graduating girls fluent in French and proficient in art, ballet, and music as well. In 1905, Adele Renard-Stonner took over as headmistress, and it was she who met Alma and Manon. Why Alma had not considered the school earlier may have something to do with the reputation it had acquired over the years. Certainly, the school was rigorous. One alumna, and Alma's classmate, the art historian Erica Tietze-Conrat, compared the school to hell. Nevertheless, she was one of several graduates whose bright future may have been due to the school's pedagogy, among them the feminist Rosa Mayreder, the writer Clara Kestranek, and the pianist Gabriele Pancera. The other reservation Alma might have had in regard to the Institut-Hanausek was that it tolerated lesbian relationships. Alma apparently was not bothered by this rumor or by the many assimilated Jewish girls who attended, despite the school's Christian affiliation. What mattered was that Manon like the school. That she could go home when she wanted proved the first boon. The second was that she could be taken out on a moment's notice whenever Alma needed Manon, too, especially when it came to being her mother's traveling companion.

By the summer of 1927 the Bauhaus campus at Dessau featured many of the new buildings that one can see now at the UNESCO world historical site—save that most of these structures had to be rebuilt or

---

22 Alma mentions this in passing in *And the Bridge Is Love* (p. 192). It is not in any of her biographies. The only secondary source is Almut Krapf-Weiler, *Erica Tietze-Conrat: Die Frau in der Kunstwissenschaft* [Erica Tietze-Conrat: The Woman in Art History] (Vienna: Schlebrügge, 2007), pp. 283–4.

recreated in facsimile after the Second World War. The main building, with its curtain glass walls, resembled a hypermodern factory and was boldly and iconically lettered BAUHAUS in the font designed by Herbert Bayer, one of the school's student-teachers. The student dormitories each had simple, identical railed balconies. Every building had a flat roof and was furnished with chairs, tables, lighting fixtures, textiles, and the like designed and manufactured at the Bauhaus—including the row of white Master Houses, where the leading faculty members lived, as did the director, Walter Gropius.

Gropius had devoted much time and energy to the transition from Weimar to Dessau, much borrowed from his personal life and his relationship with his daughter. Alma had tested his patience for years. She and Werfel had traveled through Germany in 1925 and 1926, when Werfel lectured or read from his latest book—and without bringing Manon to see her father or his new wife, even when it would have been a matter of convenience. Now, with the Bauhaus in Dessau nearly finished, and with his architectural practice in Berlin enjoying commissions from automobile design to housing developments, Gropius could at last repair some of the distance he felt from his child—and truly show her his accomplishments *in situ*, in Dessau. To make Alma at last honor her broken promise to bring Manon twice a year, Gropius had already enlisted an advocate more dogged than any lawyer in what proved to be yet another contest with Alma—Ise Gropius.

Despite the cordial encounter at Taormina and another brief get-together in Berlin during the autumn of 1925, Ise would soon come to loathe the older woman for a lifetime.[23] In the spring of 1926, Alma, with her air of *noblesse oblige*, had invited the Gropiuses to visit her in

---

23 Years later, in the margin of one of her husband's letters to Alma from 1920, which she had transcribed and translated for Gropius' biographer, Ise wrote "SIC HER, WALTER!" beside a passage in which Gropius had dropped his usual tact and chivalry about the subject of divorce and Manon.

Venice, making the point that there they—Ise and Walter, Alma and Franz—could *all* take pleasure in being with Manon. Furthermore, Venice, to Alma, was a "nonthreatening (*harmlos*)" middle ground that was hardly in the middle geographically, not only for the adults, "*but* especially for Mutzi."[24]

Gropius naturally refused the offer and stopped replying to Alma's letters. The resulting break in communication resulted in his missing an opportunity to be present for Manon's tenth birthday in Vienna. This resulted in Ise's intercession in late October 1926. She wrote Alma on behalf of her husband, taking pains to explain to her that the only solution would be to allow Manon to stay in Dessau for an extended period of time.

"Because you know Walter's heart and mind," Alma responded as though mystified, "[. . .] write to me about what has made him *like this lately*, to be silent toward me. [. . .] I understand Walter's position—less and less in regard to Mutzi. Not to mention me, whom he no longer understands *at all*.—But write me, and let me know what is making him act like this.—When we met in Berlin, you promised to come to Venice [. . .]. But *it* did not happen, so many things did *not* happen in these years! You are *young and full of energy*—not me—I am wearing down and need to rest.—That I never have this rest—is my fate. But I can do nothing *at all* about it but take more troubles upon myself. You understand me—the woman—the woman!"[25] The letter had been written on the stationery of the Hotel Atlantic in Hamburg, where Manon might have been present in the same room. And Alma had ended her letter with the suggestion that Ise write her at the Hotel Continental in Berlin. If Manon had come to Germany too, it meant she would be an hour away from her father by train or automobile.

"please don't think that someone or something has influenced walter

24 Alma Mahler to Ise Gropius, undated [December 1926], BHA.

25 Alma Mahler to Ise Gropius, November 3, 1926, BHA.

in his relationship to mutzi," Ise responded, wisely keeping herself from becoming the focus of the dispute (and without capital letters, for this new convention was as much a statement of "social leveling" as houses with flat roofs[26]). "that he doesn't *know* her is the only obstacle!" Ise continued, "and until he can have mutzi here for some length of time, this, i fear, will not change." What then emerges in Ise's words is how Alma used Gropius' work against him—and, in truth, she was right. Gropius had let his career come ahead of his child. Alma, however, had only taken advantage of this to possess Manon all the more and renege on visitations. "you should not reproach walter for neglecting human relations over an idea and his work. that is really the last thing he deserves, for i know of no one who can with such selflessness clear his head of important things when the basics of being human seem in jeopardy. *one should not be so tightfisted with him*, otherwise all is for nothing! and [. . .] he is convinced that you keep mutzi like a jewel, which you only show with fear, while he continually hopes that you will share it with him for once without restriction and with full trust. this means simply that mutzi visit us here. [. . .] *one does not learn to know a child in a matter of days,* and maintaining a correspondence with a continually growing child is impossible without the warmth of contact now and then."[27] Ise ended her letter by reminding Alma that she had not made it easy for her. The Bauhaus ("this incredibly tense business going on around us") had meant that there had been little time for her to be with her husband and, like her, Alma needed to appreciate how the school "factored in walter's behavior" and what was meant by "all is for nothing." It is one of the very few instances where Manon Gropius, the "jewel" in

---

26 In 1926, the designer and typographer Herbert Bayer persuaded Walter Gropius to introduce a lowercase system of writing and printing at the Bauhaus. Used primarily by Bauhaus masters and students, that Ise and Walter Gropius used the system in their letters to Manon is indicative of her inclusion in the Bauhaus "family" whereas for Alma it seemed, perhaps, an insolence.
27 Ise Gropius to Alma Mahler, November 1926, MWP.

Alma's tight fist, is mentioned as this human factor in the context of her father's ideas and work—what happened at the Berlin office, the Bauhaus—that she was not just Walter Gropius' little girl, but an *architect's daughter*. Or was this interjection just frustration on the part of a woman thrust in the middle of a long feud not of her making?

When the semester ended in June 1927, Ise reopened negotiations with Alma to bring Manon to Dessau, after Alma suggested that the Gropiuses come to Vienna. Their letters now were friendlier and more conciliatory. Alma even sent Gropius a package of *Oblaten* biscuits, flat sugared wafers he esteemed as much as he did flat roofs. Nevertheless, Ise did not miss the opportunity to impress on Alma the radical prominence and presence of the man who wanted his daughter. "walter is getting to be a virtually famous man," Ise wrote, "and i should be taking the greatest pleasure in performing as wife if the name were not starting to be a burden. the people whom one meets brace themselves with a visible jolt at 'bauhaus' [. . .] and yet we expect one thing sometime this year: the visit of mutzi here in dessau! it is walter's greatest desire and you cannot deny him! i fear he will only think about vienna with great displeasure! why do you sweep us aside on this point!? walter is literally sick thinking about it, wanting to have the child here [. . .] *please* make him this gift!"[28]

Three weeks later, Alma finally replied and, in a strange fit of projection on the younger woman, asked Ise to empathize with Manon. "[S]urely you were a difficult, subdued [*hartes, verhaltenes*] child too. Don't you feel that it would be proper if Walter see his child first in an environment familiar to her and then everything would develop from there." Alma wanted Ise to see it from her point of view, too. "But the shock—," Alma continued, "to suddenly put a child in a strange place—I think you would also feel as improper as I do. She doesn't know you, Walter hardly, this entire setting—the city—in short everything is

28 Ise Gropius to Alma Mahler, June 23, 1927, BHA.

strange to her. *You* understand yourself from your own childhood and judge objectively—if it would really be right." As her letter came to an end, Alma relented. She would bring Manon to Dessau in the autumn despite the inconvenience of taking her out of boarding school. And on the subject of Manon's education, Alma rubbed salt. "That Walter typically doesn't answer my phone calls about Mutzi's above-average exam *left Mutzi infinitely hurt. This he should not do.*"[29]

On the day Alma wrote Ise in mid-July, she was still haunted and feeling superstitious about nightmares in which she walked out onto the balcony of Haus Mahler in the twilight. Looking down on the garden below, she spied on a "black lady"—a lady in mourning clothes—sitting on the bench. Then the mysterious woman, whose face Alma could not see in her dream, slowly and stiffly stood up and walked backward into her house. Terrified, she went back into her bedroom, but became curious and walked back out on the balcony only to find the black lady sitting in the same place, getting up again in the same way, and walking backward into her house.[30] This episode coincided with Manon's bout with whooping cough, which kept the household awake, including Alma's houseguests, Hugo von Hofmannsthal and his wife.[31]

In the weeks that followed, Alma and Manon traveled between Vienna and Venice, including her unhappy experience at the boarding school in Geneva. In October she would have been free to come to Germany, for now she could not enter the Institut-Hanausek until the spring of 1928. Instead, Alma returned to Venice on October 5, Manon's eleventh birthday. There she saw Kokoschka at the Caffé Fenice and the bar inside the Hotel l'Europe. He looked handsome and healthy, like "Dorian Grey" to Alma—who herself had not aged so

29 Alma Mahler to Ise Gropius, July 16, [1927], BHA.
30 Mahler-Werfel, "Diary of Alma Maria," Summer 1927, p. 201, MWP.
31 Mahler-Werfel, *Mein Leben*, p. 175.

well. When he left for Paris, she entertained thoughts of suicide—but she was very much alive to receive his telegram sent from Courmayeur, at the foot of Mount Blanc, asking her to send him that family photograph he long wanted, of herself, Anna, and Manon.

Not only did the highs and lows of Alma's manic self-esteem come before bringing Manon to Dessau, Werfel's career did as well. Thus Gropius would have to wait until mid-November, when Werfel began a series of poetry readings in Berlin and in other nearby cities, before he had his daughter at last—and only for a little over two weeks. And, in all likelihood, Walter and Ise Gropius had to drive to Berlin to pick up Manon from the hotel where Alma and Werfel stayed. The Gropiuses had to know that they were little more than glorified babysitters to Alma. She would always be hovering just hours away and despite all the impassioned pleas for the girl's presence, the assertions of her father's eminence, and the Bauhaus's import, the Gropiuses knew, too, that Alma could cut the visit short at any time.

Even with such a cloud hanging over a virtually sunless visit given the cold, gray skies, Manon in Dessau delighted her father and stepmother and made for a most uncommon guest. Her father more often entertained the likes of Nobel Prize winners, notable architects, and most recently the composer Béla Bartók. None of these men meant as much to Gropius as having Manon living under the same roof at last, in a room of her own, going about the Villa Gropius, her father's *Wohnmaschine*, his dwelling system. The interior was unlike anything the girl had experienced in her mother's three homes. Her father's house would have seemed austere in comparison. The white-tiled and stainless-steel kitchen where Manon had her milk was purely functional, like a commissary in a factory. The rooms had exposed steam radiators. The plate-glass windows were framed in steel like the doors. The furniture, lighting fixtures, and other furnishings had all been designed by Bauhaus masters and students and constructed in the

Bauhaus workshops, including the steel staircase painted in bright primary colors that led to Manon's bedroom. If she took no special notice of these things and seemed perfectly at ease, it would say more to her father about the success of the design of such a living environment as the approval of the men and women who had toured these rooms. Indeed, it would have been enough for Gropius to hear his daughter's Viennese German simply calling him "Papi" under Villa Gropius' flat roof, or calling after his little dog, "Nuschi." Important too was that Manon like her stepmother, whom she called "Ischen." "Mutzi and I got along very well with each other," Ise wrote later.[32]

Over the next few days, Ise appraised the girl's conduct and what it might say about her upbringing. Gropius also studied his child—usually at the supper table and whenever he could be away from the Bauhaus. She looked taller since he had last seen her in Geneva and she now wore her long, dark hair in two pigtails—*Zöpfen*, which perhaps reminded her father of an Apache Indian and complemented the book that Manon is photographed reading in a steel and leather chair, one of Marcel Breuer's "Wassily Chairs," which furnished Gropius' study.

The worn, battered copy of *Winnetou der Rote—the Red—Gentleman I* is likely Gropius' own boyhood copy—or even Werfel's—which either man would have gladly given to her. Like so many German-speaking children who grew up in the 1890s, the first volume in Karl May's American Indian trilogy often was, and continues to be, their first "real" book followed by the German edition of James Fennimore Cooper's *Last of the Mohicans* and the like. Such adventure tales fed Gropius' lifelong passion and interest in Native Americans and the American West, which also informed his aesthetics, from the flat roof (*Flachbau*) of Villa

32 These and other observations by Ise Gropius that follow are derived from an editorial comment dated July 1974 in an early manuscript of Reginald Isaacs' finished biography ("Walter Gropius: The Man and His Work," manuscript, March 1977, p. 91, RIP).

Gropius, which owes some of its design to the pueblo, to the collection of flowering cactus plants he and Ise cultivated.

The story Manon read during her stay is for the most part about the adventures of Karl May's eponymous chief of the Mescalero Apaches and his loyal white friend Old Shatterhand. For girls, however, it featured a forerunner of today's strong female character in Winnetou's warrior sister, the doomed Nsho-Chi—and her resemblance to Manon was uncannily like the narrator's description. "The youth was beautiful, even very beautiful," Old Shatterhand observes. "European clothed, she would have certainly aroused admiration in any drawing room. She wore a long, light-blue shirt-like dress that fit closely around the neck and was gathered at the waist by a rattlesnake skin belt. There was no adornment on her to be seen, like the glass beads or cheap coins that Indian girls gladly drape themselves with. Her only jewelry consisted of her long, beautiful hair that fell in luxuriantly in two blue-black braids all the way to the hips."[33]

To encourage her to read the other volumes in the trilogy, Gropius purchased for Manon a deluxe set illustrated with color plates. This fine gift, however, may have been compensatory as well. By granting his wish to bring Manon to Dessau—but with so little forewarning—Alma had made it hard for Gropius to rearrange his schedule and commitments to the Bauhaus and his practice in Berlin. His time with his daughter was limited despite Ise's urgent pleas for him to take time off from work. Once more Gropius enjoyed little "quality time" with Manon save for mealtimes and during the evening in the hour or two before she went to bed. In his place, he let Ise fill in for him—a role that appealed to her, for she had been mother to the Bauhaus and little else. Now, however, she found herself trying to interest Manon in

33 Karl May, *Winnetou, der rote Gentleman*, VOL. 1 (Bamberg: Karl-May-Verlag, 1982), p. 308–9.

learning how to dance the Charleston and like, for the young girl seemed completely unaccustomed to such physical activities. And Ise took risks with Manon that only Alma would have allowed herself, like driving with Manon to Hanover during a "wild and frightening snowstorm" and on "less than adequate highways." The drive left Manon exhilarated and it allowed her to see her grandmother and namesake, her Aunt Manon Burchard, and her children who had never laid eyes on their Austrian cousin.

As the days passed, Ise could see that Manon "was a very dear girl and determined to establish a lasting contact with her father." This is evident by how Manon literally beams at Gropius in the photographs Ise took on one chilly day, with snow on the ground, on the "garden side" of the house. Still wearing his four-in-hand and business suit, Gropius looks the part of a doting, bourgeois father. Manon appears carefree and on the verge of laughter—her smile revealing a space between her adult front teeth. Her slim frame is kept warm by a fur coat and her only adornment is pearl ring. The rapport between father and daughter in one image—a profile of both—is plainly evident as is the stepmother, whose reflection is seen in one of Villa Gropius' picture windows.

During her stay in Dessau, Manon toured the Bauhaus campus, for her father and stepmother surely wanted the girl to see that it offered something quite unlike the world of Alma's red salon. Manon attended a concert in the *Aula*, or auditorium, designed by her father and furnished with rows of Marcel Breuer's folding chairs of canvas and nickel-plated tubular steel. In the same building was the cafeteria where the girl could be fed and surrounded by students and faculty. And to appease Manon's interest in theater, she also toured the Bauhaus stage workshop, where the master was the artist Oskar Schlemmer, whose bizarre masks and costumes for his *Triadic Ballet* (1926) and the *Figural Cabinet* (1927) would have been on display or worn, perhaps, to delight the director's daughter who, until now, had only been a photograph on Gropius' desk. And with a crucial municipal election in December—one that could bring a Nazi majority—Manon may have been treated to a rehearsal of Schlemmer's *The Weimar Affair*, for which he costumed himself in a tuxedo and tails and a red paper collar with a white cravat that read "the tie that binds us," a red cardboard dot on his shirtfront that read "the dark, sore, cardinal point," and shoes decorated with red pieces of cloth labeled "the loose tongue."[34]

Manon met her father's other colleagues, including the new young Bauhaus master, the photographer and designer Xanti Schawinsky, who took a special liking to the girl, as did Herbert Bayer. Arrangements were made, too, so that she met people her own age. Manon's shyness, which had been Alma's chief reservations about allowing her to come to Dessau, came out only when the children of the masters' families dutifully waited upon the daughter of the director. But then their visits were too brief and perfunctory for closer ties to develop with the less conventionally raised children of the Bauhaus community.[35]

During the first week of December, Manon's visit came to an end when Alma and Werfel returned for her so that they could travel on to see his family in Prague before returning to Vienna for the holidays. Ise and Walter Gropius drove her to Berlin. Before leaving her father's side, however, Manon promised to write him as he would now write to her and more fulsomely know that he had an idea of her cast of mind, her love for him, and the first signs of intellect and, perhaps, of giftedness. He began their correspondence simply though, by sending her two snapshots, pictures of his little dog standing on the supper table and playing with a ball on the porch of Villa Gropius. He taped these over a postcard, a chromo of a townhouse on a Venice canal, perhaps

---

34 Oskar Schlemmer to Tut Schlemmer, December 5, 1927, in *Oskar Schlemmer: Briefe und Tagebücher* [Letters and Diaries] (Tut Schlemmer ed.) (Ostfildern: Hatje Cantz Verlag), p. 217.

35 See Isaacs, *Walter Gropius*, VOL. 1, p. 422.

recycled from one sent by Alma months ago, one of those mailings Gropius had refused to answer. On the back, Gropius wrote, "my sweet mutzi, I miss you *very* much and dearly wish that you come back soon, 'ischen' too. nuschi is always going to your door and when we call 'mutzi'. he jumps up from the middle of a nap and runs to the door."[36]

The Stepfather

On St. Valentine's Day, 1928, Franz Werfel wrote Manon Gropius from the Imperial Hotel in Santa Margherita on the Italian Riviera. It had been nearly a month since she started boarding school and he knew the girl felt lonely. Her mother, after dropping her off in the second week of January, had traveled on to first meet Werfel and then to join her other daughter, Anna, in Rome for their journey to Sicily. "I wanted to write you a hundred times," Werfel began, "and I never got around to it. I work so much that I have written no one at all this winter . . . You, my dearest little Mutzerl, are the first one I write." As he continued, he compared himself to her—which was, in a way, natural, given how Werfel often felt subordinate to Alma—and how she considered Mutzi and "Franzl" her charges. "You know, I've got it just like you. I am also in a kind of school, a boarding school, having to study and work all day, and, what's more, am my own teacher. But work has its good side, too, as you will find out for yourself soon enough. I am all alone here now. Mommy and Annie are in Palermo. They have still sent me no news from Sicily." And so it was with Manon. Alma had dashed off a two-sentence letter assuring Manon that she would learn many new things as well as this new experience of being with girls just like her. Alma, too, had sent two boxes of fruit drops—one for Manon and one for the headmistress with an inquiry for the latter about the child's hundred-schilling monthly allowance ($14 in 1928 or $214 today).

---

36 Walter Gropius to Manon Gropius, December 11, 1927, ÖNB.

Alma did not encourage Manon to write her unlike Werfel, whose Valentine's Day letter was also a test of the girl's deepness. "In the meantime, I am enormously curious about you're being a big and studious schoolgirl!" Werfel asked. "Couldn't you send me a little letter someday and tell me a few things about your new life? I am sure you won't be too overwhelmed with work and above all you will enjoy making friends with other kids. What one must do together is a hundred times easier and more fun than that dismal studying alone! [. . .] When I get a letter from you, then in gratitude you'll get one from me much longer than this one in which I just wanted to tell you that I am still in the world."[37]

Manon likely endured the new regimen and isolation her "Onkel Werfel" knew about from his own youth in Prague, having been one of the Jewish boys who attended a Catholic school. But in March she enjoyed a long respite when the Institut-Hanausek sent its girls home for the Easter holiday. This meant Venice to Manon and, for the first time, she would fly there on March 31.

Alma had already braved air travel in February, when she and Anna took a seaplane to Sicily. Now she wanted to try the new Vienna–Venice run operated in partnership by the Italian airline Transadriatica, ÖLAG, and the Austrian Air Service. Both companies operated Junkers monoplanes, the single-engine F-13 and the G-24 trimotor (manufactured in Dessau; their designer, Hugo Junkers, attended the opening of the new Bauhaus).[38] Such aircraft could only accommodate five to fifteen passengers and the Venice run took six hours with a layover in Klagenfurt. The ticket price, based on Transadriatica timetables from the late 1920s, was 425 lire (approximately $350 today) for a seat in a cold, unpressurized cabin that offered few creature comforts but plenty of breathtaking views and snowy peaks below.

---

37 Franz Werfel to Manon Gropius, February 14, 1928, ÖNB.

38 Ironically, it was the presence of the Junkers factories that made Dessau a prime target during the Second World War, and resulted in the collateral bombing of the Bauhaus complex.

The girl's snowy journey to Hanover in her stepmother's fast car surely prepared her for the sensation of takeoff, which was uneventful. However, less than an hour into their flight, the little airliner encountered a *Föhn*-driven storm in the mountains. "We seemed to have the choice of crashing on a white ridge or plummeting 10,000 feet into a gorge," Alma wrote afterward.[39]

When the plane landed at Klagenfurt Field to refuel, the pilot requested the most recent weather reports. What he saw did not bode well for crossing the highest peaks. One of his passengers, however, was the director of the airline. He ordered his pilot to take off against his will because, as Alma later learned, this flight was to establish a record and many bets had been placed on the outcome, including those by the same London bookies who had also bet on the success or failure of the *Bremen,* an airplane that had been grounded the day before it was to make the first flight from Berlin to Ireland and on to New York.

So began the "MURDEROUS FLIGHT," as Alma called it, for upon leaving Klagenfurt, the plane met more spring storms blowing up from the south—and with radio navigation being in its infancy, there was no option of attempting to fly above the weather. Flying over the Alps in the 1920s still required that the pilot be able to see the horizon before him in order to orient the plane, which required skimming under and around the clouds. When the plane was suddenly enveloped, the pilot plunged the craft downward in order to find his bearings again on the landscape below. And this need for sight navigation and the turbulence of the storm front caused the plane to lurch and drop repeatedly as it encountered one air pocket after another. Afraid for her life, Alma promised God many things during the course of the flight, things she had been holding back, including, perhaps, rejoining the Catholic

39 The following is based on *And the Bridge is Love*, p. 192; and the passage prefaced "Stürmischer Flug" [Stormy Flight] in Mahler-Werfel, "Diary of Alma Maria," March 31, 1928, pp. 222–3, MWP.

Church and giving in to Werfel's marriage proposals. She also regarded Manon to make sure she was not afraid. But not once had the little girl shown any fear. Indeed, she had shown no emotion at all, wearing the poker face of the girl on the swing. Apparently, she just watched the clouds and mountains passing under the wing—and the theater of the Italian pilot struggling with the controls, for the Junkers likely had no partition between the crew and passengers save for a curtain that was often kept parted. Its cabin would have been filled with the near deafening roar of the motor mounted outside the cockpit.

Eventually, the storm broke. From the window the Alps rolled away below into a plain that was northern Italy and on toward Venice on the horizon. The plane circled out over the water and landed safely at the S. Nicolò Aerodrome on the Lido—the flight had become at last one of those sunlit Futurist tableaus depicted on the airline's brochures. And not only had her mother witnessed Manon's cool nerves during the flight. So did the pilot and flight officer who applauded her bravery as she, like some girl Lindbergh, stepped from their plane.

In the days leading up to her departure for Venice, Manon received a postcard from her father in Stockholm. Gropius told her the Swedish landscape was still filled with snow and ice and that he would soon sail for America. He had more freedom now after his resignation from the Bauhaus in February to concentrate on his architecture and design. One of his chief clients and patrons, Adolf Sommerfeld, the German building and lumber supply manufacturer, was underwriting the journey to the United States, not only for Gropius to study the American construction industry and market, but allow him the chance to spread his ideas in a wealthy country that had the economic might to perhaps realize his vision.

Walter and Ise Gropius departed from Bremerhaven on March 28, 1928, aboard the new German liner *Columbus*, and arrived in New York

City on April 7. The next day, Easter Sunday, Gropius sent Manon a postcard of Manhattan's skyline and a book. He now had more time to write his daughter, to make her a kind of witness to and a stakeholder in his impressions of America. But no letter exists that describes Gropius' week in the city, even though he and Ise saw the Ziegfeld Follies and the Barnum & Bailey Circus, Tiffany's (where the jewelry struck him as decadent), and various structures, such as the Pierpont Morgan Library, the Brooklyn Bridge, Grand Central Station, and Mt. Sinai Hospital, where the nurses resembled the "famous Tiller Girls" compared to their dour German peasant counterparts.

Gropius' first "real," "adult," and extant letter to Manon was written on the stationery of the El Tovar Hotel where he and Ise spent over ten days in May touring Grand Canyon National Park and nearby Indian reservations. The letter's inspiration came from what Gropius had thus far seen as the best route of rapport with his daughter. "for ten days i have actually been among indians!" he wrote, "we travel by horse and wagon through this god's country and praise the descendents of winnetou: the navaho, hopi, and supai indians. you ride day after day on horseback in order to visit them. nowadays they are peaceful with the whites, but they still very much have their dress, dwellings and customs of old! i am sending you some pictures that i did myself in part, others will follow. did you receive that indian book that i sent you from new york? In three days ise and i leave the indians and go to california—los angeles. i am back in germany at the beginning of june. i long for a message from you and mommy."[40]

Since Gropius likely sent this letter and anything else to Vienna, Manon may not have seen them for weeks given that she was traveling with her mother in Italy and eventually put back in boarding school—a vacuum of irresponsiveness that hardly prompted Gropius to write further, which created further distance, another kind of vacuum,

40 Walter Gropius to Manon Gropius, May 10, 1928, ÖNB.

between him and his daughter when she was seemingly mature enough to keep up her end of a correspondence. Indeed, in photographs that likely date from the summer of 1928, Manon looked like a small adult in a short-sleeved, floral print dress tied off with a white apron. Her hair is worn in a single long braid, which also makes her look older and closer to her final form. Her face in these images, all taken on Semmering, is not unlike the one Werfel borrowed for her character in *Embezzled Heaven*. "I shall never forget the expression on the face of little Doris, who was not yet thirteen years old at the time," Werfel's character, a writer and permanent guest of a wealthy family, reflects after he read from Adelbert Stifter's essay about the solar eclipse of 1842. "This quintessence of listening, the Platonic idea of listening, so to speak, this tense absorption, this tranquil imbibing of spiritual beauty, this pure emergence into visibility of the invisible soul—it was one of those rare moments in which a vision fills one with a profound, embracing love for one's fellow-men and for all mankind."[41]

Gropius, naturally, wanted to see this idealized person up close too—in Berlin, where he and Ise moved to a spacious twelve-room apartment at 121A Potsdamer Privatstrasse in Spandau, with two mature cedars of Lebanon towering on either side of the entrance. He moved his architectural practice to offices below, where he continued to work on new commissions, including a new touring car for the German automobile manufacturer Adler. Preoccupied once more with his work, he let his correspondence with Manon lapse until the autumn, when he learned from Alma that the girl was in Venice, which prompted him to acknowledge her approaching birthday. "just got back from zurich," he wrote Manon, "and better start cracking to send you a thousand kisses and hugs in time for your first dozen years!!!" He told her that he had already sent her a wristwatch and hoped that she had not received a dozen more because, like other adults, it was now seen

41 Werfel, *Embezzled Heaven*, p. 6.

as the right gift for a young person now old enough be cognizant of her time, her schedule, and how to organize herself. "if that's the case," he continued, "send it back to me and i will give you something else that you really want!" In the same letter, Gropius promised Manon there would be more to do in Berlin compared to provincial Dessau. He told her that he wanted to take her on long trips in the car Adler had loaned him, about his new apartment, and how Ise missed her. He described watching from his terrace the new *Graf Zeppelin* rise from the nearby airfield and fly over his building—a "glorious sight, like a silver ship glittering in the sun." He asked Manon to write him, for she had not written him a real letter yet. This he chivalrously took the blame himself "for it seems as if you have inherited my letter-writing laziness" and "so must i pay for my own laziness to you!" Gropius, too, reminded Manon that her mother would be in Berlin in November and that she should come and visit him there. He hoped, too, that she would for the present enjoy the "fun 'n' sun that you can only enjoy in venice!"[42]

Manon Gropius did not enjoy Venice much longer. She had to return to her boarding school, which often left her bored, restless, and longing for the next holiday—Christmas and the long week of bringing in the new year, 1929. Then it would be back to school and waiting for Easter and Venice—or those chance holidays when her mother took her out of school for a traveling companion. In her thirteenth year, Manon seemed to be developing, indeed, speeding along into a real person, an individual. "My sweet Mutzikind," a self-deprecatory Werfel wrote her in gratitude for one of her now lost childhood letters. "You have excellent handwriting.—When I come to Vienna the next time, you will surely be a 100 kilometers ahead once more. This Bohemian presents you with this scrap of paper as a hurried reply to your lines and as a

42 Walter Gropius to Manon Gropius, October 3, 1928, ÖNB.

small token that I am always always always thinking of you. [. . .] I did not write as beautifully as you."[43]

Her mother, too, would reach a milestone in 1929—the age of fifty, which was then considered the crest of one's life, a time to take stock, assume one's emeritus status, and accept aging gracefully. The first two Alma did naturally, but the latter was already proving difficult for Alma given her diary entries that complain of constipation, sweating, and spasmodic pain. That she had become addicted to tippling Benedictine as her favorite form of self-treatment escaped her. "Physically I was not in good shape," Alma wrote, "I was failing everywhere. My eyes would no longer keep up; my hands slowed down on the piano; food did not agree with me, standing did not, walking did not—nothing did but drinking, perhaps. It was often the only way to control the chills and shudders in my body, since I had a vagotonic disposition, a weak heart, and a low pulse. [. . .] I had to keep in step, to feign youth."[44] And what made it harder, bitterer, was the youth of her teenage daughter and Werfel, who was not yet forty.

Alma found travel to be the best way to distract herself from herself. She revived her dream of going to India. She even purchased tickets so as to present the journey as a fait accompli to Werfel. However, he found the idea of such a long trip too arduous and disruptive for his work. So Alma exchanged her tickets for a future voyage and visited Paris for its theater, opera, and high society and entertained thoughts of buying another home in Italy, a seventeenth-century castle outside the town of Comologno, where she would retire to live like a mother superior with, presumably, Manon as her one novice.

Meanwhile, Manon remained in Vienna, where she attended her boarding school during the winter and spring. There her mother wired for hugs and kisses and asked Madame Renard-Stonner in the tersest

---

43 Franz Werfel to Manon Gropius, undated, ÖNB.

44 Mahler-Werfel, *And the Bridge Is Love*, p. 197.

telegramese (REQUEST WIRE HOW MANON IS DOING, REQUEST MUTZI'S CONDITION). Alma contented herself with the idea that the Institut-Hanausek properly educated and cultivated her daughter in mind and body. Her only concern had been Manon's "innocent talk in school about 'Onkel Werfel, who is living with us.'"[45] It was this impropriety that forced Alma to finally yield to Werfel on marriage.

She had long resisted marriage for two reasons—it entailed a certain loss of existential freedom for her and it meant marrying a man who, though seemingly Christian in every way, remained a steadfast Jew. And as Alma aged, her anti-Semitism only intensified. She likely did not want a family connection to Werfel's family, too. Although she considered his mother and father "good Jews, surely meaning well," it was hard for her to reciprocate their warmth when they visited Alma, their son, and Manon during Easter in Venice.[46] Weeks passed before Alma finally agreed to end ten years of what she called "wild wedlock." She did so with her mind occupied with her regrets over Kokoschka and Werfel's lingering desire to be in "the eye than this blurry beast of class struggle—which is none of [his] business."[47] To smooth the way past such doubts, Werfel filed papers with the city of Vienna, since one's religion had to be legally declared, and resigned from the "Mosaic faith" and entered himself as "unaffiliated." He allowed for Alma to provide the rest of the leverage—Manon. Although what the "neighbors" thought of her did not matter. But it did for her daughter—especially in the future when it came time for her to marry—hopefully into Viennese society, for Alma already entertained plans and alliances for the girl, and for that "Manon perhaps [. . .] Martin Johannes should grow up in orderly, western surroundings."[48]

45 Mahler-Werfel, *And the Bridge Is Love*, p. 197.

46 Mahler-Werfel, "Diary of Alma Maria," March 4, 1928, p. 230.

47 Mahler-Werfel, *And the Bridge Is Love*, p. 231.

48 Mahler-Werfel, *Mein Leben*, p. 201.

Alma Mahler and Franz Werfel were married by a justice of the peace in Vienna's Rathaus—the city hall—on Saturday, July 6, 1929. In a matter of seconds, after the witnesses had signed the marriage certification, Manon Gropius, the architect's daughter, became the stepchild of a famous novelist, poet, and playwright, who was only one great book shy of being nominated for the Nobel Prize in Literature. Meanwhile her real father, Walter Gropius, had designed a line of modular furniture for Feder Department Stores in Germany—pieces in appearance and packaging that anticipated what IKEA stores sell all over the world today. In trying to picture his daughter in her world, he imagined her room furnished with his work.

In late July, Gropius, much as Werfel did, thanked Manon for one of her well-written letters. Though it is lost, like all the letters she wrote her father, some of her personality surfaces in her father's response, his mild defense of himself. "my dearest mutzi, you are right to berate my heartlessly lax letter-writing, which surely has nothing to do with 'forgetting,'" Gropius wrote, "for you are never so light as to slip from my mind and heart. i suffer that, for it's so terribly seldom that we see each other and this writing-paper life is only a dreary replacement. i have been in berlin for over a year, but you haven't even seen my new surroundings. i hope that you come soon someday—finally!—i am proud of you, that you have such good grades and already write like a grownup and i am happy that you're up in semmering prowling around. i will pick out a few trinkets for you here that surely won't fit into your current indian life but might later back in vienna. i will send you that picture of me again so that you will not totally forget my face during our long separations and please send a snapshot of you again as well, one that mommy has surely taken of you."[49]

Gropius ended his letter with greetings for her mother, her half-sister, and Sister Ida, which may have been his way of acknowledging

49 Walter Gropius to Manon Gropius, July 30, 1929, ÖNB.

and—as Wittgenstein says—"passing over in silence" that Werfel was now her stepfather. And with every request for a new photograph taken by her mother, Gropius might have to see Werfel with the girl as though she were his child—photographs in which it is easy to see that she hardly resembled him and would even be taller in another year or two. Although there was no longer any animosity on Gropius' part for Werfel—indeed, Werfel belonged to the Circle of Friends of the Bauhaus—Gropius surely left it to the imagination of others—including this author's—about his feelings in regard to Werfel's closeness to Manon, how much she saw Werfel as a father figure over her real one.

Ironically, Werfel, even with his frequent presence in Manon's life, felt that he neglected her too much. When he returned to her mother, after weeks of writing in Italy, he made up for it. Werfel gave Manon special attention, too, when it came to teasing her out of her shyness and cultivating her imagination, her seeming desire to be an actor, as when he prepared an elaborate entertainment intended, perhaps, for Alma's fiftieth birthday at Haus Mahler in August 1929.

Werfel had seen how the theater thrilled his newly acquired stepdaughter. Three years earlier, in March 1926, when Manon was nine, she had attended the Dresden rehearsals and opening of Verdi's 1862 opera *La forza del destino* (1862). Werfel's translation of the Italian libretto—*Der Macht des Schicksals*—The Force of Fate—proved an enormous success and the opera enjoyed a revival in the German and Austrian cities where it was performed. Set in Spain, the opera had all the death and sadness Manon professed to love in *Spiegelmensch.* The story begins as a forbidden love affair between Don Alvaro, the son of an Incan princess, and Leonora, the daughter of a Spanish marquis, and ends with her disguised as an eremetic monk, stabbed to death by her brother seeking revenge for the murder of their father.

La forza del destino, eerily in keeping with its fatidic theme of unavoidable doom, also had the reputation of being a cursed opera. The soprano who first played Leonora died of a grave illness. Over the years, other performers have suffered some bad fate. An opera house once suddenly and inexplicably lost power. And in 1960, a famous baritone dropped dead on stage after launching into an aria that begins "To die, a terrible thing!" The opera was also considered too chaotic and Verdi's black sheep. Werfel, however, saved it from obscurity—and to his surprise and personal satisfaction, *The Force of Fate*, with all its miscegenation, swordplay, bloodshed, crossdressing, and potent mix of love and religion, had rekindled Manon's interest in the theater. "Her face was no longer pale—it positively glowed instead. And she already knew the entire text by heart," Werfel recalled much later in his "Manon" necrology. Paradoxically in this account, Manon was twelve years' old according to Werfel's reckoning, which dates what came next to 1929—an adaptation of his libretto for a theatrical children's performance of *The Force of Fate* to please Alma and her guests at Haus Mahler and to showcase their talented daughter on her mother's birthday.[50]

This last assertion is conjectural. Unfortunately, Alma's published memoirs more confuse than corroborate. While she gets the costuming right, her editors seem to have comingled two separate events. Werfel's novel 1939 *Embezzled Heaven*, however, does provide a kind of reference point from which to deduce the year 1929 and an August birthday, indeed, a significant birthday and party given for Alma's character. The festivities feature an outdoor theatrical pantomime in which Manon's character, a twelve-year-old girl, performs in a period costume, a "rococo dress-coat" under the direction of the narrator, Werfel's character.[51]

What the novel, Werfel's necrology, and Alma's diary transcript agree on is the presence of celebrated guests in Manon's audience, including the Burgtheater director Franz Herterich and his companion,

50 The following account and quotes are from Werfel, "Manon," *Erzählungen aus zwei Welten*, p. 392ff.

51 See Werfel, *Embezzled Heaven*, p. 125ff.

the lieder singer Stella Eisner, Sholem Asch and his wife, and others. Werfel himself directed the play, which not only included Manon, but a playmate from the neighborhood of Breitenstein, a "little friend [who] kept Manon company there," according to Werfel, "a funny, plump-looking thing." They would not sing, but rather read their parts, which, perhaps, to Werfel obviated any curse, there would be no notes, like those in the overture believed to be *Diabolus in musica*, the notion that a certain combination of notes summoned not only evil but the devil himself. And what could be more innocent than children pretending to be actors on the porch of Haus Mahler, the porch that Gropius had designed for Alma during the war years?

"[T]hose days of preparation live on in me unforgotten," wrote Werfel (who also admitted to having a terrible memory). "I helped Manon through her role—or, more accurately, *roles*, for she performed several. I believe that no director who ever hit on such a talent for the first time, untalkative, a perfect listener, would have known a greater joy than mine." Altering some adult costumes used for other summertime family masquerades at Haus Mahler, Manon played Don Alvaro as a Spanish officer in a rococo evening coat with high-heel lady's shoes and a toy sword. She also played him as the Brother Rafaello, in a real monk's habit that had to be hemmed for her to wear.

That no photographs had been taken of Werfel's adaptation of *The Force of Fate* or the children in their costumes is remarkable given how many photographs there are of Manon at Haus Mahler. It suggests that the play had been performed in twilight, after dinner, when the light was too dim for cameras that lacked a flash apparatus.

Presumably, the double doors that led from the living room to the porch were opened in lieu of a raised curtain. The spectators sat in chairs placed on the lawn. "This audience, among which could be found theater people, was as much surprised as I was by the twelve-year-old Manon," Werfel continues. "She moved freely in her costume and with incomparable grace. She was entirely immersed into the character she played. In her dark voice, there was this sweet, child's emotion. She even made you overlook the occasional involuntary comedy of her partner, the clumsy fat girl. In that scene with the monk kneeling and begging his opponent for forgiveness, I forgot that it was a child, my child, and for a moment felt real pathos."

As a youth back in Prague, Werfel had crushes on the actresses of his day and wrote poems about how their unattainableness to him as a boy had made him into a writer, such as an early elegy to Eleonora Duse and a later poem for Marie Immisch, whose range and appearance almost seem informed by Manon. "Her hair was black. Her eyes were blue," he wrote of Immisch, "She played girl, child, and lady / In peplum, petticoat, Stuart collar, cloak. / She spoke the words in a dark contralto"[52]—and to be the mentor-father of such a talent—now *attainable*, now "my child"—surely ran through his mind on that summer evening. "From that day on for us, for my wife and me," Werfel continued in his necrology, "it was settled then and there that Manon was born for the theater and would be going into the theater no matter what. That much was understood, particularly by me, such that we did not talk about it much anymore. We did not suspect that this childhood and public performance of *The Force of Fate* would have been Manon's one appearance."[53]

---

52 Franz Werfel, "Sechs Setterime zu Ehren des Frühlings von Neunzehnhundertundfünf [Six Septets to Honor the Spring of 1905]," *Gedichte aus den Jahren 1908–1945* (Frankfurt am Main: Fischer, 1946), p. 153. The poem is based on a Prague theatre festival marking the hundredth anniversary of Schiller's death.
53 Werfel, "Manon," *Erzählungen aus zwei Welten*, p. 393.

The parents.

(LEFT) Family portrait of Manon, Walter, and Alma Gropius, December 1917. MWP.

(RIGHT) Alma Mahler and Franz Werfel, 1918. MWP.

Manon Gropius, second from left, and her half-sister, Anna Mahler, extreme right, summer 1917. MWP.

Manon Gropius in Venice, Easter 1923.

(ABOVE) With Franz Werfel and Alma Mahler in St. Mark's Square.

(LEFT) With Alma at the Caffè Florian.

Courtesy of Maria Mahler.

Manon Gropius, her grandmother Anna Moll, and Anna Mahler at Casa Mahler, Venice, 1924. MWP.

Growing.

(LEFT) In early seventeenth-century Venetian costume dress, 1924.

(RIGHT) On a swing near Haus Mahler, Breitenstein, 1925–26. MWP.

(BELOW) Manon and Walter Gropius on the porch of Villa Gropius, Dessau, 1927 (the Feininger–Moholy-Nagy master house can be seen in the background, top left). BHA.

(ABOVE) Manon Gropius reading Karl May's *Winnetou* in a Marcel Breuer "Wassily Chair," Villa Gropius, Dessau, 1927. BHA.

(BELOW) Villa Mahler, postcard sent by Manon Gropius to Leo Perutz, thanking him for a birthday gift. October 1934. DE.

_ate autumn picnic—a fifteen-year-old Manon Gropius shown with Walter Gropius and Ellen Frank in the Adler Primus, November 1931. BHA.

Visitors at Haus Mahler, Summer 1933.
(LEFT) Susi Kertész, Alma Mahler, and Manon Gropius. MWP.
(RIGHT) Alma, Julius Tandler, and Manon. Courtesy of Marina Mahler.

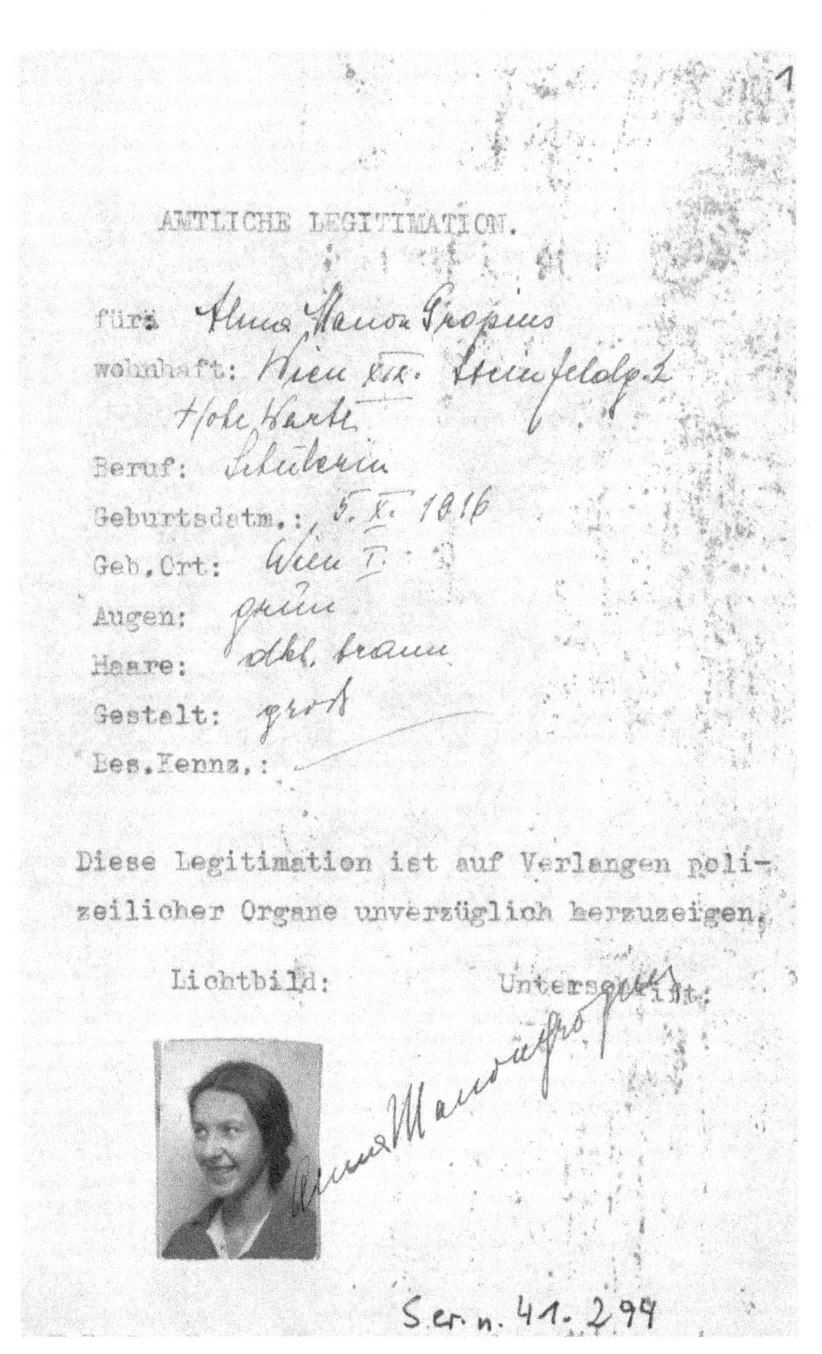

AMTLICHE LEGITIMATION.

für: Anna Manon Gropius

wohnhaft: Wien XIX. Steinfeldg. 2
Hohe Warte

Beruf: Schülerin

Geburtsdatm.: 5. X. 1916

Geb. Ort: Wien I.

Augen: grün

Haare: dkl. braun

Gestalt: groß

Bes. Kennz.:

Diese Legitimation ist auf Verlangen polizeilicher Organe unverzüglich herzuzeigen.

Lichtbild: Unterschrift:

Anna Manon Gropius

Ser. n. 41. 294

Manon Gropius's police passport during the February Uprising, 1934. ÖNB.

Manon, Ernst Lothar, Alma, and Werfel at the Caffè Lavena, Venice, April 12, 1934. MWP.

Manon's grave, spring 1956.
Walter Gropius Papers, Harvard University. WGP.

Cover art of Pinchas Zukerman and Pierre Boulez's 1986 Columbia Masterworks recording of Alban Berg's Violin Concerto. Sony Music.

THE GAZELLE

To this extent, as Alma experienced the vicissitudes of age upon her own body, she projected what she no longer could radiate herself—eroticism and sexual attractiveness—into her "pure" daughter.

—Oliver Hilmes[1]

The Palace

Three weeks after Manon celebrated her thirteenth birthday, panic sales on the New York Stock Exchange resulted in the unprecedented stock market crash that would be called "Black Tuesday." In the evening edition of Vienna's liberal daily, the *Neue Freie Presse,* for October 24, the lead editorial opined that "political tranquility" between the various factions in Austria would bring "economic calm." However, a late report from New York reported a 100-point drop in value and a sell-off of over six million stocks traded in one day, in other words, a "*finanzielle Katastrophe.*"

To Austria and Germany, the unfolding Great Depression further weakened their new and still vulnerable democratic institutions. Austria's new chancellor, Johann Schober, promised reforms that would unite his increasingly restive nation. But he was mistrusted by the powerful Social Democrats, especially for the ruthless way he suppressed the Revolt of July 1927 as Vienna's police president. And though he claimed no party affiliation, he was seen as serving the various parties and interest groups

---

1 Hilmes, *Witwe im Wahn*, p. 258.

on the right, including industrialists, the conservative Catholic clergy, the quasi-fascist Christian Socialists, and the *Heimwehr*—the Home Guard—whose troops sported feathered Tyrolese hats and hobnail mountaineering boots. To counter the latter, the Social Democrats, whose support was found in Vienna and other large Austrian cities, formed the *Schutzbund*, brigades of armed workers. And amid such a divided society, Austria's National Socialist Workers Party—an arm of the Nazi party in Germany and loyal to Adolf Hitler—found increasing support, especially in the countryside and among students.

Despite the gloomy news in Vienna's newspapers, cheery advertisements for winter vacations also appeared on the front pages for the November–January travel season to Egypt aboard Lloyd Line steamers departing from Trieste for the "the Land of the Pharaohs." Alma, however, hardly needed such prompts for her delayed honeymoon—a reprise of their 1925 journey with an extended tour of Palestine, Syria, and Lebanon from January to March 1930. This long whirlwind tour began once more in Cairo with a night at the opera again and a stay at the famous Mena House near the Valley of the Kings, where they rented a motorcycle and sidecar to ride out into the desert in the cool Egyptian winter. Alma and Werfel also traveled on to Palestine once again. They stayed at the Hotel King David in Jerusalem and explored the Old City. In Damascus, they toured a carpet-weaving factory that employed Armenian children orphaned during the genocidal deportation campaigns of the Young Turks between 1915 and 1918. Werfel's subsequent research of these events would become his next novel, for the calamity that the Armenians suffered during a virtually forgotten event in the Great War could happen again—to German and Austrian Jews. Despite the new obsession of a book that would certainly write itself after learning about how the Armenians resisted the Turks on a mountain named Musa Dagh—Mt. Moses—Werfel thought of his stepdaughter. Left behind, Manon had become a problem at the Institut-Hanausek. "Do well as usual and keep doing well,"

Werfel wrote to reassure her. "The first semester is over and we're already slowly getting closer to holiday time, that blink of an eye, when we go up to Semmering, where I already long to be. [. . .] be well, keep doing well, and take a bite of those assorted sour apples that life not only serves us in school."[2]

Werfel signed his letter with "Franzl" to soften what amounted to paternal advice from him. The tenor of Alma's telegrams to Madam Renard-Stonner, however, requesting information about Manon's health and mood revealed a more urgent situation—the first of others as the year progressed. These testify to some difficulty with traditional forms of instruction, as when Manon's piano teacher, a young woman, resigned. Although raised in a musical household founded by Alma and long exposed to young musical talents such as her half-sister and Gustav Mahler's nephew, Wolfgang Rosé—a piano prodigy who spent part of the summer of 1921 at Haus Mahler much to the delight of Alma's "exceedingly bright and dreamy daughter"[3]—Manon showed little aptitude for the piano. Alma, nevertheless, refused to abandon the idea that Manon would be musical and, as a favor to her, Alban Berg interceded. He arranged for his student, Hans Erich Apostel, to assume the duties of Manon's piano teacher because the younger man had "specialized himself in difficult pedagogical cases."[4] Manon, however, refused to keep her nails cut short and to practice "loudly and slowly" as Alma and Helene Berg had advised. She also refused to cooperate with Herr Apostel, who found the teenage girl insufferable.[5]

---

2 Franz Werfel to Manon Gropius, undated [early February 1930], ÖNB.

3 Mahler-Werfel, *Mein Leben*, p. 153.

4 Harald Kaufmann, *Hans Erich Apostel*, VOL. 4, *Österreichische Komponisten des XX. Jahrhunderts* [Austrian Composers of the 20th Century] (Vienna: Lafite, 1965), p. 57.

5 See Bernhard Günther and Andreas Vejvar, *Musik aus Österreich* [Music from Austria] (Vienna: Music Information Center, 1997), p. 92; and "More on Secret Programs," *Encrypted Messages in Alban Berg's Music* (Siglind Bruhn ed.) (New

He, too, resigned, and if Alma had any hopes of Manon Gropius having musical talent and becoming another member of her musical family, they were dashed.

Alma must have complained to Gropius about Manon and her school, which he only acknowledged to his daughter as being an impediment in their way to some life together, of even being *on the road* together. "finally i have received a small sign of life from you—via egypt from mommy—a little letter, which you wrote *her*. did you know it has been six months since your last little letter to me?" he began, still smarting after a ring he had sent to her as a Christmas present had been returned despite the correct address on the package. "you outdo me considerably in my own aversion to writing [. . .] how are things going, what are you up to, with whom do you go around—everything interests me that concerns you. i only see you from very far away, through upside-down opera glasses [. . .]," he went on. "i long for the day when you are done with school and you can divide your time more freely than you can now. Then you could surely go with me on my trips sometimes! i drive around a lot lately because i am, having become its general director, setting up a german exhibition in paris. perhaps mommy can take you there in the spring!? that would give me the greatest joy!"[6] In ending his letter, he offered her something else in place of the ring—an ensemble of his Feder furniture.

In early March, Alma and Werfel sailed from Alexandria to Venice. There Alma hoped to decorate Casa Mahler with the objects and souvenirs she had purchased during her travels. However, not long after

---

York: Routledge, 1998), pp. 51–2, in which the musicologist Gottfried Scholz describes how Apostel told him many years later that the angel of Berg's Violin Concerto was nothing but a "spoiled brat" and hardly possessed the angelic nature that Berg and his wife Helene saw.

6 Walter Gropius to Manon Gropius, February 26, 1930, ÖNB.

her arrival, she learned that Manon had developed an oral infection. Alma cabled Dr. Gertrud Bien, requesting that she take Manon to her dentist and have her braces ("*Maschine*") removed. The irony here is that Dr. Bien was no ordinary pediatrician. She came from a family of respected Jewish physicians and, in addition to being one of the few women doctors in Vienna, had proved herself an able administrator as the head of the Children's Reception Center (*Kinderübernahmestelle*), an innovative primary care and observation station for abused and neglected children established by her colleague, Vienna's Social Democrat health minister, Dr. Julius Tandler. To Alma, however, she was still seen as a mere house physician for wealthy families—and Tandler's mistress. Although Alma entertained the pair in her home, she despised Dr. Bien. But Manon trusted her and Alma did not want Manon pressuring her half-sister into helping her during this crisis, for she blamed Anna for making her older sister Maria sick and still considered Anna contagious with scarlet fever after nearly a quarter of a century!

What also bothered Alma about Anna Mahler was her third marriage—to Werfel's publisher Paul Zsolnay, whose family derived its wealth in part from tobacco imports and whose mother, Amanda "Andy" Zsolnay had a salon of her own and whose patronage of the arts trumped Alma's many times over. "Strangely," Alma wrote in her diary in August 1930, "Anna is now a rich woman—in her palace, with a host of servants, thus a so-called grand life. Poor child! I would not want to trade with her, I'd rather reduce my standard [of living], not raise [it]."[7] Even so, Alma had always envied her wealthier Jewish friends and how they made her feel unworthy—something that Anna's new mother-in-law must have apprehended, for she encouraged Alma to go house-hunting for a villa that suited her station as Mahler's widow, the wife of Austria's leading author, and for Manon, who could not be presented to the eligible bachelors of good families in a flat, no

7 Mahler-Werfel, "Diary of Alma Maria," August 8, 1930, p. 242, MWP.

matter how quaint or beautifully decorated. "I will not have myself fixating this way on material things," Alma told herself in her diary.[8] Nevertheless, she did and found a mansion she knew well.

Haus Ast, at Steinfeldgasse 2, was around the corner from her mother and stepfather's villa at Wollergasse 10. The great Secessionist architect Josef Hoffmann had designed the building for Eduard Ast, a construction engineer whose company had built virtually everything made of reinforced concrete for the Austro-Hungarian Empire's infrastructure, from railway bridges to mountain tunnels. Completed in 1911, Haus Ast was the last mansion in Hoffmann's "villa colony" on Hohe Warte (a placename not unlike Watch Hill or Mt. Lookout) in the suburb of Döbling. As with his other villas, Haus Ast featured site-specific furnishings and motifs found in the woodwork, tile, and other furnishings. Indeed, no expense had been spared on this architectural jewel of the Wien Werkstätte, and its sand-colored mortar exterior and concrete fabrication bespoke Eduard Ast's wealth and its source. The villa's grounds encompassed a beautiful flower garden in the back with a pergola and reflecting pond bordered by forest, which adjoined the Moll property. From its third story, one had a breathtaking panorama to the west, with views of the Vienna Woods, hills gently sloping upward covered with vineyards to the horizon, and such prominent landmarks as the Orphanage for Jewish Girls and the Gothic clock tower and red-tiled roof of St. Michael's Parish Church. Yet despite the suburban, even bucolic setting, Haus Ast was connected to Vienna proper, for Woller- and Steinfeldgasse formed part of the terminus for the Number 37 streetcar, which circled and returned to the heart of the city—the Schottenpassage on the Ring. Less than a kilometer downhill was another even more imposing structure, the world's largest apartment building, the Karl-Marx-Hof, the pride of Red Vienna's efforts to provide working class families with affordable housing.

8 Mahler-Werfel, "Diary of Alma Maria," August 8, 1930, p. 242, MWP.

Eduard Ast's firm had been greatly impacted by the increasing effects of a now worldwide depression. To remain solvent, he put the house on the market in late 1930 and Alma and Franz Werfel purchased it in January 1931. However, even at a comparative bargain, it would be a costly purchase for Alma and Werfel. Fortunately, Werfel's father transferred forty thousand schillings into his son's bank account as the down payment.[9] More money, however, would be needed to pay the legion of interior decorators, carpenters, and like craftsmen who now transformed Haus Ast into "Villa Mahler," which Alma wanted to be a virtual museum of her life and her possessions, from her father's paintings to Auguste Rodin's bust of Gustav Mahler, which would greet guests in the grand entrance hall. And as work proceeded, Alma took Manon out of school in early February and mother and daughter traveled to a thermal mud spa in Italy to treat Manon for back pain, likely due to an accident she suffered after tripping over the runners of a bobsled and a broken nose as well—injuries that may have been self-inflicted to get away from Madame Renard-Stonner.

This therapeutic vacation lasted for several weeks and included side trips to Venice and Santa Margherita, where Werfel was writing his sixth major novel, *The Pascarella Family* (*Die Geschwister vom Neapel*, 1931). They also stayed at Casa Mahler for the rest of February before returning to Vienna in early March, when Manon received a letter from her father, who had seen her "inner portrait" in an X-ray that Alma sent. He commiserated with his daughter, described his newly designed Adler "Primus" cabriolet, and acknowledged the impending move to her new home. "with satisfaction i see you're sauntering about in the riviera sun, i'm glad that you succeeded in unscrewing yourself away from the iron directrice, which certainly tested the courage of the whole family! [. . .] i'll soon be getting the enclosed bed car that i designed, which made a big impression here at the international auto show. you

9 Around $5,700 at the 1931 exchange rate.

can sleep in it on the go. if the factory puts the car at my disposal, as i expect, then i really must take you for a drive in it once this year. it is a beautiful car that looks marvelous, i have attached a photo for you. — so now you're moving into your fancy chateau! you must send me the exact floor plan of your room so that we can install everything correctly and then i will gradually send you the additional furniture, a wardrobe and bed and what else you still need in fabrics, etc.!"[10]

While Gropius voiced only enthusiasm for his daughter—and with only a mild trace of irony or resentment that she would live in a style and setting that dwarfed his—Alma dwelled on what was wrong with the impending move. Herr Ast and his wife Marie had lost their two adult children in the villa—indeed, in one of the rooms that would be Manon's quarters. Eduard Ast II had died of leukemia in April 1923, a week after Easter Sunday. Then a year later, in May, his younger sister Grete died at the age of twenty while giving birth.[11] Alma repressed her misgivings, but at last they surfaced on her final day—March 29, 1931—in her beloved apartment at Elisabethstrasse 22.

That Sunday had been an eventful day of snowstorms in Vienna, made all the more dramatic by the early morning overflight of the *Graf Zeppelin*, which had been lit up by searchlights. At noon, to mark International Women's Day, socialist and communist groups had organized a mass rally of working-class women and children who braved the driving snow. They formed a column and marched in the Ringstrasse carrying red banners and signs with slogans that read "Against the Social Reaction!" and the like, all a show of strength against Austria's increasingly militant right-wing. For Alma, however, it was a quiet day

10 Walter Gropius to Manon Gropius, March 5, 1931, ÖNB.

11 Margarethe Ast Bernatzik was the first wife of the anthropologist–ethnophotographer Hugo Bernatzik (1897–1953), the founder of the concept of alternative anthropology. Her portrait by the Austrian Expressionist Anton Kolig, which depicts her pregnant, hangs in the Belvedere.

spent with Manon alone, for the servants had the day off. Undoubtedly, seeing her child healthy, happy, and very much alive both comforted Alma and weighed on her. She worried about what their life would be like in the new house haunted by the dead children of its former owners. Ever superstitious—especially when it came to herself, of being cursed, a "*jettatore*," Alma wrote in her diary that she would "have to muster a lot of strength to battle the deaths there," whatever force had killed the Ast children. "Will my cheerfulness," she asked herself, "be able to dry the tear-soaked walls? It is perhaps no accident that I am so—totally alone. Is it the end of the past or the beginning of the future? I would like to hear a human voice and even if it were the stupidest, the furthest away!"[12]

Alma and Manon moved to Steinfeldgasse 2 the next day. Her fears during the sleepless hours of the night before faded. She now felt welcomed by the great house. "The untold work," however, undertaken by the movers and Alma herself—still nursing a badly strained shoulder from the previous days of packing—left her exhausted. By evening, she could think of nothing but going to bed. But she was restless and so was Manon. Both felt too far away from each other, too isolated. They were no longer just a few rooms away. Unfamiliar steps and long corridors separated their quarters. Unable to sleep, mother and daughter crawled into Alma's king-size bed and slept their first night together in what was now Villa Mahler.

Alma's friend, Felix Salten, the author of *Bambi* had suggested that she throw a party to help dispel the loneliness and the onus of any family curse. So, during Holy Week—and before she left for Venice—Alma gave a proper Viennese house-warming, with plenty of *Gemütlichkeit* provided by herself and her guests, mostly theater and film people, including the director of the Burgtheater, Georg Reimers, and

---

12 Mahler-Werfel, *And the Bridge Is Love*, p. 204; and "Diary of Alma Maria," March 29, 1931, p. 257, MWP.

the screen actor Conrad Veidt. Such parties went on until dawn with plenty of music and conversation, food and drink—surely enough for Alma to exorcise the ghosts of the dead Ast children. Certainly some of the good cheer came, perhaps, from seeing Manon descend Villa Mahler's great staircase like Ernst Lothar's heroine-daughter in *Little Friend*, "as she tensed her bare, pretty, long-shanked legs, in white anklets and narrow Mary Janes, almost teetering on every stairstep."[13]

Amid the powder snow and pine trees of the Riesengebirge in the Sudeten region of northern Czechoslovakia, Walter Gropius saw Manon, too, during the first week of April. He imagined her on a ski slope, learning to go downhill with him. In a postcard signed by Ise, Herbert Bayer, and his wife Irene—missent to Elisabethstrasse—Gropius suggested that Manon accompany him on a ski trip in the near future. He had made such requests in the recent past, for skiing had become one of Gropius' favorite pleasures in his middle years, as it was for his wife Ise and the *Bauhäusler* of their inner circle.

"Greetings to the Vienna branch office" read one such request—in Xanti Schawinsky's hand—from an earlier road trip to Ascona, Switzerland, this on the face front of a postcard depicting one of the architectural wonders of Germany, the Ulm Minster, which once boasted the world's tallest steeple. For the added amusement of the recipient, Schawinsky drew a little Charlie Chaplin-like caricature clinging to the bell tower. Bayer inscribed his own greetings for Manon and added an angel in flight, holding up a swallowtailed lancer's flag in one hand and the other thrusting a lightning bolt at the church.

In asking Manon, Gropius reminded her that she would need her mother's permission. But it never came, for Alma, vigilant and overprotective of what was hers, likely forbade Manon and could point to the girl's sled accident as a reason not to risk further injuries that often

13 Lothar, *Kleine Freundin*, p. 96.

left victims paralyzed given what the newspapers reported. Then there was a diagnosed minor defect in Manon's right foot, discovered by the physical education instructor at her boarding school. "We have two underage persons to look after," Alma wrote in the days before the twentieth anniversary of Mahler's death. "Werfel and Mutzi—and nothing else is more important to us now."[14]

Though Alma had no desire for Gropius to help her with the one charge they had in common, she nevertheless reproached him for neglecting their daughter. In June, Gropius endured one of Alma's letters in which he learned that Manon had left school. This prompted a long letter to her in early July. Much weighed on his mind. The German republic, like Austria, was now in the throes of the Great Depression. Banks had closed, a monetary crisis had ensued, and the unemployed were taking sides, more so with the Nazis than their Communist adversaries in the ongoing street fighting. And he had only scraps of information from Alma about his daughter—and hardly any images of her, ones that he could have latched on to, like the snapshots taken of her new wigwam on Semmering, in which she slept out at night during the summer, for she still loved and identified with American Indians. And Gropius still lacked an address for the new house! He had little to go on but that and his imagination as he suggested an alternative plan for her future. "you're probably already fatalistically resigned about your letterless papa," he began, disparaging himself,

> right now i'm outside on our balcony, in air that is finally getting cooler, to devote myself to you, my darling. you can hardly imagine the difficulties that have beset me in the last months in this battered and impoverished germany. being true to my plan to simply live and work for things that look important to me and worth my effort, i've fought hard to exist, for a 'decent'

14 Mahler-Werfel, "Diary of Alma-Maria," April 30, 1931, p. 258, MWP.

living, the kind we all would love to have, but i can tell you that it's more gratifying in the end to live by ones ideas, to be a pioneer, than to only think about what makes money. i'm writing you about awful grownup things, but i remember that you're so smart. i feel that i'm more a friend to you than a father, and already i think you will follow after me when I tell you something of my life. before you know it, you'll grow up yourself and you'll picture the world for yourself and make your own decisions. at the moment i'm happy here, where i can once more talk to you and learn about your life, how you are coming along, what occupies you in *particular*, and what, in the person of mutzi, is beginning to express itself as *uniquely* distinctive! i'm astonished to read that you're already done with school! why? it's not time yet, what are you going to do now? i'm very interested in knowing this. call me tomorrow [. . .], then i can hear your voice again [. . .].

Gropius then told Manon about the great success of his Adler Primus at the "big beauty contests" in Wiesbaden and Berlin, where the car had won the best-in-show prizes. He imagined that she would have more time for a road trip with him if she were out of school as he returned to that topic. "did you finally leave over your good old dragon, the headmistress, or did you get into a seminar? i would like to give you some advice, do whatever you can to learn other *languages*! i really have come to see the way foreign language is a wall between people. the world is getting smaller and communication possibilities constantly increase. you'll be supreme among men if you have a command of their language [. . .]."

What Gropius meant by a "seminar" is not the famous Max Reinhardt-Seminar for young actors. He meant a Berlitz school and the like as his endorsement of learning foreign languages suggests, which is in keeping with what Alma wanted Manon to do if she intended to leave the Institut-Hanausek. The rest of his letter reminded her of his work, of his controversial ideas for mass housing, a new book on the subject, that he was wanted for lectures in the United States, and he reminded her of his importance chairing a recent meeting of CIAM—the Congrès internationaux d'architecture modern—which represented Europe's most prominent modern architects who saw building and design as necessary for social progress. "so, my sweet mutzili, this time there is something more than a postcard, pick up the thread and spin it back to me," Gropius ended, asking for more snapshots with her in the picture rather than her pet turtle, the one she had adopted in the garden pond behind Villa Mahler.[15]

Gropius had no idea how much the turtle meant to his daughter or that she had other such pets. A word, albeit rare in usage, had already been invented for her preference in animals, *herpetophile*. As such Manon surely would have been surprisingly conversant about, say, the midwife toad with Paul Kammerer were he still alive. She subscribed to the monthly *Kosmos,* the official publication of the Friends of Nature International, founded by the head of Austria's Social Democratic Party and the first chancellor of the republic, Karl Renner, to promote not only outdoor recreation for city dwellers, but also the humane treatment of animals and environmental awareness. Manon took a special interest in the pictures and articles about amphibians and reptiles and had already revealed herself to be their special advocate.

This Werfel well knew. He had killed a snake in Manon's presence, thinking, perhaps, that its bite, even if harmless, posed a danger to the fearless girl. But as he fetched a hoe from the garden shed, Manon began to protest and weep inconsolably. She had to be carried away kicking and screaming before he did the deed, still playing the part of the brave and noble stepfather rather than the poet who had once expressed an empathy for serpents, snakes, the form the devil took, and

15 Walter Gropius to Manon Gropius, July 31, 1931, ÖNB.

even a blindworm crushed under a wheel, which he remembered from boyhood, in his verse.

Manon's feelings for such creatures provided Alma with a cruel joke in July 1931, when Arthur Schnitzler came to stay at Haus Mahler. Apprehending that the playwright and author of the notorious *Traumnovelle* (Dream Novella) seemed lighthearted and witty after a long period of mourning, Alma quipped that she intended "to stab" some turtles—likely caught during Manon's favorite road trip in the summer, to the lakeshore of the Neusiedler See—in order to make turtle soup in his honor. Unfortunately, Manon would not allow for it. "[K]nowing our dog [the Irish setter Harro] as well," Alma wrote, Schnitzler said, "I should be happy that I'm not getting a dog biscuit."[16] Then Schnitzler made further light, wondering aloud if turtles hibernated without suffering "winter insomnia." But this strange, even awkward exchange with Alma must have been bittersweet for him.

If Manon were present—she was undoubtedly nearby—his late daughter, Lilli Schnitzler, could not have been far from his mind. He had lost her in Venice three years earlier. After an ill-fated marriage to an Italian army officer, the young woman, at the age of eighteen, shot herself in a gondola in front of her husband. Days later, she died in the care of her friend, Anna Mahler, who washed and prepared Lilli's body for her father to take back to Vienna.

Alma had offered her home and sympathy to the Schnitzler family on the day of the funeral. In the time after, she wrote in her diary of the bond she felt with Lilli—and how the dead young woman haunted her dreams while trying, but unable, to speak. Yet seeing Lilli's ghost had more to do with Alma's feelings of mortality. "I feel very ill," she wrote in her diary. "I can see what Werfel and Mutzi will do without me [. . .] take comfort in enjoying their newfound freedom."[17]

---

16 Mahler-Werfel, "Diary of Alma-Maria," July 15, 1931, p. 262, MWP.
17 Mahler-Werfel, "Diary of Alma-Maria," July 1, 1931, p. 260, MWP.

In late September, however, Alma sought relief not only for her aches and pains—and drinking too much Benedictine—but for her daughter's back as well at Abano Terme, a spa town in the hills of Padua known since Roman times for its salt and sulfur hot springs and thermal healing mud baths, or "fangotherapy."

Since the summer of 1931, Ise Gropius had been living in Switzerland with Herbert Bayer, enjoying what Gropius ruefully called her "asconian joys," for which he blamed himself. Like his relationship with his daughter, he had let his work take over too much of his life and he had not been attentive to the needs of his younger wife. Fortunately, Ise returned to her husband in time to welcome Manon when she came to stay with them in Berlin. Meanwhile Alma traveled with Werfel on a speaking tour during most of November that took them to various lecture halls and radio stations throughout Germany. Although Alma claimed that she and Werfel had been invited to a "100 places" such as operas and concerts galas, they didn't always feel welcome. In an East Prussian townhall, a hostile audience of Nazi university students—the radicals of their time and place—blew whistles to drown out Werfel's voice and force him off the stage.

In a series of photographs taken between a road and a fallow field, where Gropius had parked his Adler for a picnic lunch, Manon already looks like a young woman in her ankle-length fur coat and madcap tilted to the side. Walking beside her father, she is tall enough to look Gropius in the eye. In beauty and poise, she complements a special guest of her father and stepmother, Ise's younger sister, the actress Ellen Frank. Her presence strongly suggests that the Gropiuses knew that Manon wanted to be an actress, and Ellen would have provided a perfect mentor for her. She had studied with the German theater director Erwin Piscator in the 1920s and performed as cabaret dancer and singer in the Katakombe, a notorious Weimar Berlin nightclub. Now,

Ellen was a rising film actress, who had made her debut in a film career that would span sixty years.

The shadow of a male photographer appears in one image, perhaps betraying the presence of Xanti Schawinsky, who took several portraits of Manon during her visit to replace the dated portraits Alma had sent, but also to give her father images that had a Bauhaus aesthetic. Schawinsky did not fail in this respect, taking a close-up of Manon's face surrounded by a chiaroscuro-like shadow with the viewer drawn to her eyes looking upward and to her left (two o'clock). Another image in which the light and shadow is as carefully composed as the subject is a group photograph of Manon in which she emerges from the background, and looks much like the three other adult women posed with her in a group portrait that includes Ise's sister Hertha, Ine Burchard, the wife of Gropius' nephew Jochen, and the curved-creased paper sculptor Irene von Debschitz, Schawinsky's future wife.

The illusion of family life for Gropius ended abruptly, even as it seemed to promise Christmas with his daughter. (Schawinsky's photographs are mistakenly dated "Weihnachten 1931.") While apparently still at her father's Berlin apartment, Manon took a telephone call from Andy Zsolnay, her sister's mother-in-law. Then came an urgent telegram with "Job's tidings" (*Hiobsbotschaft*) for Alma: Anna had swallowed Veronal tablets after her husband had discovered her affair with one of his authors, the cultural historian René Fülöp-Miller. Within hours, Alma fetched Manon and took the earliest express train to Vienna in order to care for her older daughter—and put an end to the scandal that not only embarrassed the Zsolnay family but put at risk Alma's new namesake, Anna's infant daughter Alma Zsolnay, as well as Werfel's income that supported her three households.

Gropius' disappointment in seeing his daughter leave turned to pleasant memories and possibilities, for it would be so very long before she could, of her own free will, be with him. "my dear, sweet long-legs," he began his next letter to Manon, still impressed by the physical change he had seen in her. "i sit in -20° in a white, divine landscape; where the sun is hot, such that you could undress, yet freeze in the shade one step away." He further described his setting—Haus Gadenstaat, a ski lodge in Arosa, Switzerland—the terrace restaurant and the view of the Weisshorn. He encouraged Manon to imagine herself on the slopes with him, taking in the breathtaking beauty—and "on skis speeding down the mountain." He wrote of the progress on his enormous "soviet palace," for Manon had very likely seen not only its drawings in his apartment and office, but an impressive scale model of the building. If the design won, the Soviet Union's legislature would meet in the first avant-garde government building of its kind or size and he might get other commissions from the huge, developing nation. After "some insane night work," the project was "happily finished," Gropius reported to Manon, an heir and stakeholder who might have to play Ise's role if she were to leave him. "my entire office is flattened out after that save for your tough old man," he continued. "now i enjoy double the splendors of my christmas vacation." In closing, Gropius called Manon "lazybones," for leaving Berlin without a note or some other token of affection for him, and wished her a pleasant holiday in her "splendid marble palais."[18]

In his letters, Gropius asked his daughter about her friends, her milieu. That he asked repeatedly suggests that he did not learn very much, but he did seem aware that she was no longer the shy and virtually friendless girl of her early childhood. In the Austrian National Library, there are dozens of postcards from people her own age, whom she had met in boarding school and afterward at her language school, at various cotillions and dances, the holiday parties and teas that prepared young people for their social responsibilities as adults—and which allowed for the opposite sexes to meet.

18 Walter Gropius to Manon Gropius, December 22, 1931, ÖNB.

Typically, Manon's male chaperone was her older cousin Willi Legler, Alma's nephew and the son of her sister Grete and the landscapist Wilhelm Legler, one of Carl Moll's students. That the younger Legler wanted to be an architect surely would have flattered Gropius. So, too, would knowing that Legler's friend, Walter Jaksch, the son of Hans Jaksch, one of Red Vienna's leading architects, began to call on Manon in the winter-spring of 1932. That he was four years older than her reveals that Manon could interest and hold her own with a young man presumably more mature. And this was true of her closest girlfriends, such as Agathe Lothar. Like Manon, she had been introduced to the theater early in her life. Ernst Lothar, after all, was the theater critic for Vienna's liberal daily and, unlike Werfel, encouraged his daughter's desire to be a stage actor. Naturally, Agathe was sympathetic to Manon's ambitions and both undoubtedly attended the matinee performances at the Burgtheater and Josefstadt.

No one, however, was as much a confidante as Sister Ida, who was still "Schulli" to Manon. Although she had returned to nursing at the Leopoldstädter Children's Hospital, Sister Ida still remained in Alma's service, filling in for Villa Mahler's butler, Spitzer, whom Alma called her "*Hausjuden*"—house Jew. Sister Ida, too, received an annual honorarium for her services, and though it was not always forthcoming given Alma's cutbacks to keep her two housemaids and cook, she was still always there for her former charge. In an April letter to Sister Ida, one of the very few in Manon's hand to survive, a brief snapshot of a girl on the verge of womanhood is revealed, with the splendors and excitement of the eighteenth Venice Biennale in the background, with its pavilions and galleries on the island of Sant'Elena, with exhibits of *aeropainting* by the Italian futurists and German and Austrian artists increasingly labeled as inauthentic and decadent in their homelands.[19]

---

19 Had it not been for Carl Moll, the yellow "Germania" pavilion might have remained closed. He found the funds that the German and Austrian governments

In words dashed off—and in chicken scratch for which she apologizes with a colorful German expression—Manon Gropius seems aware that others are vicariously taking pleasure in the faster pace of her life, what Gropius called her "lidoesque experiences":

> Dear little Schulli,
>
> How are you? You naughty thing, didn't even write me once, so now I (mind you, "Me") have to sit down and write you! It's lovely here (it's a shame you're not here) but it is not so warm yet. Isn't that terrible? Jaksch has already written me a very nice letter! Were you with Affi? She is sweet! I have this great longing for her every day! Excuse my handwriting (like a rooster on the dung heap [*Hahn am Mist*]) but I am in a big rush! Many parties here lately. The king and the queen with two princesses were here at the opening of the Biennale. It was fantastic. Dear God made some lovely weather for it! No one can imagine the color, the joy.[20]

Another friend that Manon made in the spring of 1932 was a seven-year-old boy named Erich Rietenauer, who had been seen loitering near Villa Mahler with an autograph book and pen, hoping to meet one of Alma Mahler-Werfel's famous guests.[21] A handsome child whom Thomas Mann compared to Tadzio in *Death in Venice*, Rietenauer met Alma in early December 1931 at a charity concert for Winterhilfe—Winter Aid—which distributed clothes and shoes to Vienna's disadvantaged. Dr. Tandler officiated the event, a recital by the Vienna Choir Boys, and had selected Rietenauer as a special case, for Rietenauer had lost his father, who had been mysteriously poisoned

---

refused to spend on exhibits in in a time of bread and soup lines.

20 Manon Gropius to Ida Gebauer, undated [28 April 1932], ÖNB.

21 The events in this passage are informed by Erich Rietenauer, *Alma, meine Liebe* [Alma, My Love] (Vienna: Amalthea, 2008), pp. 25ff.

with Lysol that he mistook for stomach bitters. The tragedy left the family impoverished and ostracized, for the mother had been wrongfully accused of her husband's murder. Now the boy desperately needed shoes for his first Communion, a pair to replace the high-topped lady's shoes that he now wore, which made him waddle about like Charlie Chaplin. After reciting a Christmas poem, Alma Mahler-Werfel rose and gave the boy a hug, pressing him into her breasts and belly that, as he learned later from Sister Ida, were so soft and enveloping because Alma never wore a bra or corset. The boy was also treated to a noseful of her intoxicating perfume and a gift box with a pair of black shoes that she herself presented.

Months later, the boy joined a soccer team that practiced at the Sportplatz, which was directly downhill from Hohe Warte. By getting off the No. 37 streetcar early, at the corner of Wollegasse and Steinfeldgasse, he could observe the taxis and fancy automobiles that arrived at Villa Mahler, and seek an autograph. One day he noticed an Irish setter behind an iron fence and walked up to get a closer look. When he attempted to reach through the bars, an older gentleman with a long white beard shouted at Rietenauer and warned him not to pet the dog. Then an old woman and a teenage girl with long dark braids came from the house. Seeing the dog lick the boy's hands—and her husband Carl degrading a mere child—Anna Moll interceded and invited Rietenauer into her kitchen. There she served him hot chocolate and cake and he dutifully answered the questions posed to him about where he went to school, who his parents were, and how he had lost his father. Turning to her husband, Anna Moll scolded him for being mean to the boy and pointing out that the dog "Harro" knew a good child from a bad one.

Manon, too, took her grandmother's side. She addressed him as "Burschi"—"boy" in dialect—and it soon became apparent that she was the daughter of Alma Mahler-Werfel and that he had already met her mother at the Winterhilfe concert. "Oh, you're the little boy with those hideously tied shoes," said Manon. "She told me that she had never seen such horrible, far-too-big shoes on such a little kid. She had given you your package and had to leave right away, otherwise she would have wept in sympathy for you before all the people there. Julius Tandler—I call him 'Jolli'—you know—he did not think that was right. Mommy should have stayed longer, until all the children received their packages. But then she told Tandler why she had to go, and he understood. Tandler often comes to see us, you can meet him again, if you'd like." Manon also told Rietenauer that Harro belonged to her and that he could come and play with the dog whenever he wanted.

Soon after the boy began to appear regularly in the neighborhood, made welcome by Manon and her grandmother. While the latter fed him sweets, Manon let him play with Harro as promised. She also let Rietenauer accompany her on a shopping trip in Grinzing, and while his photographic memories of Manon seem too "good" to be true, such as the long string bag she carried and how she had to muzzle and leash the dog before taking it on a walk, these small details suggest a certain authenticity. So do like microhistoric details of life in interwar Vienna, which included the craze for collecting celebrity autographs. Rietenauer's book of signatures is almost a log of his presence at Villa Mahler, where he further made himself a fixture by running errands for its residents. Werfel relied on the boy to fetch cigarettes, for which he received not only one of Werfel's fountain pens, but a piece of the True Cross that the writer had brought back from the Holy Land—and Sister Ida made use of the boy as the unofficial photographer for the Mahler-Werfel family.

Having learned how to take pictures from his uncle, who ran a photography studio, Rietenauer proved himself to be an expert with Sister Ida's Zeiss Ikon Box-Fix camera, which took high-quality images with small-format roll film. This came as a surprise to Werfel, who thought the little camera was a toy, a piece of trash (*Dreck*) until he saw the flattering pictures the boy took. Unfortunately, Rietenauer never handed over his camera to another. There is no visual record of his presence at Villa Mahler. From the little rolls of film, he produced some incredibly detailed images, many of them with Manon, on whom he developed the kind of crush that very young boys have for unattainable teenage girls.

In May 1932, with the collapse of another Christian Socialist government, the president of Austria, Wilhelm Miklas chose the Minister of Agriculture and Forests, Engelbert Dollfuss as chancellor. A former seminarian and a highly decorated war veteran—despite being five feet tall and under regulation height—Dollfuss spent the greater part of a day praying for guidance on how to lead a nation divided between the Social Democrats and Communists on the left and the clergy, paramilitaries, industrialists, and the growing Nazi menace on the right.

Since the Catholic faith was an expression of Austrian patriotism, Alma, who had long seen herself as a pagan, decided to return to the Church, a decision that would be made for Manon as well. Though nominally a Protestant like her father, Manon had attended Catholic services with her mother and Werfel, but she had little if any formal religious upbringing. This and the state of her soul surely came as a surprise to the clergymen Alma invited to Villa Mahler, among them the Prelate Karl Drexel and the elderly Monsignor Engelbert Müller of St. Stephan's Cathedral, whom Alma now consulted on the matter of her and her daughter rejoining the church.

Werfel, for his part, had once more declared himself Jewish. He had also returned to writing about the current and perilous situation that Jews in Germany faced, for he had taken all his research on what became known as the Armenian genocide and began drafting *The Forty Days of Musa Dagh*. In addition to the atrocities that the Ottoman Empire had inflicted on its Armenian citizens, Werfel developed human and personal stories to bring this history to life. Not only were the Armenian characters based on people he knew from his own life, many of them intellectual Jews he had known in the cafes of Prague and Vienna, he had also borrowed from his immediate family and environs, for there is much of life on Semmering that could be read as a subtext of *Musa Dagh*. After much discussion with Alma about the nature of the novel's hero—she wanted a kind of Nietzschean-Wagnerian superman—Werfel settled on a man who had many of his own defects, due in part to being from a wealthy, assimilated Armenian family—Gabriel Bagradian. And like Werfel, Bagradian was married to a woman who would further assimilate him, Juliette Bagradian, based on Alma herself, albeit much younger.

Between them would be Bagradian's love interest—and the person to detach him from his assimilation—a nineteen-year-old Armenian beauty, Iskuhi Tomasian. Much of her reticent character and inscrutable qualities as well as her appearance, Werfel based on the teenage Manon Gropius. He lightened Iskuhi's skin (not unlike Karl May's literary—colonial hybridization in creating a fairer sister for Winnetou) and gave her light-colored eyes and a boarding school background. Werfel even gave her a vocation not unlike the one for which Manon now studied, as the French instructor of an Armenian orphanage. Iskuhi, too, exists in this threshold state, between "of her people" and not of them along with the other boundaries over which she hovers. She has a "fairytale delicacy" (*märchenzarte*). The set of Iskuhi's mouth is a thing out of German Expressionist poetry. "It was not surprising that Iskuhi should have inspired love [. . .]," Werfel writes in the finished novel. "Apart from her magnificent eyes, the most beautiful thing about her was her mouth. Her deeply tinged lips had always a moist, smiling, luster that penetrated like the pupil's of one's eyes."[22] Iskuhi is an *exaltée*

---

22 Franz Werfel, *The Forty Days of Musa Dagh* (Geoffrey Dunlop and James Reidel trans) (Boston: David R. Godine, 2012 [1934]), pp. 102–3. This detail is lacking from the 1934 translation, which was restored with other missing passages devoted to the Iskuhi character.

and the object of desire not only for Bagradian, but for his son Stephen, her Protestant minister brother Aram Tomasian, and the feral orphan girl Sato.

Iskuhi is their fetish and her "lame left arm"—an injury suffered while being raped by a Turk—becomes one of her most alluring attributes (a kind of chaste *acrotomophilia*) in addition to her small breasts and "priestess" voice. Even Iskuhi's confirmation bible becomes a fetish object. In a passage omitted from the original English translation of *Musa Dagh*, Stephen—an alter ego of Werfel as a boy—keeps it hidden in his bed. There, under his covers, he clasps the bible between his legs the same way an adolescent might stuff a pornographic picture or a pillow on which to act out his fantasy. Incredibly, Werfel's obsessive regard for his first Manon character does not take over and is largely lost in a novel nearly a thousand pages long. However, if one expends the effort to read the book *looking* for Werfel, Alma, and Manon on Semmering, he or she will find it running throughout a narrative that is the *War and Peace* of the Armenian genocide, the novel that so much predicated and predicted the Holocaust of the next world war.

Manon was hardly one-armed as she practiced her serve and backhand in June. She could have been the revenant of a Jewish teenager, Maria Glaser, whom Werfel longed for during his Prague youth whenever he saw her playing tennis—the inspiration of a poem and elegy—and whose pet name "Mitzi" echoed Mutzi. Such athleticism inspired her father to write from Berlin, where he nursed a broken foot that had him "hobbling around on a cane like an old general." With six million Germans unemployed, Gropius, too, felt the vicissitudes of Depression. Nevertheless, he enclosed photographs of the prototypes of his new copper-sheathed, prefabricated houses for low-income families. He also responded dutifully—and rather cerebrally for a teenage reader—to her last letter, in which she must have complained about her body. "i am enormously pleased that you are training for the tennis championship," he continued. "it is surely the best massage for your long legs, which you mention, and the best exercise for sanity at the same time. it has always impressed me about the greeks, how they managed to simultaneously practice philosophy and sport in their palaestras[23] and to reach the height of human harmony by so doing. [. . .] i'd also love to know how your studies are going, the direction your mind is taking, it interests me; are you being faithful with your italian?"[24]

In a subsequent letter, Gropius hoped there might be a father–daughter "rendezvous [. . .] during the fall or christmas holidays [. . .] so i can teach you to love the snow."[25] Alma, however, had need of Manon, whose growth spurts and first flashes of adulthood and wit made her the kind of female traveling companion and confidante Alma had not enjoyed since Lilly Lieser, despite her lesbian proclivities. In September, mother and daughter spent ten days at the Schloss Velden, the famous resort hotel on the lakeshore of the Wörthersee in the Austrian province of Carinthia. There Alma also learned the pleasures of having a younger, pretty variation of herself and how it compensated for her own lost charms, which had become almost a self-deprecatory theme in her diary. She saw the men staring at Manon as they entered the hotel's grand ballroom. Among them was Austria's new Minister of Education, Anton von Rintelen.

Alma knew he was a powerful figure in the Christian Socialist party, an open fascist whose right-wing politics complemented her own views now that Austria needed a dictator like Italy. Unlike Mussolini in his generalissimo uniforms, Rintelen assumed a presence that was part strongman, given his powerful build and close-cropped hair, and part university professor with his pince-nez. Over the years, Rintelen had built a base of power in his native Styria, where he had been the governor. Long a foe of the Social Democrats, he also had strong links

---

23 Ancient Greek boxing and wrestling schools.

24 Walter Gropius to Manon Gropius, undated [late June 1932], ÖNB.

25 Walter Gropius to Manon Gropius, July 22, 1932, ÖNB.

to the most militant and anti-Semitic elements of the Home Guard, whose ideology of unification with Germany and swastika flags differed little from those of Austria's Nazis (who had only days before hosted Joseph Goebbels to speak before 20,000 party members in a Vienna stadium). Many Austrians saw Rintelen as a future chancellor, one they nicknamed—or ridiculed—as "King Anton"—for he would more likely crown himself, coming to power not from fair elections but from his political intrigues. For this reason, Chancellor Dollfuss wanted Rintelen in Vienna and his chief political enemy closer—and once there he became something of a hero to the devoutly Catholic Austrians. When Julius Tandler forbid crucifixes in the public hospitals in Vienna and priests to have access to patients beyond visiting hours, Rintelen responded to such secularization by making religious services compulsory for schoolchildren.

"Inexplicably, he had fallen in love with me," Alma wrote in her diary. "He followed me into my bedroom and pulled me out onto the balcony and courted me passionately like a little boy [*Bengel*]. Something he saw as love. [. . .] Mutzi and I laughed half the night over this clumsy old fool."[26] Soon after, however, Rintelen began sending notes to Manon, and Alma, rather than discourage such contact, pushed her daughter on him "with guile and skill" and allowed Rintelen "to fall in love with Mutzi, whom he had not considered at first."[27] Without realizing that she could be entirely wrong about this last point, Alma tried explain it away as a game, something for her and Manon to enjoy at the expense of King Anton. What goes unsaid is her desire to be a player in Austria's politics, and how she had no conscience when it came to exploiting her child.

While Alma surely prompted Rintelen to wish her daughter a happy birthday on October 5, the newly minted sixteen-year-old wrote her

26 Mahler-Werfel, "Diary of Alma Maria," September 23, 1932, p. 268, MWP.
27 Mahler-Werfel, "Diary of Alma-Maria," October 22, 1933, p. 285, MWP.

father to inform him that he had forgotten her milestone. Though horrified by his negligence, Gropius defended himself and accused her of having not written him *for a year*. He more than saved face, however, in recognizing that his daughter was now an adult and, with a choice Gallicism, praised her as his equal in maturity and intellect. "i just got back [. . .] from paris, where i spent 10 days at the salon d'autos, and found your little letter! you really doubt my paternal feelings, my precious, since i wrote and sent nothing on your 16th, but you will soon see otherwise. [. . .] i simply feel terrible that the natural relationship that should exist between us always encounters such enormous impediments *because we so seldomly get together!*" Gropius blamed their "life *in letters*" and the lack of frequent personal contact that distorted their relationship. "i am *never* mean to you," Gropius continued. "in childhood, a person doesn't know their obligation to others. he lives more carefree then and doesn't dwell long on the feelings of his fellow men. but now you are 16 years old, cultivated by nature out of intelligence and an environment of enormous quality that very few have! so i must make up my mind to see you as a grown, finished person from now on and without reservation deal with you en camarade"—meaning as a friend, as no longer a stranger. Gropius told Manon how much he looked forward to one day enriching her with all he experienced, which included, too, his all-important work, to make of her his daughter, too, not just Alma's. He admitted that it all seemed a vain belief. "i have already waited long to someday achieve this atmosphere between us both that places me outside of the center—to impart—the quintessence of this, what i know and am as an older person—! this can't be forced, but i have this positive need to someday be so near and dear together with you such that you not only have some inkling of me but really come to know me."[28]

Not long after posting this letter, Manon came down with mumps—*Halsdrüsen*—which left her face distended (and documented

28 Walter Gropius to Manon Gropius, October 14, 1932, ÖNB. Unmentioned is a third Nobel winner, Gerhard Hauptmann, who Alma fêted in October 1932.

by Rietenauer's camera with the subject's cooperation). Weeks later, in November, she wrote her father about her illness and that she had met Sinclair Lewis. "sorry that i missed you when I called, but it made me very happy that you're going out again for that letter gave me such a terrible scare. please write soon, what was the reason for the gland trouble, what did the doctor say? has the fever gone, or did it come back again?" Gropius asked, telling Manon of Ise's bout with the same symptoms. Then he schooled his name-dropping daughter on her conduct in the company of Nobel Prize-winning authors who had been recent visitors to Villa Mahler. "your visitors are a choice lot. you are being spoiled rotten getting to meet this intellectual elite in mommy's company, make sure you don't lose proportion, you certainly don't treat thomas mann with much respect, it's not always the measure of a man if he glitters in conversation with others. by the way i know the wife of sinclair lewis was she with you?"[29] Gropius wrote, inquiring after Dorothy Thompson, who was the first American journalist to write about the Bauhaus. Then he suggested to Manon a belated birthday gift, a desk lamp—perhaps the signature Christian Dell design produced by the Bauhaus—or some other finishing touch.

Manon had indeed also met Dorothy Thompson and found her wonderful. When she asked the boy Rietenauer if he did not think so too, he answered: "Mutzi, when I am with you, I don't see other women."[30] The flattery earned the boy a pat on the head. And when Manon brought him to Sinclair Lewis for an autograph, the author of *Arrowsmith* and *Elmer Gantry* noticed the loyalty in the boy's eyes and kidded them both, saying that if little Rietenauer wished to be Manon's boyfriend, he needed to grow faster if he did not want to remain her dwarf.

---

29 Walter Gropius to Manon Gropius, November 17, 1932. ÖNB.
30 Rietenauer, *Alma, meine Liebe*, p. 89.

In the late autumn, Manon would tour Italy but remained in Vienna when her mother left with Werfel for his annual reading tour of Germany, which saw an emotional leavetaking on the part of Alma and Manon. Werfel had intended to read a finished, and controversial, chapter from his novel-in-progress that could easily be interpreted as a criticism of Nazi anti-Semitism—and a reminder of the empathy Germans had shown to the Armenians in the First World War. Given the reports of German Jews being accosted, of "un-German" lectures and performances being interrupted by brown shirts blowing police whistles, and the like, Alma feared for her husband's life. Manon, too, may have been similarly overwhelmed, for as the Berlin express left Vienna's North Station, she stood transfixed as though in a dream. Unable or unwilling to leave, Manon had to be guided from the platform to a taxi by her Grandmother Moll and Sister Ida on either side of her.[31]

In Breslau, Werfel and Alma stayed at the same hotel that hosted Adolf Hitler and his retinue on a campaign swing through the city for the coming German parliamentary elections. While drinking champagne in the hotel lounge, Alma waited to catch sight of the "face that had subjugated 13,000,000 people [. . .] And true, it was a face! Kind, soft, but sweeping eyes, a young scared face. No Duce! But a teenager, one that will find no seniority, no wisdom." Werfel stood beside her and she quoted him saying "Not too unsympathetic." [32]

Although Alma took the time to see Hitler, she made sure to avoid Walter and Ise Gropius—who Alma more feared—instructing Manon not to say anything to her father about Werfel and her mother being in Berlin. But Gropius was resigned to the fact that his daughter had other travel plans and that her return to the Institut-Hanausek would also get in the way of their being together. "since your gastronomic tour

---

31 See Rietenauer pp. 90ff. His chronology is corrected with other sources.

32 Mahler-Werfel, "Diary of Alma Maria," December 16, 1932, p. 273, MWP.

of italy," he wrote Manon in December, "i have heard nothing save that you are back in vienna and am quite curious as to how you are and how you look. i was hoping that in the coming year i could once more give you a hug here in berlin, but i realize that you have to be in school again after what has been such a nice long break for you. i followed you and your trip in my thoughts and it made me think of my first impressions when i toured northern italy, part way on foot, with two friends not long after high school. these first heavenly experiences live with one forever! your girlfriends at the institute will envy you and you will soon make them mad with your experiences in the world! are you getting along with them and do you like it there now?"[33] As Gropius continued, he told Manon that he would send a "charming device," manufactured by a Swiss friend, a camera to replace a windup motion picture camera that he and Ise had sent earlier that proved too difficult to operate. To ensure that Manon would not suffer any further frustration, her father spent the rest of his letter in explaining how the new one worked.

On the first day of 1933, Gropius wrote Manon a letter from Arosa far different in sentiment from his prosaic instructions for her Christmas present. "my gorgeous daughter of whom i only have a premonition!" he wrote. "i telepathize [*telepathisiere*] you to me, but you don't become flesh and blood! how you look, how you wear your hair, how you dress. you appear to me now as a christmas angel such that my fatherhood is given impetus beyond writing letters."[34] In Hanover, Gropius' mother also wrote Manon. The two had corresponded over the year and had, at last, become close. For this reason, the elder Manon's New Year's letter was more special than the ones she likely wrote her other grandchildren. She inquired after Manon's health and "glandular problem" and requested her namesake and eldest son's only child come

33 Walter Gropius to Manon Gropius, December 18, 1932, ÖNB.
34 Walter Gropius to Manon Gropius, undated [January 1, 1933], ÖNB.

to Timmendorf this summer, where a family reunion of four generations would gather. And despite the optimism she expressed for the younger Manon, the elder did not hide that she was not well, that "winter—even this mild—is always my foe."[35]

A week later Grandmother Gropius had to sleep upright in a chair so as not to suffocate or cough through the night. Her son, back from Switzerland, kept abreast of her condition and hoped for the best during a necessary business trip to Osnabruck. "i hope," he wrote his mother, "that you will already be over it. we always marvel at your invincible style with which you meet adversity."[36] His encouragement, however, was not enough. When Gropius visited his mother on January 20, he wrote Manon as though his life were as normal as ever, segueing from the sickroom in Hanover to brighter topics in a tone both blithe and weirdly detached. "my mother is very ill," he wrote from Berlin, "such that i barely have any hope of seeing her again. she asked about you a lot and so i am really asking you to write her a letter. she enjoys it immensely when you tell her about your life and she will no longer be able to share in it for long. [. . .] it made a sad impression on me to see her so poor and sick.—i hope for you my dear that things still go well!?" Gropius continued, hardly aware that by the time his daughter read his letter she would have no chance of leaving for Hanover immediately or of planning to attend a funeral. He told her about his travel plans for the coming week, when he would travel to the Soviet Union for the first time to give a lecture in Leningrad. He asked for news about her and invited her to come skiing with him in the second half of February. "i sit with my head painfully thick with flu and you will scold your old man for not writing with more humor," he closed, "but these germs are crawling throughout your loving papa!"[37] Less

35 Manon S. Gropius to Manon Gropius, December 30, 1932, ÖNB.

36 Walter Gropius to Manon S. Gropius, January 7, 1933, WGP.

37 Walter Gropius to Manon Gropius, January 20, 1933, ÖNB.

than forty-eight hours later, on Sunday morning in Berlin—a day marked by loud and enormous Nazi and Communist party demonstrations as the German elections neared—Gropius began a new letter, informing her that his mother died in her sleep.

Manon's response to her father's letters, which included a copy of the newspaper obituary, can be inferred from his reaction. Knowing that Alma had likely advised Manon on how to be incensed and insulted for being kept in the dark about her grandmother, Gropius wrote her like a man caught out as too preoccupied with himself. "you and mommy are thoroughly mistaken if you think that I have neglected anything. [. . .] the doctor was of the opinion that she would pull through this illness or it would at least not last very long. however, when i visited her, my personal impression and her subjective feeling were not [. . .] that i had no more hope of ever seeing her again and i wrote to you *straight away*. [. . .] it makes me *so* sad that you can't see her anymore. i read in her diary yesterday the great joy she felt from last seeing you in berlin."[38]

Mother Church

In the spring of 1933, at the age of sixteen, Manon Gropius converted to the Roman Catholic faith. She took little part in the decision. Her mother made it for her and Manon dutifully complied. The only person who could hesitate was Alma, whose return to the Church had been delayed by her vanity as much as by any real intellectual reservations—for she still saw herself as Nietzschean, for whom being fearless and cheerful, according to *The Gay Science*, is knowing that "God is dead."

Alma enjoyed the attention the churchmen paid to her at Villa Mahler and her conversion had become a kind of courtship rite. Among the priests taking a great and personal interest in these conversions was

38 Walter Gropius to Manon Gropius, January 26, 1933. ÖNB.

Vienna's new archbishop, Cardinal Theodor Innitzer. Alma and Werfel had attended his installation at St. Stephens Cathedral in October 1932 and, at one of the grand dinner parties to celebrate the new prelate, Alma confided to him that she still had many reservations about the church and its liturgy. Sympathetic to her, the cardinal knew of someone with more expertise in matters of faith, a priest who often counseled other priests when they, like Alma, suffered from religious doubt. The cardinal introduced her to Father Johannes Hollnsteiner, a thirty-eight-year-old professor of theology at the University of Vienna.

In appearance, Hollnsteiner was unprepossessing, a bespectacled and balding cleric of a type that seemingly represent a *genera* unto themselves regardless of race and religion. Nevertheless, Alma found him both interesting and pleasing. Hollnsteiner seemed to always say the right thing when she expressed some religious doubt, as when he did not deny the pagan roots of the Church but elucidated on them. And Hollnsteiner complemented her politics, for he saw a restored ultra-Catholic Austria as a bulwark against the new evil from the east, Bolshevism. Instead of the legions of Janissaries, Austria must protect the world from liberal Jews like Julius Tander and Karl Renner. Hollnsteiner entertained the notion of a "healthy anti-Semitism" (*gesunden Antisemitismus*) as simply a kind of acceptable suspicion. For Alma, this had to come as absolution for the things she had long thought and expressed herself.

During the winter–spring of 1933, Hollnsteiner became a regular visitor to Villa Mahler.[39] His constant presence caused young Rietenauer to think that Alma was dying and needed the priest near to confess her sins and take last rites. Sister Ida, however, saw that Alma and

39 Part of this account is informed by Friedrich Buchmayr, *Der Priester in Almas Salon: Johannes Hollnsteiners Weg von der Elite des Ständestaats zum NS-Bibliothekar* [The Priest in Alma's Salon: Johannes Hollnsteiner's Path from the Elite of the Ständestaat to Nazi Librarian] (Vienna: Bibliothek der Provinz, 2003).

Hollnsteiner had fallen in love and were taking advantage of Werfel's frequent absences—a suspicion confirmed by Alma herself. "Every word from him," she wrote in her diary, "is a hymn to me." And she enjoyed thinking of herself as the priest's first intimate contact with a female. "J.H. is thirty-eight years old and has not yet met a *woman* until now. [. . .] He sees me differently, and I bless him for that. He said: Never before have I been close to a woman."[40] But as with her similarly effusive remarks about Rintelen's attraction, Alma did not consider that her professor of theology may have been attracted to Villa Mahler by the other presence at his meetings with Alma—a strikingly beautiful teenage girl, who he also tutored for her conversion to Catholicism.

For his part, Werfel did nothing to discourage Alma's dalliance, for Hollnsteiner provided Alma with a companion while Werfel finished his Musa Dagh novel. Writing from Santa Margharita, Werfel told her that Hollnsteiner was a "blessing" and one of the few "*genuine* and *serious* priests."[41] But such an endorsement hardly confirmed the brilliance of her spiritual advisor. Alma sought that from Arnold Berliner, sending the great physicist Hollnsteiner's multivolume history of the papacy.

Berliner had been a friend and patron of Gustav Mahler and, after the composer's death, he remained close not only to Alma but to her daughter Anna and later Manon as well. As the editor of the renowned journal *Die Naturwissenschaften* (*The Natural Sciences*), Berliner loomed large in the world of science, having published some of the most important scientific works of the twentieth century, including papers by his colleagues Albert Einstein and Max Born. But among his many interests, and although Jewish, Berliner was an authority on the history of the Catholic Church, and for this reason Alma believed he would

40 Mahler-Werfel, "Diary of Alma Maria," early 1933, p. 248, MWP.

41 See Jungk, pp. 210ff.

be ideal to appraise Hollnsteiner's scholarship. However, before he turned to the subject of Hollnsteiner's pedantic prose, Berliner needed to mention a gift for Manon, one that presented the scientist with an unusual problem—giving a pocketbook to a teenage girl. On the matter of the purse, he deferred to Alma's "higher authority" on whether he had shown good taste. His criteria were not only those of fashion, but for practical and ingenious features, too, such as the pockets for lipstick and a compact, which elicited from him a parody of concern for openly discussing the new purse's intimate compartments and the propriety of an older gentleman sending a girl such a gift. "In your wisdom," Berliner confessed, "you will interpret all correctly such that the Mörikesque poem is spared these lascivities beforehand." Alma knew that the "poem" was Manon herself and that Berliner's rather amatory allusion was to Eduard Mörike's "willing maiden" verses in his famous "Peregrina" poems. But he was not finished with making allusions. "[H]ow shall I get this white leather wonder to you? Could there be, perhaps, a smart lady of your acquaintance here [i.e. Berlin] who could bring it? Or should I let it go as parcel post, which would be quite inconvenient for you (given customs)? Letting it go as printed matter is too risky. 'Do you know what happened?'" The fateful question he posed to Alma was not just about the exorbitant duty that Austria had placed on German goods. Berliner had quoted the First Norn in Wagner's *Gotterdammerung* to reveal his anxiety over the recent Reichstag Fire and other dark events in Germany that would soon overtake him.[42]

Berliner was less nuanced in regard to the priest's writing, which caused him much eyestrain and tact on his part given Alma's sensitivities. He suggested that her nevertheless "readable pastor might work toward a good, readable two- or three-volume work." Fortunately for Father Hollnsteiner, his appeal was not in reading him, but in his

42 Arnold Berliner to Alma Mahler-Werfel, March 8 [*c.*1933], MWP.

religious instruction, such that Alma and Manon willingly fell into their roles as his "school girls" (*Schülerinnen*) and "protégés" (*Schützlingen*).[43] He went along when Manon called him "Holli," and he shared his passion for collecting stamps with her and helped her improve her own collection by sending her rare stamps. The priest also enlisted the boy Rietenauer at Manon's behest and made him his altar boy whenever he said mass at the nearby parish church, where Alma, Manon, Sister Ida, and Grandmother Moll often sat together in their family pew.

Manon Gropius was rebaptized on April 13, 1933, Holy Thursday, in a private ceremony at St. Augustine's—the Augustinerkirche—in the Josefsplatz, next to the Hofburg, the former winter palace of the Habsburgs. Father Hollnsteiner officiated, receiving Manon clothed in either a white alb or dress. A chapel veil covered her long dark hair. The priest, no longer dressed in the black clerical garb of the theology professor, would have worn a white cassock with a violet stole. Unlike an infant baptism, Manon followed a different but no less beautiful rite, without the proxies of godparents.

As an adult catechumen, Manon mostly likely could have stood on the threshold of the church's entrance rather than before the baptismal font, and would have responded to a series of questions asked by Hollnsteiner. Her rote answers were memorized and delivered in Latin, addressing such matters as personal salvation:

Fides, quid tibi præstat? (What does Faith offer you?)
Vitam æternam. (Life everlasting.)

This inquiry continued. Then the priest then performed the *exsufflation*, in which he breathed three times over Manon in order to remove any unclean spirit and infuse in her the Holy Ghost. The rite continued with much touching on the priest's part, such as making the sign of cross on the girl's forehead and breast and laying his hands on

---

43 Buchmayr, *Der Priester in Almas Salon*, p. 78–9.

her head. He also put a little salt in her mouth, the symbol of Gospel's wisdom and he may have performed the *Ephpheta*, in which he took a little of his own spittle and touched Manon's ears and nostrils.

Before the catechumen entered the church itself, Hollnsteiner made the sign of the cross three times and spoke the formula that cast out any lingering demons in the girl's body. In her own words, too, Manon would also have to formally renounce Satan. Then Hollnsteiner anointed her heart and head with oil and led her to the baptismal font, where he put on a white stole and completed the ceremony, and she, the new member of the Catholic Church, made various responses in testimony to her new faith. Finally, the priest poured holy water over the head of his candidate three times. He also applied the *chrism*, a fragrant substance made of oil of olives and balsam, to Manon's forehead. She then took a lighted candle given to her by the priest.

Gropius learned of his daughter's conversion from a telegram she sent, but it took days to reach him in Timmendorf. While he was virtually a fellow-traveler of Ise's atheism, he rationalized Catholicism on aesthetic grounds. "your becoming catholic surprised me," he wrote Manon on May 17, the day before his fiftieth birthday, "i myself am totally unchurchlike, but every visually and sensually talented person naturally prefers the catholic church with the pomp and circumstance of its ceremonies to protestantism's arid austerity, i can well understand why you have crossed over." In his letter, Gropius apologized for having taken so long to write. "it's not going very well for me in these bad times and i do have this tendency toward silence," he confessed, blaming it on his disappointment in Manon not answering his invitations to ski in Davos. "i wish i could for once spend a lovely time with you without work, without letters, entirely in the present, perhaps it will be possible this year?"

Gropius also hinted at his lack of income, admitting that he was in Timmendorf to rent out his late mother's summerhouse rather than continue with the family reunion. His work had long been anathema to the Nazi's conception of what German architecture should be, and, with Adolf Hitler as chancellor, he was now blacklisted. "i suffer very much under the circumstances that are now in germany," Gropius continued, "i am ashamed of what is happening here and to my personal work where every possibility seems to be blocked for now."

Perhaps realizing that he dwelled too much on himself, Gropius asked his daughter to tell him more about her life and about what he called her "inner person." He did so while conceding that she kept her own company and arranged her own "cercles" of friends, the French word an acknowledgement of her ability to read and write in French (which she practiced with her pen pals as far away as New York City). Gropius hoped her milieu conformed to her mother's "lofty school" and ended his letter by asking about her Italian exam and whether she thought she would do well. He reminded her of his significant birthday, too, and that all of his friends would be with him, "not just you," his clever way of saying that he did not exclude her from his *cercle*.[44]

In the same letter Gropius had inquired about Manon's new girlfriend, "this susi," a name he must have heard in a phone conversation or read in a letter. Born Suzanne Kertész in December 1914 to an assimilated Hungarian Jewish family living in Budapest, her father was an agent for a large German textile firm, which provided him with enough income to send Susi to boarding school in Lausanne after the family moved to Sofia, Bulgaria. After his death in 1931, she rejoined her family in Vienna, where she attended the Institut-Hanausek and met Manon there when the latter returned to finish school in 1932.

Like Manon and Agathe Lothar, Susi also wanted to be an actor and enroll in the Max-Reinhardt-Seminar. All three girls were very serious about their futures on the German-speaking stage. According to Rietenauer, Manon spent much time with Agathe, memorizing

44 Walter Gropius to Manon Gropius, May 17, 1933, ÖNB.

lines, learning parts, and putting on informal theatrical performances—which surely helped her play her role in her baptism ceremony. Presumably both did the same with Susi—and all three knew the importance of being multilingual, for it would serve them in taking roles not limited to German theater or cinema. That Manon studied to be a foreign language teacher and could express herself in French, Italian, and English as well, was not to simply appease her parents but rather for a personal and heartfelt ambition. With Agathe, whose family also spent their Easters in Venice, Manon both practiced her Italian and acting skills. In their respective homes, at Villa Mahler or in the Barichgasse, the girls performed scenes from Venice's street life, with Manon on one memorable occasion playing the stock role of an Italian fruit vendor and Agathe as the customer. For an encore, Manon, too, imitated the great Italian tragedienne Eleonora Duse reading a letter to her scorned lover, a performance that her Anna Moll described as "heartrendingly beautiful."

The commitment of all three girls could be gauged in the youngest, which came to light during Manon's crush on Raoul Aslan, one of the Burgtheater's greatest actors. Known for his resonant voice and delivery as well as the *Weltschmerz* of his dark piercing eyes—which betrayed his Italian-Armenian heritage—Aslan had sex appeal for young females. Manon's appreciation, however, was far more mature for her age. It was enough to deal with Carl Moll's insensitive revelation that Aslan was a homosexual and that a pretty girl like her had no chance. Undeterred, she wrote the actor a sonnet in which she bared her feelings for him and her goal to be a stage actress:

To my dearest actor Raoul Aslan

You are a giant for me, one divinely inspired, a lord!
You are gifted in the theatre, like a kind prince.
You are generous as well—that is why I adore you.
I love how you speak, which lends your soul

the gripping mellifluence of soaring music
The smile on your lips moves me
Your eyes are unlike the eyes of other people.
I too would like to tower in the theater—like you!
To be able to step before you, to say to you
that it all happened because of you alone.
I want to become as pure and great as your eyes
command my soul.—The one who knows your soul—
but seeks my own way!

Your Manon Gropius[45]

Surprised and quite moved by this epistolary verse, Aslan wrote back. His candid response suggests that he was unaware that Manon was the daughter of famous parents and that this unknown female protégé had given him an awkward surprise that called for both encouragement and humility. "To the actress-to-be Manon Gropius," he replied, "I gather from your ode to me that you seriously wish to become a good actress. To be honest, I don't know if I should congratulate you on this wish, for our vocation requires from us considerably more, much more than we get back from the public. Such problems the actor has with his calling that you, as a clever girl, surely know about by now. By no means do I want to discourage you for every person who strives to greatness is doing the right thing. Saying "yes" to every joy and sorrow in life, such that "no" is driven from the world, is the right course in life—for the eternal "no" makes our life pointless and worthless. In your ode to me (if you'll let me call your verse that) you write that you want to step before me after attaining your goal to say: 'That it all happened only because of me.' You won't be able to do this for my insignificance can contribute very little to fulfilling your desire. At most I can inspire you toward it. Whether your desire fulfills itself only depends on you and you alone. You've given me a big problem.

45 Quoted in Rietenauer, *Alma, meine Liebe*, p. 111.

Nevertheless, you may not have expected me to send you this picture of an elder actor as a gift in kind for your charming affection with the dedication: All the best for your future!"

Although Aslan enclosed a standard autographed glossy of himself, he found a better gift for her "Ode," for the one who knew his soul. This other gift made them virtual contemporaries, friends, and suggests that Aslan's sexuality was hardly the impasse of ill-mannered minds. "To be halfway fair to your being so kind," Aslan continued in a postscript, "I must come up with something else! Before me is my first passport. In the picture I am 18 years old. About the same age as you I guess. At about this time I had this strong desire to be a good actor. That was not really easy for me. But I took on every adversity and became, as you say, a good actor. I am taking this ancient photo from my old passport in order to send it to you. If you're ever down and out, look at this photo. At that time the young man had the same problems as you as a young actor. Yet he achieved his goal as an actor according to your opinion. 'I believe in you!'"[46]

If Raoul Aslan's photograph and belief in her encouraged Manon to pursue acting, she would need it facing her mother and stepfather whose support of her seemed to lessen, as though they had merely indulged her over the years and never really felt confident in her talent, not enough to risk their own reputations. In his "Manon" necrology, Werfel incredibly stated that her "passion for making speeches and playing on stage seemed to flicker out in her more and more" during this time when she had her heart set on taking acting lessons. She seemed to be nothing but a "girl, shooting up tall," one who "often displayed a submissive leeriness and lightness" in sharp contrast to the precocious child she no longer was. "I began to accept that for Manon it was nothing more serious than the usual phase that children go through with acting," Werfel wrote, as though describing a changeling.

46 In Rietenauer, *Alma, meine Liebe*, p. 112.

"I paid little heed that it might be the embarrassment of self-expression, the shyness from self-exposure that all sensitive natures experience beset, as she was, by puberty. To us Manon appeared to have become quite shallow. One had the impression that she was only interested in clothes. For hours on end she sat poring over fashion illustrations. 'Unfortunately,' we said of her, 'she has no intensity.'"[47]

Lichtbild

Anna Mahler saw Alma and Werfel actively frustrating Manon's aspirations. Since Anna now lived at Villa Mahler, following another separation from Paul Zsolnay, she saw her half-sister's growing pains firsthand as she herself grew as an artist, having become a student of the Austrian sculptor Fritz Wotruba. In hindsight, Anna considered what her mother or Werfel said that trivialized Manon as simply their bad conscience talking, their self-defense. And she was not alone in seeing Manon as repressed. Her friend, Elias Canetti, also noticed the thwarted person as well as an ethereal, indeed, liminal being, as some-one—or some*thing*—more than the victim of her mother and Werfel.

Canetti, a future Nobel laureate, was still a relatively unknown writer when he first saw Manon in the summer of 1933. At the time Canetti had been involved in a brief affair with Anna Mahler, who offered to help advance his career by arranging for an afternoon audience with her mother. He needed such an advocate to succeed as a young writer with a chemistry degree. Born in Bulgaria to Ladino-speaking Sephardic parents, Canetti spent much of his childhood in England. There he learned English and his mother taught him German—the very skills with which Canetti began his literary career translating Upton Sinclair's *Love's Pilgrimage*, *Money Writes*, and *The Wet Parade*. A natural polymath, Canetti also developed a passion for crowd psychology—and the psychopathology of Viennese themselves—after witnessing the

47 Werfel, "Manon," *Erzählungen aus zwei Welten*, pp. 394–5.

infamous July Revolt of 1927 and the torching of the Palace of Justice, an event that inspired his novel *Die Blendung* (The Glare, 1935), better known in English as *Auto-da-Fé*.

For Alma, Canetti would have been another strain of the assimilated Jews she collected around herself, and she could help open doors for him or, at least, not stand in the way. Meeting Werfel might also help Canetti, even though he, the younger man, like other modernists in Vienna, disparaged Werfel's success and his work as sentimental trash. (Robert Musil even made a satirical character of Werfel, the poet Felix Feuermaul, i.e. "Lucky Firemouth," for his novel *The Man without Qualities.*) And as much as Canetti might be a bad human specimen to Alma, her reputation also served to whet Canetti's curiosity when Anna introduced him to her mother, ensconced on her divan in the so-called Blue Room of Villa Mahler.[48]

At their other meeting, Canetti could see that Alma was already inebriated from Benedictine. Like another younger man, Ernst Krenek, Canetti could not believe that Alma had once been considered the most beautiful girl in Vienna, now gone to fat and giving him a creepy, treacly smile. And to her—even without the least mention in her diary—he would have been another "nihilistic Jew," another disreputable young *Dichter* picked up by her troubled older daughter. Thus, they suffered one another in Alma's reception room, which to Canetti was laid out in such a way that it directed, like a musical score in itself, where the eyes of her visitors should fall upon the major movements in her life. His eyes fell on Gustav Mahler's death mask in yellowing plaster, various musical scores by Mahler, including the unfinished Tenth Symphony in a vitrine, with the page open to where the composer had penned a love note to his "Almschi," and the only copy of

48 The following account is informed by Elias Canetti, "Trophies," in *The Play of the Eyes* (Ralph Manheim trans.) (New York: Farrar, Straus & Giroux, 1986), pp. 50–5.

Bruckner's Third Symphony. As Alma pointed to these objects and explained their significance, Canetti began to see them as trophies. The Blue Room became the hut of a headhuntress and her displays, fetishes, or cult objects. No less menacing, too, was Kokoschka's 1912 portrait of Alma. It dominated the room and to Canetti the narrowed blue eyes in the portrait followed him around, projecting a dangerous, murderous quality underscored by Alma pointing out for Canetti what was already obvious and did not bear repeating, that Kokoschka had painted her as the notorious Renaissance beauty and poisoner, Lucrezia Borgia. "That painting really frightens people," Alma told him, or, at least, the one he had exaggerated no less than the artist.

At some point during Canetti's audience with her, Alma "clapped fat hands" and in a loud voice that reached into the garden summoned Manon, "Where's my kitty cat!" Soon there appeared, with a "loose stride and light step," an "easy, brown creature," one only "pretending to be a young girl." She "radiated timidity more than beauty," Canetti waxed effusively, "an angelic gazelle not descended from the ark but rather from the sky." He claimed that he had jumped to his feet, not to greet her, but rather as her rescuer, "intending to keep her out of this den of vice or at least block her view of the poisoner on the wall, Lucrezia who never ceased playing her role as she, unstoppable, took center stage." This is likely contrived, more what Canetti wished he had done but was too late. "Pretty, isn't she?" said Alma. "This is my daughter Manon. By Gropius. In a class by herself. You don't mind me saying so, do you Annerl?"—a diminutive of Anna and, to Canetti, indicative of her lower status as a child of Alma. "What's so wrong with having a beautiful sister?" Alma continued, but what seems more from anecdotes learned from Anna herself and after. "Like father, like daughter. Have you ever seen Gropius? A tall handsome man. The real Aryan type. The only man who was racially suitable to me."

Alma soon dismissed Manon with instructions to fetch Werfel so as to show off this last trophy. "With this commission Manon, the third trophy, slipped out of the room, as untouched as she had come," Canetti observed, or rather projected, "her errand didn't seem to trouble her. I was greatly relieved at the thought that nothing could touch her, that she would always remain as she was and never become like her mother, the poisoner on the wall, the glassy, blubbery old woman on the sofa."

That Canetti did not see Werfel's imagined changeling but rather a girl pretending to be a girl is telling, for it does not deny that she is a performer. That he saw a girl with an animal nature, as a gazelle, hearing her referred to as Alma's pet rather than daughter, too, is in keeping with what we already know about Manon Gropius thus far; testified to those who witness her rapport with animals, which became another kind of theater around her, the way she could become the mistress of someone else's cat or dog, or the way she could master a frightened drayhorse one day on Steinfeldgasse, as witnessed by the boy Rietenauer.

He also took the photographs of Manon when two roe deer, a buck and a doe, came out of the woods behind Villa Mahler, also witnessed by Alma, Werfel, and the conductor Bruno Walter from Alma's music room. The teenager could be seen through the glass doors that led outside to the terrace and garden. "I'll always see this unearthly apparition before me," Walter wrote in his memoirs, "which offered itself to us as we sat there still at brunch, an angelic, beautiful girl, [. . .] with a deer at her side, appeared in the doorway—she had her hand on the delicate neck of the deer, smiled at us unshyly, and vanished again."[49] Alma, thinking the deer might eat her flowers, ordered Manon to lock the animals in the garden tool shed and have the humane society take them away. Manon refused, claiming that animals are intelligent and if one projected tender thoughts toward them, they would respond in kind. She said that she could read their minds and that they could hers. Thus

---

49 Bruno Walter, *Thema und Variationen: Erinnerungen und Gedanken* [Theme and Variations: Memories and Thoughts] (Stockholm: Bermann-Fischer, 1947), p. 411.

she fed and watered them—and played with them as though they were tame, which they were not, for the little buck charged Rietenauer when he ventured too close with his camera.

As Alma watched, she said to Walter, "I don't want any of this in my head. I have no mystical child. I don't see anything." The conductor, however, in a voice he used to carefully contradict her, still believed that Manon had supernatural abilities. This shared experience was one he would never forget until the day he died. "It was like a mystical visitation, unreal and yet wonderful and beautiful. Your daughter Manon must be an exceptional person to have these animals obey her in such a wonderful way. It was like being an uninvited spectator to some fairy world, eavesdropping on the elf queen consorting with the animals of the forest. Alma, I'm not pulling your leg, understanding this experience was a balancing act for me and inexplicable. I am thankful to have experienced this event with you."[50] Werfel agreed, saying that she was in some way akin to Francis of Assisi.

Although Manon left the impression that she was this fairy, or even airy-fairy being given her sensitivities, shyness, and remoteness—to some adults who engaged her in conversation, their words did not reach her, "that she was far away"—she was still quite human and made of far harder stuff. Manon's reserve, however, owed something to being wary of grownups. This may have been especially true for her mother, who claimed to "know" her daughter's heart.

According to Rietenauer, Manon believed her mother had always been behind reinforcing Gropius' impression that his daughter did not care for him. The boy learned this upon finding Manon distressed outside Villa Mahler and waiting for a streetcar. "Are you in a hurry or do you have time for me?" she asked the little boy.[51] He said no and agreed to accompany her into the city, for he would never pass up

50 Quoted in Rietenauer, *Alma, meine Liebe*, p. 129.

51 The following dialogue is after Rietenauer, pp. 144ff.

spending time with his crush. She paid his child's fare and found two vacant seats so they could sit together. "All hell has broken loose at home," Manon told her young confidante. "Mommy won't let anyone use our telephone or telephone from grandmamma's either. I know exactly why she is making all this theater, since today my father is fifty years old. It's to make it look like I forgot papa's fiftieth birthday. That's not true! If I cannot see him, I want to at least call him."

When the streetcar stopped before Vienna's main post office, Manon and the boy Rietenauer got off and went inside. There she entered one of the telephone booths while the boy waited outside. When she pushed open the folding doors, Manon left in tears, dabbing her eyes and nose with a handkerchief. She could not get through to her father. She went to the counter to pay for her telephone call and send a telegram. Rietenauer offered her a schilling, but Manon laughed and said they should get ice cream instead.

"Listen, Burschi," she said as the two friends sat on a park bench by the Danube Canal, "I have a very wonderful father. He is smart at his job. He is a person with a good soul and a handsome man as well. Only he's in Berlin and can't get commissions from the new government anymore. His finances aren't very good. The worst of it is I can't go to him in Berlin and he can't come to me in Vienna. I have, in my seventeen years, perhaps seen my father for a total of four weeks. Can you imagine that?"

The boy could, for his father was dead. Manon pressed his hand and spoke about how much she regretted missing her father on his birthday and what he might think. She wondered if his telephone had been disconnected.

"You have a lot of love for your papa," said the boy.

"I love my father above all else," Manon replied and then she wondered aloud about her mother's reasons. She told Rietenauer that she and her father suspected that Alma kept many of his letters from her. So he began inserting notes in the trade journals he also sent. "For fourteen days he had secretly sent me these messages," Manon continued. "I read them over and over again." At this point in Rietenauer's account—written during his early eighties—he quotes Manon Gropius quoting from one of her father's letters verbatim, which reveals how his memory of a day in May 1933 after more than sixty years is not reliable in the usual sense that biographers would like. They are perhaps *impressions* of what happened and very likely good impressions if not good memory. For Gropius did send magazines and textbooks and when he responded to his daughter's letters in his, he is aware that Alma read them, that she is heavy-handed in influencing her against him. Even though Manon may not have really repeated his words to Rietenauer ("my gorgeous daughter of whom i only have a premonition!"), she surely knew how out-of-focus she was to her father. If she did not tell a little boy eating an ice-cream cone of her real feelings ("This is why my father is so sad. Because he can't see me. Everything is just terrible—for me as well!"), he would have no reason to tell this story—and it may be mostly *story*—that Manon Gropius had this pathos for her father, one no less strong than what she felt on the death of his mother, for a pair of deer, for a garden snake.

Stories of Manon—whether factual, myths and legends, probable and outright lies and falsehoods, and simply the mistakes of poor memory—inform this text for the portrayal of her portrayals, the *mutable* portrait that is achieved. For that reason, they are more interesting as mistakes than Gropius' official biographer placing his subject in Vienna to visit Manon in mid-June when such an encounter was impossible. First, Gropius could ill afford the exorbitant bond the German government placed on its citizens crossing the Austrian border—this in retaliation for Dollfuss outlawing the Austrian National Socialist Party. Second, Gropius' letter of June 17 to Manon was posted from Berlin—and with no mention of any birthday telegram, but rather a letter that began with an acknowledgment of her apology for her very human handwriting. "i found your letter not the least bit 'scrawly,' Gropius began, 'but am surprised at how your writing gets ever more unabridged and all your own; i am following your development closely, and of course i don't place any value on calligraphy and [. . .] that you just have me in mind pleases me deeply; they are the only pearl points which i can follow the progress of your lifeline.[52] i would love to know more about you and the things going on inside you, sometime give your old man a more intensive hour, will you?" Gropius then listed his plans for the summer, which included a stay at Dartington Hall, a school and planned community inspired by the Bauhaus in part, founded by Leonard and Dorothy Elmhirst, he the former personal secretary the Rabindranath Tagore and she a wealthy and progressive American socialite. Gropius also told his daughter about a new "job opportunity," most likely from Harvard University, an exhibition devoted to his work in Milan, and the upcoming CIAM meeting in Athens. Nevertheless, he confessed to Manon that he had much time on his hands. "i've been taking so many long walks like no other time in my life," he wrote, and putting his "mother's estate in order, a contemplative task as you can imagine. your desire to have a picture of her i have not forgotten, but it is very difficult, there are only small photos and these i have to try enlarging now to get the relative best, which i will then send to you."[53]

Gropius also desired photographs—new ones of Manon. When he wrote her near the end of the summer, he contemplated the one on his desk, taken on Christmas Eve 1931, in which her eyes look knowingly upward to her left. "you look at me so matter-of-factly because, since the last time you left here, xanti schawinsky—now he too is mountains away—made me a life-size enlargement of your head, which is beautiful and is always sitting on my desk. visitors always ask who is this girl with the interesting face! but now it has been almost 2 years and i am

52 *Pearl points*, a term from palmistry.
53 Walter Gropius to Manon Gropius, June 17, 1933, ÖNB.

sure there are new photos you have been keeping from me. I would be pleased with anything you send." The rest of his letter lamented his fallen status since the Nazi rise to power. He had no commissions, had sold his beloved Adler in which he had proudly driven Manon, and contemplated emigration, which did not appeal to him, for he still felt himself to be a loyal German and akin to many Jewish Germans, too, given the uncensored way he commiserated with Werfel, whose books were being burned throughout Germany. 'tell franz that right now i feel especially close to him,' he wrote, 'and have half a mind to get myself circumcised out of sympathy! hony soit qui mal y pense.[54] [. . .] where are you and what are you up to? still on semmering? [. . .] all my friends are gone, it is very lonely."[55]

Between Gropius' two letters, Manon suffered the loss of Agathe Lothar, who had contracted poliomyelitis—*Kinderlähmung*—in the "bloom of health at a holiday resort."[56] At first, she exhibited the classic flu-like symptoms of headache and fever. Then, two weeks later, she became paralyzed from the neck down. During July, according to Rietenauer, Manon visited her sick friend—likely against her mother's wishes, even though such physicians as Dr. Tandler and Dr. Bien knew the disease was no longer contagious. Eventually, Agathe was transferred to a clinic in Innsbruck, where she died of a massive infection on August 13, just three days after celebrating her eighteenth birthday. In an obituary for his eldest daughter—a heroine of his novels—Ernst Lothar revealed the cruel nature of polio, an "insidious infectious disease," of how his Agathe, this "angel on this earth," the "dearest person in the world," seemingly on the verge of recovery, had died of "untold

54 The motto of the Order of the Garter, "Evil be to him who evil thinks."

55 Walter Gropius to Manon Gropius, September 11, 1933, ÖNB.

56 Todesfälle [Deaths], *Neue Freie Presse* [Vienna New Free Press], August 15, 1933, p. 7, ANNO.

suffering" and been "snatched away from us by a cruel fate."[57] She was buried in the churchyard in the suburb of Morzg outside of Salzburg, which had recently been named "Austria's City of Beautiful Girls."

Agathe's death was not the only heartbreak of the summer. Manon's Irish setter Harro died after being fed poison under mysterious circumstances. Alma recorded ominous events, too. When she and Manon had been returning from church, a gang of drunken men accosted them. Fortunately, their screams alerted two mounted policemen to intercede. Then a crazy "gypsy" woman appeared outside Villa Mahler, giving the house the evil eye and cursing "mal oki, mal oki" and forcing Alma to chase her off with the Steyr pistol she carried in her purse.[58]

Travel had always been anodyne to unhappiness in Alma's family and, in mid-September, she, Werfel, Manon, and Susi Kertész went to Velden—where Manon received a letter from Sister Ida, who was taking care of Manon's new Siamese cat "Toifi" (another name for Krampus from Austrian folklore), as well as photographs of a litter of kittens. Then the Mahler-Werfel party traveled on to Haus Mahler on Semmering for the first week of October to enjoy the autumn leaves and to celebrate Manon's birthday. When they returned to Vienna, it was in anticipation of seeing the final page proofs of *The Forty Days of Musa Dagh*. According to Alma, the entire household waited with breathless expectation until he came down from his atelier and pronounced the book finished. Nearly a thousand pages in length and in two volumes, Alma wrote how it was a gigantic accomplishment for someone Jewish in such a time, for it could still be sold in Germany, albeit without his name anywhere on the book.[59] Although the book was ostensibly about the Armenian genocide, German readers—and Nazi censors—could

---

57 "Agathe Lothar" (obituary), *Neue Freie Presse* [Vienna New Free Press], August 17, 1933, p. 10, ANNO.

58 Rietenauer, *Alma, meine Liebe*, p. 131.

59 Mahler-Werfel, "Diary of Alma Maria," October 10, 1933, p. 285, MWP.

see parallels with their own Jewish minority as well as a condemnation of German nationalism. In this Werfel had been carefully provocative rather than a provocateur, for he wanted to elicit what he imagined to be an essential and German humanitarian quality, for such might forestall the German leaders from embarking on persecuting Jews.

While such an ambitious work of literature might mean a Nobel Prize in Werfel's future, it also meant much needed income to maintain Alma's three houses, the servants who staffed them, a stepdaughter, and her new French governess. Mademoiselle Nadé not only would serve to tutor Manon in French, but provide her with a chaperone and companion more suited than Sister Ida for cultivating the daughter of Alma Mahler and Franz Werfel of Hohe Warte. Having turned seventeen, Manon's birthday presents acknowledged her status. Among the fine clothes, shoes, and accessories, she received a new bible. On the flyleaf was verse 1:27 from Paul to the Philippians in Latin—"Walk worthy of the gospel of Christ."—as though she needed to be more mindful of her conduct and virtue. And with fewer strings attached, Manon also received a porcelain Chinese figurine to go with her other fragile miniatures—a gift from one of Anna Mahler's new lovers, the novelist Leo Perutz. Also made of glass was Gropius' grownup gift, a Jenaer tea service designed by the Bauhäusler Wilhelm Wagenfeld. It consisted of a round, heat-resistant kettle as well as cups and saucers. His letter of October 3 told her that the set would soon arrive, as well as the story of how he had experienced her coming into the world. "yesterday i found among my mother's correspondence the first letter i wrote her following your birth and everything came back to me," he wrote. "i had traveled to vienna to be there when you first drew near to us with your presence, but you would not be separated from your mommy, so i had to go back to the front [. . .] bemoaning my fate and waited with beating heart until you could bring yourself into beginning your autonomous existence. and after many weeks, when i was at last allowed to espy my sweet production on mommy's changing table, mommy was like a lioness defending her cub from someone who wanted to wrest it from her. then came a couple of beautiful holiday weeks during which you accepted me as your father and let me swaddle you daily as your features and character began to peep from the blanket—i have not seen you for so terribly long! those sporadic encounters during the war have remained chronic between us."[60]

Manon may have never heard her father's story before. If it came as a surprise, it only measured how far back his despair went and her mother's role in causing it. Ironically, Gropius could not keep up his daughter's need for more contact from him. "really now it is not so bad after all, your imagination running away a little," Gropius wrote in his defense, " because, since my last letter of 10 october, i have only received the one from you of 19 oct. but you are right nonetheless, i am a dog for letting you go so long without news. but you know communication across the frontier is a little difficult and i cannot write as much as i would want." Gropius then described how he and Ise now lived in reduced circumstances, having given up half their apartment and getting by with just two rooms. Although it surely hurt him that he could do nothing for her in the way of financial support, he refrained from bringing up what was so implicit. Instead, he put on a good face in his letter, responding to her far better circumstances—and the breakage of one her new teacups despite being as sturdy as Pyrex. "i am happy because your news sounds good, because you sail with the wind at your back and enjoy your life, my dear; it's a crime that i cannot see that up close. at least send me another picture of you.—how are preparations going for your interpreter's exam? i would be so proud of you if you succeeded in taking that exam at such an early age. [. . .] did the replacement come for the broken cup? [. . .] write me my angel, with no hard feelings."[61]

60 Walter Gropius to Manon Gropius, October 3, 1933, ÖNB.
61 Walter Gropius to Manon Gropius, December 12, 1933, ÖNB.

Throughout 1933, Alma obsessed over politics, especially German politics and what Hitler and National Socialism—to her an "*Ersatzreligion*"—would mean to Austria, to her husband, and to other Jews. Despite her many Jewish friends—so many that she tactlessly contemplated titling a memoir *My Life among the Jews*—Alma, with just Julius Tandler and the other architects of Red Vienna in mind, believed their progressive ideas would bring about their demise. For Austria, she found Dollfuss weak and vacillating and looked to his rival Rintelen, who had been sent to Rome as Austria's envoy to the Vatican in late October—a move to keep him from conspiring against the chancellor. To celebrate this "promotion-as-exile," Alma gave a party for Rintelen at Villa Mahler and continued to encourage the married politician to "court" her teenage daughter. The boy Rietenauer had even seen the two together on a wooded path near Villa Mahler, talking earnestly and intimately "face to face," as though in love. Rintelen tenderly put his raincoat over the girl's shoulders as it began to rain lightly. The boy, who saw himself as one of her suitors, found the sight of an older man flirting with Manon disturbing. He was more appalled when Carl Moll told him not to say anything about what he had seen, for he and Alma saw Rintelen as a modern Arminus, the great German chieftain who defeated the Roman army in the Battle of the Teutoburg Forest, and that his falling in love with Manon would gird him into a like victory over Austria's internal enemies.[62]

What Rietenauer witnessed nevertheless spread and led to an uproar at Villa Mahler. Father Hollnsteiner was so shocked by Rintelen's presence that he ceased calling on Alma and Manon for a time. In all likelihood, however, nothing scandalous took place. Like her mother when she was much younger, Manon had developed a rapport around older men and "seemed unperturbed" by them.[63] And Rintelen had to

62 See Rietenauer, pp. 155ff.

63 Hilmes, *Witwe im Wahn*, p. 257.

compete for her attention with his political opposite, Julius Tandler. Before Tandler left for China in the summer, he posed for photographs on the porch of Haus Mahler with Manon on one arm and Alma on the other. He also established three o'clock in the afternoon as that special time of the day—his "rendezvous"—when he would write Manon a letter or postcard, which she looked forward to more so than any assignation with the ludicrous Rintelen.

Manon, too, picked up a third admirer in Max Reinhardt, who now lived in Austria. He had left Germany in March in protest despite being offered the title of "honorary Aryan" by the Nazi government if he would return. After producing Goethe's *Faust* for the Salzburg Festival during the summer, he had turned his attention to future projects, including a Broadway play based on the Old Testament and intended to highlight the struggles and contributions of the Jewish people. For this project, Reinhardt enlisted Werfel to write the oratorio and Kurt Weill for the score, which entailed more contact between Reinhardt and the Mahler-Werfel household. Thus, sometime during the latter half of 1933 and, perhaps, as late as the holiday parties leading up to Christmas and the New Year of 1934, Reinhardt reacquainted himself with the little girl he knew traveled to Berlin with Werfel and Alma over the years.[64]

But now Manon Gropius was a beautiful adolescent girl whose height and waist-length hair gave her a certain grownup presence at gatherings with her mother and stepfather that obscured the fact that she was still a minor. "Reinhardt," Werfel wrote, "is the greatest seer of acting talent that I know. His eyes are like a divining rod for this capacity. They see and remain fixed on a face, knowing all there is to

64 The approximate timeframe for this encounter must be triangulated from Werfel's necrology "Manon," which seems too late—March 1934—and Rietenauer's memoir. The latter states June 1933, which is more likely, but Reinhardt was staging his production of *A Midsummer's Night Dream* in Oxford, England at the time.

know. It isn't necessary that one act or read some lines for him. On seeing her for the first time, Max Reinhardt said to Manon: 'I'm going to do Calderón next—in a revival of Hofmannsthal's Theater of the World. And I want you to play the part of the First Angel.'"[65] This was a plum role. Reinhardt meant the *Salzburg Great Theater of the World*, an adaptation of Pedro Calderón de la Barca's Baroque-era original, *El Gran Teatro del Mundo*, which he had premiered at the 1922 festival. The play was overdue for a revival and would honor the memory of Reinhardt's great friend and late collaborator, Hugo von Hofmannsthal.

Werfel, despite the trust he placed in Reinhardt, was shocked by the offer. The First Angel was no minor part. It was a demanding and integral role that required a forceful, authoritative young woman. Manon would have to talk down to the World in this elaborate allegory, and play other archetypal characters, such as the Wiseman, Beggar, and King. This angel would need to talk to and for God, the Master, and against the Adversary. She led the angelic cohort on the upper stage and gave many short but dark and powerful speeches that would need to project for festival performances that took place outdoors. According to Werfel, he became increasingly agitated and apoplectic given the importance and beauty of the First Angel. "I thought it an absurd idea. It would be a dangerous experiment to entrust such a role to a gullible young thing who knew next to nothing about the stage," he remembered. "My eyes saw less than Reinhardt's eyes. I violently advised against it."

Although Alma had no objection, Werfel overruled her. He remembered how he had overheard Manon singing in her room with a full-blown soprano voice with an astonishing power for reaching the high notes. But when asked to sing for her mother, who tried to

---

65 This account is informed by Werfel, "Manon," *Erzählungen aus zwei Welten*, p. 395ff; and Rietenauer, *Alma, meine Liebe*, pp. 134ff.

accompany her on the piano, Manon could produce nothing more than a warbling little girl's voice. No coaxing or begging helped. "I can't do it any other way, she cried, and she did cry for such attempts typically ended in tears." For something like this to happen in private was one thing. In Austria's theater world, it would be an embarrassment suffered by the whole family.

In Werfel's account, his refusal to let Manon audition for the First Angel supposedly had no effect on her. "Manon seemed to suffer not at all under my strict 'No,'" he wrote. "Easter was near. We always went away to Venice for Easter." However, according to Rietenauer, Manon had been deeply hurt and disappointed by losing this chance of lifetime. She left the party to sit and sulk in the garden, where the boy allegedly took a surreptitious snapshot of her with his miniature camera. "With his stupid gob," Carl Moll said, "Franz has now ruined the poor girl's career."

Although it would not have been a consolation for her, no other young woman would be the First Angel in the 1934 festival. Max Reinhardt abandoned his revival of *The Great World Theater*, for Austria's continuing cold war with Germany made it impossible for Germans to attend—as did the aftermath of the Austrian Republic's civil war, known as the "February Uprising."

The long-awaited showdown between Dollfuss and Vienna's Social Democrats and its legions of supporters in Austria's major cities had been festering for months, ever since the chancellor began ruling Austria by decree. Called the "Millimetternich" for his diminutive stature—and for the reactionary Austrian statesman and architect of the Congress of Vienna—Dollfuss now wore the same feathered alpine paramilitary uniforms of the Home Guard. His so-called Fatherland Front had effectively welded together the interests of the Christian Social Party, the Roman Catholic clergy, the military officers, and various other right-wing factions save for those loyal to Berlin. With the Nazis and Communist parties outlawed, the only real opposition to finalizing an Austrian fascist dictatorship were the Social Democrats and their own paramilitaries.

Throughout January and early February 1934, with Werfel away at St. Margherita, Alma sensed an "atmosphere pregnant with danger" in Vienna, especially in the "proletarian" neighborhoods when she drove down to the city in her car, accompanied by Manon (still called "my little daughter" in her diary). In her favorite cafe, she pored over the Viennese dailies on the right and left to get a clear picture of recent events, such as the "secret telegram" that had been intercepted, decoded, and interpreted by the Dollfuss regime as proof the Bolshevists in Moscow intended to overthrow his government. On February 12, the Home Guard found a cache of arms inside the headquarters of the Social Democrats in Linz. The next day martial law was declared. Although Karl Renner pleaded for calm and reason under the headline "Quo vadis, proletarians?"—thousands of workers walked off their jobs at the power station, the telephone exchange, and other key places, and took to the streets. Many also took up arms and began fortifying predominantly Social Democrat neighborhoods in Austria's cities.

Alma and Manon experienced the first signs of the revolt when the electric lights flickered out and the phone line went dead at Villa Mahler. Then came the sound of gunfire from nearby Karl-Marx-Hof, where truckloads of government soldiers, militia, police troops and an assortment of armored cars and "mountain guns," small but devastating artillery pieces, were positioned around the vast apartment complex. Despite the proximity of danger, for which Alma packed a small traveling bag for herself and Manon should they need to accept the invitation of the justice minister, Kurt Schuschnigg, to stay with his family, she decided to wait out the fury of the three-day siege and protect her house, as it was a virtual museum filled with precious objects. Alma also found the *Schadenfreude* thrilling as the socialists got their comeuppance, to her fascist way of thinking. To celebrate and shore up her courage, she sent a maid to the wine cellar to fetch a bottle of good champagne to toast "qui vive"—be on the lookout—with Mademoiselle Nadé against any stray bullet or artillery shell—or the armed workers retreating down Steinfeldgasse.

For Manon, the adventure continued for four weeks, during which she had to carry a police passport for moving about Vienna. Although bearing an official stamp, the document seems almost perfunctorily typed on ordinary stationery. It included her full name ("Alma Manon Gropius"), birthdate, address, description (Eyes: green, Hair: drk. brown, Stature: tall), and her occupation ("Schoolgirl"). The identification photograph (labeled *Lichtbild*, a nineteenth-century German word loaned from the slides of magic lanterns) reveals a young woman who had matured in the last nine months, with her resemblance to her father even more pronounced, and a smile that seemed both amused, by the formality of being photographed just to travel to the city center, and looking forward—as Werfel said—to Easter in Venice.

IN SICKNESS

When a child is sick, everything loses its meaning.[1]
—Ernst Lothar, *Children, First Experiences*

She loved everything that Nature created, except, I think, the polio virus.[2]
—Albrecht Joseph

"[T]errible days are behind us and what may come!!!" Alma wrote Anton Rintelen near the end of February, still filled with trepidation over the recent civil war upon her return from three days in Venice. Like her other letters to the would-be dictator of Austria, she mentioned how much she and Manon missed seeing him in person. To further ingratiate herself, Alma also encouraged Manon to add a fawning postscript and sign it "Sissy" for Rintelen's delectation, since that was the pet name of the late Empress Elisabeth of Austria, the wife of Franz Josef I. Elisabeth was a model of beauty for Austrian males born in the late nineteenth century and Manon Gropius' resemblance to her was rarely lost on men of Rintelen's generation. He had apparently made the comparison himself. "How much I would love to come to Rome with Mutzi," Alma continued, "but our funds are rather scarce

1 Ernst Lothar, *Kinder, erste Erlebnisse* [Children, First Experiences] (Vienna: Paul Zsolany, 1932), pp. 28–9.

2 Albrecht Joseph, "Zu Besuch bei Alma Mahler-Werfel" [Visiting Alma Mahler-Werfel], in Weidle, Barbara, and Ursula Seeber (eds.), *Anna Mahler. Ich bin in mir selbst zu Hause* [Anna Mahler: I Am at Home in Myself] (Bonn: Weidle and Seeber, 2004), p. 86.

at the moment! Where are they to come from?—For Mahler is not being performed and Werfel not read—and we have all survived on Germany!"[3]

Not long afterward, in early March, Franz Werfel also returned to Vienna and life at Villa Mahler. He had been in Italy writing poetry for most of the winter and had no desire to turn around and go back in a few weeks. He suggested to the family that they might stay home for Easter. This did not go over well with his stepdaughter. She had spent Easter in Venice for practically her whole life. She had new clothes and hats in which to be seen in St. Mark's Square. She had gone to Rietenauer's uncle's studio and had a new passport photo taken in which she wore makeup and no longer resembled the "schoolgirl" of a few weeks earlier. And, she had endured a depressing winter of wanting to be an actor with seemingly no one to believe in her. "Word for word," according to one of Villa Mahler's maids who had overheard her and gone to Alma, Manon said, "I think if I don't go to Venice this year, I will die."[4]

Although alarmed that her daughter would speak of suicide, Alma likely had no intention of staying in Vienna. "Like clockwork," she wrote in her diary, the family would celebrate Easter in Venice as always.[5] As a special privilege, Manon invited a friend, Antoinette Cavin, a classmate from Switzerland, to stay for the holiday.

Pina Belloto, Alma's housekeeper in Venice, and her husband Carlo, had Casa Mahler ready when Alma, Werfel, Manon, and Mademoiselle Nadé arrived in late March for Holy Week and Easter Sunday, which fell on April 1. The early date made Alma think of her first trip to Venice and Italy in 1899 and how Gustav Klimt had lured her to his

3 Alma Mahler-Werfel to Anton Rintelen, February 23, 1934, WSA.

4 Werfel, "Manon," *Erzählungen aus zwei Welten*, p. 396.

5 Mahler-Werfel, "Diary of Alma Maria", March 28, 1934, p. 290, MWP.

hotel room. Manon would receive the same attention from Anton Rintelen, the irony being that Alma now found a fascist politician as worthy as an artist. She had her daughter at the airport in time so that her "statesman with farsighted eyes" did not have far to look for the revenant of the beautiful and long dead empress.

Rintelen was not the only one looking for Manon as he entered the Lido terminal. His entourage included a young Austrian bureaucrat, Erich Sepp Cyhlar, who already met Manon in December, when he attended an intimate gathering of the "the elite of intellectual Vienna," hosted by her sister Anna and Paul Zsolnay in a candle-lit Baroque salon with music provided by the Tautenhahn Quartet.[6] Cyhlar certainly belonged at this tea party, having earned a reputation as a lecturer for such groups as the Free Association for the Political Education of Women. Having made a good impression—and not necessarily on Manon—he then attended a Christmas Day gathering at Villa Mahler in the company of his friend, Albert von Trentini's son, Johannes, who was also one of Manon's admirers.[7]

Ten years older than her, Erich Cyhlar had been a centrist in the Greater German People's Party. But since 1930 he moved to the right and was now a paramilitary advisor to the Fatherland Front, even though hardly a man in uniform. With his degree in economics from the University of Vienna, Cyhlar had been a government consultant and was now in line to be the personal secretary of the Minister of Social Administration. As the image of a young bureaucrat, he looked the part with his blandly handsome features, light, wavy hair parted in the middle and *runde Brille*, the round celluloid eyewear that was stylish among European men in the 1930s.

---

6 The Zsolnay party is reported on the society page of the *Neue Wiener Journal*, December 19, 1933, p. 5, ANNO.

7 The pair are identified as Erich Chillar (*sic*) and Dieter (*sic*) Trentini, see Rietenauer, *Alma, meine Liebe*, p. 158.

Alma saw that Cyhlar was smitten with Manon, but she recorded nothing on the part of her daughter that suggested any reciprocation. Instead Manon seemed to only venture forth with her mother. Together, they attended Easter Sunday mass at St. Mark's Cathedral, where the pomp and circumstance rivaled that of the Vatican's celebration of the resurrected Christ. The ritual and ceremony took four hours, from nine in the morning until one in the afternoon. "You would have been happy with us,"[8] Alma wrote of her own and Manon's piety to Father Hollnsteiner.

Easter Monday brought Rintelen to Casa Mahler, where he expounded on his political ideas. There followed, too, the usual Easter week gatherings, house callings, and chance meetings with new and old friends while strolling, dining, or simply watching people on St. Mark's Square. Alma saw the young Prince Albrecht von Urach, who had rented out Casa Mahler the year before, his new his English wife and baby girl. Alma, Manon, and Werfel also visited their friend, the art and antiques dealer Adolph Loewi, his wife Katherine, and their two daughters, Kay and Marlene, who lived in a *palazzo* on Canal San Trovaso. The Loewi girls had long known Manon, considered one of the "older girls" and now one of the adults in the way she dressed and followed the grownups' conversation. This was evident when Manon delivered a sly and inappropriate retort while sitting perched on the armrest of a sofa beside her mother. Taken aback, Alma responded, "Mind your tongue, Mutzi, or I'll dedaughter you!"[9]

Meanwhile, no one seemed to notice that Manon barely touched a thing on her plate at mealtimes, or that she sometimes vomited whatever she did manage to eat. Nothing belied her enthusiasm for being in Venice. No one noticed her nausea, headaches, and panic, or think any-

---

8 Alma Mahler-Werfel to Johannes Hollnsteiner, April 9, 1934, quoted in Buchmayr, *Der Priester in Almas Salon*, p. 78.

9 "Sag das nicht, Mutzi, sonst enttochtere ich dich!"

thing was wrong with how much Validol (menthyl isovalerate) she was taking. This common sedative treated the aforementioned indications as well as for the discomfort of seasickness and menses. But Alma did notice something odd about her daughter, especially when Manon declined going to Milan for a weekend on the pretext that it would be cruel to leave her governess alone.

On Friday, April 6, Alma and Werfel took the morning train to Milan.[10] They visited Ricordi's, the famous music publisher, and attended a thrilling performance of *La forza del destino.* Alma, however, still felt heartsick for not insisting that Manon come. Even though Manon's telegram on Saturday imparted there was nothing to worry about, she wondered if her daughter might be lying.

On Monday, April 9, Alma returned to Venice and found Manon looking pale but otherwise well. However, on Tuesday afternoon, when Alma hosted a luncheon for the actor Max Pallenberg and other guests at Casa Mahler, she noticed that Manon had not touched any of the sandwiches that had been served. What she did consume was more Validol, nine tablets on top of the four she had taken that morning. When Alma asked her what was wrong, Manon complained of a head cold. And Alma took her at her word, for Manon seemed to converse normally at lunch. Pallenberg, one of Reinhardt's favorites and a person whom Manon would want to impress, even found her fascinating.

Pallenberg stayed long enough to be invited to dinner with the Werfels at the Ristorante Fenice. There, too, Manon exhibited the same poor appetite and blamed the food, which she said nauseated her. This too only left Alma mildly concerned and it was forgotten while strolling with Pallenberg, Werfel, and Manon in St. Mark's Square. If there was

---

10 The narrative that follows, covering the events leading up to Manon's illness, are drawn from the 1935 entries of Alma's diary transcripts ("Diary of Alma Maria", pp. 293b–4b) in which she recalls April 1934 and Alma's two published memoirs (*Mein Leben*, pp. 243–7 and *And the Bridge Is Love*, pp. 221–3).

something to worry about now, it was the loss of Alma's emerald cross, which she always wore. "We searched the square, every alley, in vain," Alma remembered. "Then a terrible fear overcame me. I don't know why, it was an evil premonition. I was so miserable that I had to stay in bed late into the day."

Werfel, too, had his own suspicions. On Thursday morning, April 12, he met Ernst Lothar for breakfast at the Caffè Laverna on St. Mark's Square. "Warm-hearted as always, he wanted to know every detail of Agathe's illness," Lothar later wrote, "who, being almost the same age, had been his stepdaughter Manon's friend."[11] This was difficult for Lothar, since he had come to Venice alone, to forget the pain of his daughter's death, which had come on the heels of his divorce from her mother and his marriage to the actress Adrienne Gessner during the previous year. Lothar hoped to enjoy the company of Werfel's family. Alma, too, had come to breakfast, but apparently did not hear the conversation between Werfel and Lothar, and there was another guest, the composer Gian Francesco Malipiero.

The outdoor tables afforded a marvelous view of St. Mark's Square, dominated by the great dome of the basilica, its lions, and its great clock tower. Soon Manon emerged from the crowds in the sunlit plaza. Lothar was still relating what had happened to his daughter when "the beautiful girl arrived—or rather [. . .] rushed toward us when she saw us." Here their conversation ended, as Werfel rose and called out to his stepdaughter, "Don't skip so!" The reprimand was "in the apparent wish" that Manon's seeming health and entrance should not upset Lothar, that he should not "have to see so flagrantly the contrast in plain view."

---

11 Ernst Lothar's account is from his memoir, *Das Wunder des Überlebens. Erinnerungen und Ergebnisse* [The Miracle of Survival: Reminiscences and Results] (Vienna: Paul Zsolnay, 1961), pp. 68–9. In Lothar's account, he identifies the restaurant as the Quadri.

Alma did not see the reprise of a little girl that Werfel saw. She saw how elegant and svelte her daughter looked and walked. The photograph taken that day speaks for such an elegant entrance, for Manon's long figure seems more draped than sitting in her wicker chair. She wears the latest couture and millinery—a sleek, swept-back beret. The wide cut of her overcoat's round, standup collar, casually open to the cool spring weather reveals a wide turtleneck blouse and a small but proportionate bust vis-à-vis her narrow waist and one long leg crossed over the other. Such an eye for style—indeed, self-design, would not have displeased her architect father so far away from her now, skiing again with Ise and her boyfriends in the Sudetenland.

This photograph would be the last ever taken of Manon Gropius. Its setting, with the tables and chairs, the other diners and the archways of the Procuratie Vecchie in the background, evokes the atmosphere and ambience of the moment. The easy give and creak of the wicker furniture can almost be heard, the flap of the awnings, muted conversations, the footsteps of passersby, the flutter of the pigeons. Manon looks across at the squinting, myopic Werfel. Alma looks over her left shoulder, from under her straw sun hat. Malpiero's seat is empty (perhaps he took the photograph). And Lothar sits facing the lens, smiling weakly with a half-empty glass.

Alma had noticed his pained, unnerving expression as he watched Manon's entrance that morning. Alma took it to be envy, for her daughter was alive and Lothar's was dead. She had no idea what he really felt. "Common sense," he wrote in hindsight, "prevents considering such coincidences possible. But death has none."

That evening Alma and Werfel packed for a long weekend in Vienna in order to attend the first concert in a Mahler festival, *The Song of the Earth* conducted by Bruno Walter. Manon had once more asked to remain behind. With a heavy heart, Alma agreed.

Manon threw up in the early morning hours of Friday, April 13. Instead of returning to bed to sleep late, as was her habit, she insisted on accompanying her mother and stepfather to the railway station. Once there, however, she suddenly said she felt sick again. Torn between going home and waiting for the train to leave, she clung to Mademoiselle Nadé. But she forced herself to stay and left Alma with the charming memory of seeing her wave good-bye with her long hand. "That was the last time I saw my Mutzi well," she wrote in her diary a year later, "walking, standing in her unbelievable beauty. But we had erred, she was already sick at the time. We would have taken her back to Vienna given the way she was. And indeed I wanted to, but when she wanted something she had a strong will. The entire day en route I had this feeling that I should have taken her. Mutzi is sick. I told Werfel, who tried to calm me down."

On Saturday, Alma endured various social engagements. Nevertheless, she worried about her daughter and her mysterious illness. She cabled Manon on Sunday morning and requested that she give her an honest assessment of her symptoms and how she felt.

"Stomach upset almost better, come hopefully Tuesday," Manon wired back.

"This 'hopefully,'" Alma wrote, "I could not shake off, but it was not enough, what was I to do, it was Sunday. No flights were leaving." So Alma and Werfel attended another Mahler concert in the afternoon. Then they had supper with the Walters and attended an evening performance of Tchaikovsky's opera *Eugene Onegin* at the invitation of the justice minister, Kurt Schuschnigg. This was followed by cocktails at the Grand Hotel before returning to Villa Mahler. Once home, the parlor maid informed Alma that there had been a telephone call from Venice with news that "Mutzi was not well," that it was something with her head. Talking among themselves, Werfel, Alma, Schuschnigg, and Anna Mahler discussed the nature of her illness and what it might be.

At midnight, Alma telephoned Sister Ida, whose nursing skills and presence had long been trusted when it came to making her former charge feel better. She agreed at once to return to Venice with Alma the next day.

On Monday morning, April 16, the telephone at Villa Mahler rang again. It was Mademoiselle Nadé screaming and crying over the receiver. Alma could barely understand a word of the woman's French—but finally the word *camphor* had been blurted out and Alma had heard enough to know the situation was dire. She quickly dressed, met Sister Ida, and arrived at the airfield. Despite having left her passport behind, Alma was allowed to board the plane.

Alma and Sister Ida stared out the window through much of the flight and prepared themselves for the worst. At the airport, Prince Urach met the two women. He looked despondent and volunteered his opinion, that Manon might have meningitis, for she had all the telltale symptoms—the nausea, fever, the severe headaches. "I don't know how we got back to the house," Alma remembered. When she rang the doorbell, Manon's governess cried for joy from the upper window. Manon hugged her crying, saying again and again: "Everything will be fine now that mommy is here."

Two doctors came to see Manon. With grave expressions, they informed Alma that her daughter must undergo a lumbar puncture—a spinal tap—for a proper diagnosis. The procedure required Alma's permission, for it entailed certain risks, including brain herniation, which was nearly always fatal. The procedure, too, would be excruciatingly painful and for the patient as much a violation as an insult to her body, for Manon would likely have to lie naked in a fetal position on her bed, the front of her body covered by a sheet at most or just her dress clutched over her. The doctors might have also made her bite down on something for the pain, as one would do for an epileptic going into a seizure. Then the skin would be swabbed with alcohol and the correct site found between two lower vertebrae. Manon would have to be held and braced—by one of the doctors, Sister Ida, or both—while the other doctor forced a long, thick hypodermic needle into her spine accompanied by a sickening crunch.

To deduce meningeal inflammation, the pressure at which the fluid exits (or rather spurts) from the spine must be noted. Then a large sample must be drawn. Today a lab test would be performed to identify the presence of bacteria and viral particles as well as testing for other possible diseases such as toxoplasmosis, Epstein-Barr virus, even a fungal infection. In 1934, however, the clinical processes would have been less comprehensive and the equipment would have been no more sophisticated than a centrifuge to produce sediment and a microscope to examine it for abnormal globulin content and the like. Given that Manon's doctors were probably Italian or even German internists, the kind of attending physician called by a hotel to treat a sick tourist, they would have relied on the gross appearance of her spinal fluid. This could be done under black light in a darkened room or without any apparatus at all—the fluid would simply be held up to the light as one might appraise a glass of rosé wine. Clarity, in this case, would not denote quality. A healthy turbidity of the white and red blood cells would have been reassuring.

Alma did not assist in or watch the procedure. She went upstairs to the Molls' apartment and paced about her mother's bedroom like "a crazy woman." For comfort, she tried to read *The Cherubinic Wanderer*, a collection of inspirational aphorisms by the seventeenth-century mystic Angelus Silesius. But she grasped not a single word.

Meanwhile, a proper Austrian physician had been found, Dr. Hermann Friedmann, a *Nervenarzt*—a neurologist. His reputation was well-known to Alma, for he was attached to the Rudolfinerhaus, Vienna's most prestigious private hospitals and had treated her friends, such as Alban Berg for his many chronic illnesses. Given that it was

Alma Mahler-Werfel's daughter, Dr. Friedmann soon departed on the afternoon flight accompanied by Werfel, Anna Mahler, and her husband Paul Zsolnay. On seeing them all, Manon found some humor in being the unaccustomed center of attention. "I never knew that you're all so fond of me." And as news of her illness spread, messages of concern came along with real help. Adolph Loewi lent his personal water taxi, a kind of elegant motorboat with a town car compartment. He also sent over its "chauffeur," Luigi, who remained nearby should Manon need an ambulance to negotiate Venice's canals.

The delirium and seizures that usually come from a tubercular meningitis infection failed to manifest themselves in Manon. Instead, the patient was alert and in good spirits. Tuesday passed uneventfully, but on Wednesday morning she could not get out of bed. Her legs were paralyzed and the paralysis spread upward. Dr. Friedmann could now make the proper, indeed, obvious diagnosis. Manon had polio. The disease had followed its classic course after the brief respite of its initial symptoms, the bouts of nausea and headaches Manon had suffered during the week before.

Dr. Friedmann explained to Alma and Werfel the nature of their daughter's disease and her prognosis, for in 1934, in the prevaccinal era, a great deal was already "known" about polio and how to treat its effects, but much of that knowledge was still conjectural, tentative. In Europe and North America, many researchers believed in a nasal port of entry for the disease's pathogenesis. Others saw polio as an intestinal disease. This line of research eventually proved to be correct in 1937, when it was discovered that the polio virus could survive in stool—i.e. raw sewage—samples for weeks.[12] This research confirmed what many physicians suspected, that polio was a waterborne disease, like cholera,

---

12 John R. Paul, M.D., *A History of Poliomyelitis* (New Haven: Yale University Press, 1971), p. 283. Many of the facts and hypotheticals that follow are supported by this invaluable monograph.

and whenever there was an epidemic, the amount of the virus escaping into sewage and possibly contaminating water—even drinking water—exponentially increased.

For this reason, one only had to look at Venice's canals. They served as the city's sanitation sewers, flushed out only by the tides. For centuries they had been seen as a source of disease. Everyone knew to be careful given the legacy of cholera and the pervasive presence of flies and mosquitos, especially in summer. On some days, the foul smell of the canals got into one's clothes. Given what Dr. Friedmann knew of polio, the canals would be a seething broth of the virus in an epidemic. One had to beware of everything here, from the spray churned up by a motorboat to the holy water font of the churches, to the water that washed the drinking glasses at the cafes, the lettuce leaves of a salad. Indeed, one should avoid such a scenario—and this Werfel seized on the most. But whether there had been a real rumor of an epidemic or the well-kept secret of one may have been his own invention. "The newspapers were not allowed to print anything about the epidemic raging in Venice," he wrote later, blaming the city's government.[13] To him the Fascists would do nothing to jeopardize the lucrative Easter tourist season and the opening of the Biennale.

Given that the polio virus can incubate from less than a week to as long as a month before its early symptoms become manifest, Manon Gropius could have brought the disease with her from the seemingly hygienic and safe space of Vienna's suburbs to the so-called epidemical hotspot of Venice. In one of the most mystifying inconsistencies in Rietenauer's loving memoir, he writes that Manon had contracted the polio virus from Agathe Lothar! This was impossible but illustrative that Manon's polio vector could have been someone as close to her as Agathe, in their circle of friends, in her mother's household, and so

13 Werfel, "Manon," *Erzählungen aus zwei Welten*, p. 396.

on. Some of the most aggressive forms of the disease occur in transmissions from younger children, in whom the symptoms are mistaken for stomach flu or colic, to adolescent siblings. Such a child existed at Villa Mahler when Alma Zsolnay, Manon's niece, was there. (Even Rietenauer, as a young schoolboy, could have left the polio virus on something as innocent as a piece of cake shared with Manon. Alma's staff all had contact with her daughter—the gardener who cleaned the pond in which Manon's turtle swam, the women who prepared the food, washed the china and crystal, who scrubbed the bathrooms—and used them too—and touched every kind of common surface. Then there was that legion of anonymous passengers reaching for the handrails of streetcars from Hohe Warte to the Ringstrasse, the servers in coffee-shops, milk bars, pastry shops, sharing a cigarette with a boy, all of these people just as capable of transmitting the virus as their counterparts in Venice and anywhere in between and in any way possible, say, the porter who handled Manon's luggage at the point of departure, who had soiled just one fingernail after his morning stool. The carrier of the polio virus need only facilitate enough virus-infected fecal matter—simply put, the shit that found its way past Manon's lips—for it to enter a human mouth via food, water, or like contact, with the last step almost always involuntarily performed by the next human host.

The vector need not be sick in any apparent way. "Most individuals have no symptoms at all, while others experience only the minor illness of poliomyelitis, a brief, mild, febrile episode that might ordinarily be disregarded and does not go on to paralysis."[14] This is one of the main traits of poliomyelitis, an opportunistic virus that spreads from one susceptible child to another—and what made the majority of infections of a limited nature were the lymph nodes, especially the tonsils. Indeed, many doctors and researchers had already made the connection

14 Paul, *A History of Poliomyelitis*, p. 3.

between polio epidemics and the increasing number of tonsillectomies. As early as 1916, Dr. Max Talmey, an early polio researcher and polymath (who had once mentored a ten-year-old Albert Einstein in science) saw that recent epidemics in New York City may have been caused by the rise in tonsillectomies. He decried the campaign to exterminate the tonsils and seeing tonsillar tissue as this so-called cobra's venom of scarlet fever.[15] By 1929 Talmey's theory found support by such researchers as by Dr. William L. Aycock of Harvard. During the 1930s, the "Talmey-Aycock thesis was proven correct both epidemiologically" and ultimately "experimentally by Dr. Albert Sabin."[16]

Manon had had her tonsils cauterized in 1921. Thus, what had been done to protect her from what killed Maria Mahler left her vulnerable to the polio virus. Furthermore, Manon lacked "immunological maturity," that is, an immunity that builds over time, due in part to breast milk and some exposure to contaminated water. While drinking such water could make a child sick, it left it with an ever-growing store of immunities, which for centuries had included one for polio. But this immunity to polio had been lost or weakened by something. Many researchers by the 1930s saw this to be the revolution in clean municipal water supply. Although it had virtually wiped out cholera in the West, it had allowed another disease to slip through yet another well-intended prophylaxis—and that made it far more threatening.

In Saturday's mail, a letter arrived at Casa Mahler addressed to Antoinette Cavin. The sender, a young admirer named Frédy Passek, assumed that she was now Manon's guest. In his "simple but sincere" French, written "sans un dictionnaire" at a table in Vienna's Theatre Café, he confided that a mutual friend telephoned him about Manon's illness and hoped that she felt better. He also sympathized with

15 Quoted in Paul, *A History of Poliomyelitis*, p. 188.

16 Marc Shell, *Polio and Its Aftermath: The Paralysis of Culture* (Cambridge: Harvard University Press, 2005), p. 46.

Antoinette, now "doubly abandoned" with her friend sick and left among strange adults in Venice.[17] Antoinette, however, likely never saw her suitor's letter. Manon would have been under quarantine, for her condition worsened.

As the polio virus reproduces, it penetrates the central nervous system, which is a paradox given evolutionary efficiency, for the spinal fluid is a dead end and the virus can no longer be expelled in stool. In severe cases, lesions form on the anterior horn cells of the spine, which spread hour by hour as the virus floats through the spinal fluid. For this reason, the need to perform a spinal tap, so as to diagnose the disease and rule out other causes, can hasten the final insult to the body: paralysis.

Dr. Friedmann administered twenty-one injections to Manon. Morphine and curare were likely used to numb the excruciating and spasmodic muscle pain that accompanied the spreading paralysis. The drug that he brought with him that held the most hope was convalescent serum.[18] Made from the blood of humans or primates convalescing from polio since the 1920s, researchers hoped that such sera could prevent paralysis when injected into a person diagnosed with polio. By the mid-1930s, however, medical journals were already questioning the efficacy of convalescent serum in clinical trials, either as a polio vaccine or therapy given with the first signs of paralysis. For Manon, it would be no magic bullet. The dreaded *sequelae* of the disease only worsened. Her breathing became increasingly labored.

As the weekend passed, Manon lost the use of the intercostal muscles of her ribcage and the diaphragm. The rhythm, depth, and quality of her respiration became increasingly irregular. Her breath became increasingly shallower with prolonged lapses—*apnea*—in the ability to inhale and exhale. She exhibited *hypoxia,* the inability to oxygenate the

17 Frédy Passek to Antoinette Cavin, April 19, 1934, ÖNB.

18 Ernst Lothar describes the use of convalescent serum on his daughter Agathe in *Das Wunder des Überlebens* (p. 68).

blood, which results in nervousness, excitability, the inability to sleep, distended eyes, and fits of choking. These symptoms are traumatic and, like the attending physician in Kafka's story "The Country Doctor," Dr. Friedmann certainly labored on, appearing as though he were "doing something," even though much of it was for effect as his patient went through the inevitable phases of the disease. Manon's lips and skin began turning the blue of *cyanosis*. She desperately needed an oxygen machine to survive and her sister Anna Mahler volunteered to find one.

In the cold April rain, using Adolf Loewi's motorboat, Anna and his man Luigi went from one apothecary to another, purchasing every oxygen bottle they could find as well as the machine and mask to administer them. By nightfall, they returned to find Manon literally drowning in her bed. What Werfel saw—from dragging the heavy metal cylinders across the floor of Manon's room and the "horrifying change" in her features—is recreated in the novel *Embezzled Heaven*, where he describes a young man in the throes of pulmonary edema. "His mouth gaped wide open and he was gasping helplessly for air," Werfel wrote, where one can easily insert Manon. "His eyes were rolling and his hands, which had grown emaciated, clutched the coverlet convulsively. Every now and then unintelligible syllables or incoherent words struggled painfully from his throat. He had almost crossed the last abyss. At last the oxygen hissed into the glass mask [. . .] held in front of the suffocating boy's face."[19]

During "an inconceivably terrible hour," Werfel witnessed Manon stop breathing for as long as a minute and those around her bed seemingly gave her up for lost. "It was an utter death before death."[20] This is the second part of the virus' major insult to the body, known as "Wallerian degeneration," when the gray matter in the spine swells inside its bone casing and turns the pink of boiled pork, which

19 Werfel, *Embezzled Heaven*, pp. 109–10.

20 Werfel, "Manon," *Erzählungen aus zwei Welten*, p. 397.

damages or kills the ganglia that enervates the limbs and then compromises the phrenic nerve that controls the diaphragm that inflates and deflates the lungs.

As the virus followed the template it had followed for millennia and documented in the withered limbs of Egyptian wall paintings and mummies, Alma's friends followed a social template of a comparatively more recent vintage, of social customs that evolved in the previous century with its revolutions in communication and medicine's increasing ability to make people well. Get-well cards and flowers began to arrive at Casa Mahler, making for a surreal contrast between Manon's room and the desperate measures to save her life. The bouquets included one from Anton Rintelen. That he did not know the gravity of the situation is attested by the note Alma dashed off to him. "Sissy—our *Sissy*—is terribly ill! Send prayers and wishes!"[21]

The oxygen machine saved Manon's life and her crisis passed. During the first week of May she was transported to Vienna for further treatment. As a favor to Alma, Kurt Schuschnigg requisitioned a military railway ambulance for her daughter. The Pullman car had once been assigned to Emperor Franz Josef's private train and was a hospital on wheels, equipped with a compact operating theater and, most importantly, an oxygen tent.

Adolf Loewi's servant Luigi carried Manon down the steps from Casa Mahler to the water taxi. Normally, the boat ferried pieces of antique furniture, fine art objects, terracotta saints, bolts of medieval textiles, illuminated books, and like chattels purchased from the estate sales of the financially impecunious nobility of Northern Italy. Thus, Luigi was an expert in sailing the craft when overloaded with expensive goods, a skill that served him well given the sick girl, her mother, Werfel, her half-sister, and others among the travelers bound for the

21 Alma Mahler-Werfel to AR, undated [April 1934], ASA.

S. Lucia station on the Grand Canal. The little gasoline engine struggled under the weight and was nearly swamped by the wakes of *vaporetti*, the motorboats that served as buses in Venice.

In Berlin, Walter Gropius had at last learned of Manon's illness parsed from Alma's telegrams and a telephone conversation. Despite his daughter's grave condition, he took an optimistic view from what he had been told—a view necessitated too by his inability to travel to Austria or cancel his lecture before the Royal Institute of British Architects. His letter of May 6 to Manon relayed his confidence that she would pull through and that he need not change his travel plans. "finally you are close enough and i could finally telephone and get details about how you are and how wonderfully you have come through this ordeal," he wrote, "because of your illness, which naturally had me not a little frightened at first, I asked around here and have been reassured that not only your doctors in vienna but those here, consulted hypothetically, are quite satisfied with the progress you are making and give a favorable prognosis for a speedy recovery. for all that you have endured, my sweet mutzi, our human nature is admirably adapted, especially if one is young, such that i see you rising from this insidious illness like a beautiful phoenix; i have this fervent wish when i *finally* see you again, my sweet, my precious!" Knowing that Manon would be restricted to pastimes suitable for bedrest, and that philately transcended politics, Gropius admitted to not finding the Hitler series she wanted. As consolation, he sent a commemorative set of Wagner stamps and ended his letter with more encouragement. "don't lose patience, my angel, convalescence is the boring part [. . .]," he continued, "on thursday i go to england and come back on pentecost sunday, then i hope to hear there is significant progress in your condition."[22]

Gropius departed for England on May 10 with news from Alma that his daughter's illness was far worse than he understood and that

22 Walter Gropius to Manon Gropius, May 6, 1934, ÖNB.

he had shown himself to be insensitive once more, that he had put his ambition before his child. With no time to spare, Ise Gropius wrote Manon—and Alma—in his place to justify his actions. "walter has just left for england utterly despondent. he is deeply grieved that it's not going well with you and that he can do nothing at all to ease you through this abominable time," Ise began, "if only this absurd blockade would be lifted soon so that he could come at once to you! the thousand-marks penalty that one still has to pay has always prevented him since we've become rather poor people due to the local conditions. but while he is in london i will make sure to inquire once more about getting an exemption. for the time being surely you have to be busy with your therapy such that a visit would be too much for you." Then she stated what her husband hoped would have been understood. "walter accepted this english invitation with a heavy heart, but he could not really reject it, for little by little he has had to rely on whatever foreign commission there is. [. . .] here every path is blocked and we stand before a vast field of rubble. now he has suffered the added blow of news that you have to still struggle with this."[23]

The Cranking Bed

In the days and weeks after Manon's return to Vienna, Nazi terrorists planted bombs in and around city and elsewhere in Austria, for they hoped to depress the Austrian economy further by frightening away the many foreign tourists who arrived for the summer's music and theater festivals. One of the first bombs had exploded in the Südbahn station on May 6, where and close to when the paralyzed young woman had arrived back from Venice. On May 9, another device exploded on the Philadelphia Bridge over the Danube, wounding two people. Despite the terror campaign, however, the justice minister and Dollfuss'

23 Ise Gropius to Manon Gropius, undated letter [about May 11, 1934], ÖNB.

immediate subordinate, Kurt Schuschnigg, still found time to dash off a quick note to Alma letting her know that he was gladdened to hear that "her darling patient" was back home and feeling better.

Unlike Agathe Lothar, Manon did not go to a hospital or sanatorium. Instead, Austria's best physicians and specialists came to her, for it was seen as privilege to serve Mahler's widow and her daughter. And no one felt as duty-bound as Alma herself in nursing her child back to health. She had the temperament and patience. Given her sense of self-importance, Alma considered Manon's paralysis a personal affront, almost a contest between her and God as much as a lowly virus. Alma had cared for her first-born and her second through their illnesses. To the point of exhaustion, she stayed at Mahler's bedside during his last weeks, a time that still haunted her whenever its May anniversary loomed and passed as it recently had. She had done all she could for her baby Martin Johannes and, only three years ago, she had cared for her friend and admirer, Albert von Trentini, when he was dying of stomach cancer. That experience made her promise herself to be on guard for her own nearest and dearest. "We have two minor children to look after" was still her code, "Franz Werfel and Manon. And nothing else is of more importance."[24] Thus, what finally dedicated Alma to Manon's care and cure was to make up for her lack of vigilance.

Alma met this latest challenge with cheer and fortitude. Her tendency toward self-pity, however, meant that she entertained other thoughts not unlike those Max Phillips imagined for her in *The Artist's Wife* ("And she'd still need someone to dress her and undress her and wash her, and give her an enema when she couldn't move her bowels, and wipe her when she succeeded. There'd never be an end to it, and every year she'd get uglier.").[25] That is, what life would be like if Manon's illness dragged on, when Alma was sixty and the patient twenty-three.

24 Alma Mahler-Werfel, *Mein Leben*, p. 226.
25 Phillips, *The Artist's Wife*, p. 220.

Such a prognosis must have already been voiced by some who observed Manon in May and early June, which Werfel saw as "a period of the most agonizing pain." From her doctors, he learned what a post-polio patient endured, how the "inflamed nerves die out, the muscles atrophy," and the constant pain is the only "cruel sign of life." When it ceases, "its destructive work is done."[26]

The aftermath of *bulbospinal polio* not only posed a steep curve for Manon's recovery in time, effort, and therapy, any setbacks could be fatal. An opportunistic illness such as a chest cold would be enough to give Manon pneumonia. An iron lung would have been an appropriate form of therapy, but these were not used in treating post-polio patients in Austria. Eating and drinking risked choking to death—*aspiration pneumonia.* Being bedridden left Manon open to bed sores, kidney stones, urinary tract infections. These and the difficulty of passing stool would test her resiliency and youth. Polio, too, has an emotional dimension for its young victims. It is "a major insult to developing personality," as one American psychiatrist observed, meaning the will to overcome, to live.[27]

To maintain that will at Villa Mahler, the patient, family, friends, and visitors adopted Alma's imperial hubris that her daughter would walk again. Although Werfel thought otherwise, he played the role of optimist. Like his character in *Embezzled Heaven* when confronted with a hopelessly damaged young person, Werfel too "was compelled to dissemble and pretend."[28] The chief actor in this theater, however, would be Manon herself.

Hubris requires a propagandist, and Alma filled this role. "Mutzi," she wrote Rintelen, "is on the road to recovery. Up until the last moments in Venice, your flowers were by her bed. She thanks you 100

26 Werfel, "Manon," p. 397.

27 Edward Strecker, cited in Paul, *A History of Poliomyelitis*, p. 337.

28 Werfel, *Embezzled Heaven*, p. 133.

times for everything."[29] Alma, too, had also changed the setting of her daughter's recovery and had her carried upstairs to Werfel's study on the top floor, which he so rarely used. In addition to the beautiful views of the surrounding wine country, Alma hung up several of her prized Emile Schindler landscapes and had the room decked with a "sea of flowers."[30] She also ordered a hospital bed with a crank to lift Manon up so that she, too, could play her role facing her first visitors.

The makeover of Werfel's study had also been necessitated by the pending arrival of Walter Gropius, which came with little notice. "i'm quite upset about you since i've had no news whatsoever since my last telephone call," he wrote, informing his daughter that he had posted the thousand *Reichsmark* bond and secured his travel papers. "i'm so filled with hopes and wishes for the best for you," he continued, assuming the role of a philosophical cheerleader for her, "everything is behind you now after this horrid trial by fire you had to go through."[31] Gropius promised Manon that he would leave Berlin on Saturday, May 9, unless told otherwise. On learning this, according to Rietenauer, Alma threw a "royal fit" and then hurriedly prepared Manon and her room as though a Kaiser were coming to inspect a field hospital.

Gropius checked into the Hotel Bristol in the Kärntnerring and promptly arrived at Villa Mahler on Sunday morning. He found his daughter sitting upright in a gold-leafed wing-backed chair, a gift to Werfel and said to have been from the Imperial warehouse and used by Tallyrand at the Congress of Vienna. For a moment, the architect was left speechless by the sight of his daughter, the paintings, the flowers, the balcony, and its view of the hills beyond. Alma sat next to Manon, holding her hand to convey not only affection between mother

29 Alma Mahler-Werfel to AR, undated [late spring 1934], ASA.

30 The following account of Walter Gropius' visit is informed by his letters and Rietenauer's account (*Alma, meine Liebe*, pp. 177ff.).

31 Walter Gropius to Manon Gropius, June 6, 1934, ÖNB.

and daughter but to foil Gropius from doing likewise and, perhaps, to obscure how severe the paralysis was.

All this and what passed between the three seemed to have the desired effect. However, like Werfel, Gropius had found his daughter's condition disturbing and took little comfort in what her physicians told him over the next six days, that she would recover and possibly walk again. Nevertheless, he expressed nothing but confidence and optimism to Manon, to the point that his upbeat mood seemed reprehensible to his former mother-in-law, Anna Moll, for "his child was now an incurable cripple."

What amused and saddened Gropius during his visits to Villa Mahler was how he had virtually no time alone with her. He was just one person in a queue outside her door. To Alma, however, Manon's callers were therapeutic, more so than her family, the servants, the nurses hired to care for her around the clock, the doctors, and the priest from Heiligenstadter church who gave her communion. Indeed, as soon as Manon could talk again and be made presentable, the visitors came every afternoon. She resented being shown like this. When young Rietenauer was allowed to enter her room and found himself staring at her, she said, "I'm not an animal in the Schönbrunn!"[32]

In his correspondence, Gropius does not mention the doctors he met at Villa Mahler. But among them was Alma's long-serving pediatrician, Wilhelm Knöpfelmacher, who had more time to make housecalls on Manon, having been dismissed from his post as head of the Karolinen Kinderspital, the main children's hospital in Vienna. As a prominent Social Democrat, Knöpfelmacher had been purged by the Dollfuss government after the February Uprising—a purge that, because its

32 Quoted in Rietenauer, *Alma, meine Liebe*, p. 179. The Tiergarten Schönbrunn, which serves as the "Vienna Zoo," is located on the grounds of the former imperial palace of Schloss Schönbrunn.

victims were Jewish, resembled the mass dismissals of Jewish professionals taking place in Germany.

In early June, and days before Gropius arrived, Dr. Knöpfelmacher wrote Alma a thank-you note for a bouquet he had received. The flowers may have been an apology, for his choice of words suggest that Alma had vented her frustration on him for Manon's lack of progress—or some candid remark he had made in her presence. "[T]here stands the beautiful bouquet and above all are the kind sincere words that you wrote me," the doctor began, "[. . .] I was so dejected, for I [. . .] would never consider not doing everything for your child that the situation demanded. And I would like it even less that you, dear madam, might have such a feeling. There was and is in this matter but one leitmotif: that this child who is such a charming, gentle creature will be helped in every way possible. Will you not believe that?"[33]

Dr. Knöpfelmacher was but one of the small cadre of Vienna's leading physicians who treated Manon Gropius. Dr. Bien saw her regularly for ancillary illnesses. Dr. Friedmann, however, was succeeded by another leading neurologist, Prof. Dr. Otto Pötzl, the dean of the University Clinic for Neurology and Psychiatry. Having succeeded his superior, Nobel Prize-winner Julius Wagner-Jauregg, Dr. Pötzl now oversaw the research, experiments, clinical trials, publications, as well as the hospital patients of his colleagues and students. A psychiatrist, too, he had made his estimable reputation as a member of the Vienna school of psychoanalysis. Pötzl's lectures on dreams—there is even a "Pötzl phenomenon" named for him—had been praised by Freud.

By 1933, however, Pötzl left the Vienna Psychoanalytic Society and distanced himself from psychoanalysis in favor of therapies that might yield more immediate results of the kind Alma (and, later, Nazi hospital administrators) desired. He and his subordinates had performed lobotomies and tested new drug therapies, such as insulin shock

33 Wilhelm Knöpfelmacher to Alma Mahler-Werfel, June 10, 1934, MWP.

for schizophrenics and cobra venom for degenerated spinal nerves. They conducted studies of failed suicides, dipsomaniac women, and amputees with phantom limbs. For treating the neurological damage of polio, Pötzl favored a range of magnetic, electro-, and radiotherapies to speed up the natural healing process—and had surely informed Gropius of this line of attack on the insult to Manon's body, which her father compared to a demon, one that she would have to mostly exorcise herself. "at least i have a concrete idea of you and the aura around you now and feel [. . .] reassured once more," he wrote upon his return to Berlin. "i rest in the knowledge that the angels will not let you fall as much as put your and our endurance to the test. i am so happy with your cheerful calm in the face of illness and truly marvel at your confidence against this trial by fire, my beautiful one! please, please sharpen your own inimical opposition too against this beelzebub within you. you will see the powers you give off are much more brilliant than any shortwave, faradic, and magnetic rays." Gropius—being diplomatic—praised Alma, whose "matchless verve" he knew would "rouse the inner mutzi."

Knowing she could not hold a pen, Gropius asked his daughter to dictate a letter about her treatments. "i want to know every detail, my precious, from the magnetic foot massages to the electrical stimulation!" He told her how much he looked forward to her walking, taking a "1st class trip out onto the balcony." He wished, too, that he could still be there to help, "to reinforce with an army of heinzelmännchen [helper gnomes] to do the scratching and push back the folds in your sheets to give you some relief,"—an allusion to the legendary worker elves who he knew to be Anna Mahler and the nurses—and an awareness of his daughter's still hypersensitive skin, even to a wrinkle in the bed where she was confined.[34]

Very gradually, Manon regained some use of her upper body and arms. With the encouragement and assistance of Julius Tandler,

34 Walter Gropius to Manon Gropius, June 20, 1934, ÖNB.

Dr. Bien, and her sister Anna, she held a pencil and drew simple, sinuous shapes that resembled snakes, as well as vestiges of her old poor penmanship, in a small sketch book. She had to be helped, too, and her first lines looked faint, ghostlike. The goal of this drawing therapy was that Manon write Dr. Tandler a letter, for he intended to depart again for China.

When he heard that his beloved "niece" was sick, Tandler had delayed his journey in May and began paying regular visits to Villa Mahler in May and June. Like his colleagues, Drs. Knöpfelmacher and Bien, he had been persecuted by the Dollfuss regime. During the February Uprising, he had been arrested and imprisoned in the "Liesl," the central police station on the Danube Canal. *Persona non grata* in his homeland, under surveillance, and with nowhere to work save private practice, Tandler decided to resume teaching anatomy at the Yale Hospital in Shanghai and to establish a network of hospitals in the rural districts of Hunan. And once more, Tandler swore to Manon he would think about her at their "rendezvous" time of three in the afternoon in Vienna—or wherever he might be—what Manon called "Tandler time"—and write her a postcard or letter. Although none of her letters to him have been discovered, his are a record of how one could talk to her, and from that some shape of the real person can be seen, albeit as faint as the lines in her sketchbook.

On June 6, Tandler had breakfast with Werfel and sent his first postcard from Innsbruck and the second from Cherbourg, where he boarded the RMS *Berengaria*. Each sending was written at the appointed time, even aboard ship during a storm. "The pains will likely be over by now," Tandler promised in his first letter, in which he called on those he knew would be at her bedside, including Susi Kertész. "I not only send Anni [Anna Mahler] my love but beg her to take down your dictated answer and send it to me. I cannot expect this from Mommy. She has too much to do. And Franz is away, writing of little import and kosher tales [i.e. the bible play] at that. So only Anni remains like it or not. But ever since Venice everything has to my surprise shown that she is capable, may she write as well. The next letter you will write m.p. [*manu propria*, i.e. in your own hand]."[35] And in his first letter from New York he reminded her of her share in her own recovery, that "70% is your work. You know very well."[36]

During the second week of July, while still in New York, Tandler received a sample of Manon's handwriting, a short note enclosed in one of Dr. Bien's letters. Elated over his correct prognosis, that she would be able to write by mid-July, Tandler confessed that weeks ago "a nagging doubt overcame me for a second. Now it's ceased nagging. I embrace you in spirit, a rather sterile realm for this activity—and I feel the strength of your arms. I am willing to endure this test of strength in silence too. And now I wait for the much heralded long letter."[37] The philosophical note in Tandler's sentiment—not being able to touch her save in spirit, the "sterile realm"—betrays a certain playful innuendo that the virginal Manon was expected to apprehend here as in other letters in which Tandler indulged in what he called "true love." Too, he saw this milestone—her handwriting sample—to be a sign that she had avoided crossing the border where a person becomes an "unworthy life."

Tandler arrived in San Francisco at the end of July and checked into the Hotel St. Francis. There he wrote Manon again, as though entirely occupied with her and not the dire news from Vienna that Dollfuss had been murdered by Nazi assassins. He told her of his itinerary, that he would board the Japanese liner *Asama Maru* on August 1 and arrive, via Hawaii, in Yokohama in sixteen days. In an afterthought to his wish for her complete recovery, he saw them someday talking

35 Julius Tandler to Manon Gropius, June 12, 1934, ÖNB.
36 Julius Tandler to Manon Gropius, June 21, 1934, ÖNB.
37 Julius Tandler to Manon Gropius, July 14, 1934, ÖNB

and laughing about her "disabilities & incapacities [. . .] all in the past."[38]

While Dr. Tandler waited for her to reply in her own hand, Manon Gropius wrote her father in Berlin. "My dear little Papa," she wrote. "I thank you very much for your very good long letter. From me there is very little to report. Things are progressing relatively quickly. I work frantically on getting healthy, am in treatment all day long. I hope that in 4–6 weeks that I can begin trying to walk. I am already halfway standing up." Looking up from this brief letter, Gropius surely knew—perhaps knowing himself and his famous inability to draw his own designs—that the handwriting was not entirely his daughter's, that someone helped her the way he needed help putting his designs on paper, that, in effect, he was an "idea man," ultimately. Had he compared the letters she sent him from before her polio, he would know. And by "halfway standing," Manon had stretched the truth. She could sit, but only with her hospital bed cranked into an upright position, and in her new wheelchair, in which she was carried downstairs by the gardener and other strong backs. Manon had nothing to stand on for her legs were as useless as a mermaid's tail on land. But what her father wanted to know was that she was getting well, and this she confirmed, for it was in keeping with the optimism he, her mother, and others encouraged. "It's a shame that you saw me so miserable and unhappy," Manon reminded him.[39] By midsummer, her hips, thighs, and calves had lost their muscle tone and began taking on a withered appearance. Her ankles and feet may have contracted into the classic "equinus deformity" of polio patients if splints had not been used to restrain them from resembling horse's hooves. So as not see or show them, Alma made her

38 Julius Tandler to Manon Gropius, August 1, 1934, ÖNB.
39 Manon Gropius to Walter Gropius, undated [July 1934], BHA.

daughter cover her legs with a blanket or an Oriental rug. Photographs were no longer taken.

What comes across in Manon's letter is the serenity others saw in her. "One must treat the sick with the greatest sensitivity, especially paraplegics," Werfel remembered, thinking of how he steeled himself for the worst in his stepdaughter as her body and sense of personhood were radically transformed. "[T]hey tend to very soon take on what one calls the *psychology of the cripple*. They become suspicious, jealous, egocentric and they try to oppress and torment those around them."[40] But as she lay in her bed or sat upright in a chair, she seemed lovelier. Given her appearance, she had changed from the shy teenager destined to grow up a nonentity, a cipher. Her face now "showed an entirely new kind of transcendence, sometimes almost a quality of relentless acuity. Everything that was said in her presence expressed the most smiling hope that she would make an early recovery. She fully agreed to this tone. And so far I could never tell whether she shared this optimism or knew the truth." In private, Werfel had asked "the great doctor and specialist" for the full truth, and Pötzl told him without a hesitation: "The lower limbs are totally dead. Experience shows that in spite of all our modern therapies, any improvement is illusory. Your stepdaughter, unfortunately, will never walk again. Nevertheless, you should be happy that she has regained the use of her arms and hands."

Hearing this left Werfel speechless and he kept it from Alma. "With all my heart I tried not to believe it, holding that great neurologist to be the blackest of liars." Gradually, Manon recovered enough use of her upper limbs to impress another renowned physician who came to see her, Dr. Martha Brunner-Orne, a psychologist and neurologist, who had successfully treated cases of partial paralysis with fever therapy (and who, twenty years later, treated the American poet Ann Sexton for postpartum depression). She wrote that "Manon's lovely arms and

40 Werfel, "Manon," *Erzählungen aus zwei Welten*, p. 397.

hands were spared," such that she "was able to use them gracefully," which suggests that she was on the road to recovering enough upper body strength to wheel herself around unassisted.[41]

Undoubtedly, Dr. Brunner-Orne would not have been so grim as her colleague Dr. Pötzl. She might have been no less honest with Alma, that while Manon would never walk again, she could still enjoy some quality of life with physical therapy. Such gentle honesty might dissuade Alma as well from her unhealthy denial, which the physicians did not want to facilitate. But her denial may have become a charade in itself. Three years later, Alma recorded a dream in her diary that reads like a repressed memory of the brutal honesty she had already internalized. In her dream, an unidentified doctor told her that Manon "would have to die" and that any plans had to be canceled to make her daughter's last days holidays with "Paris, lovers, if she wanted . . . everything, everything, so that she had not lived in vain."[42] To some extent this is the course Alma took.

The Philosophical Newborn

Like Rilke's archaic torso of Apollo, whose missing arms and legs conveyed—"You must change"—so Manon Gropius' damaged limbs inspired those around her with an ultimate, even sacred meaning from her

41 Dr. Brunner-Orne's comments appear in an undated, unsourced newspaper clipping ("A beautiful child who inspired a concerto") from 1980 in the papers of Louis Krasner at Harvard University. Presumably printed in the *Boston Globe*, the article describes the "angel" of Berg's Violin Concerto, recently performed by the Boston Symphony Orchestra under the direction of Seiji Ozawa with Itzhak Perlman as soloist. "I felt," writes Dr. Brunner-Orne, "like having visited an angel every time I saw her. She was so beautiful and accepted patiently her illness without giving up hope [. . .]."
42 Mahler-Werfel, August 31, 1937, "Diary of Alma Maria," p. 306, MWP.

poetry of virtual helplessness. She had to be bathed and her hair combed. Whenever she was dressed, her now thin arms had to be threaded through the sleeves. A nurse or a housemaid had to pull the hem over her waist, work it over her hips, and pull the flounce over her ragdoll legs. These would have to be pulled straight for her, as one would for a corpse to be laid out. A corpse, however, cannot pick the clothes she might want to wear. From her cranking bed, Manon could sit up and feed herself a little from a tray. She could certainly turn the pages of books and magazines that made her an "*Expertin*" on snakes. To Werfel, Manon came to life when she pored over reptile literature.

The color Werfel saw in her face, however, surely came from the effort of breathing. It was another reason why visitors often saw Manon in makeup. Conspicuously missing from them was Anton Rintelen. He had little time for Alma and the now damaged "Sissy" during the early summer and would have no time after the failed Nazi coup of July 1934. Rintelen's complicity had been discovered and he was arrested. Instead of forming a new government, in which he would be Hitler's willing puppet, Rintelen was jailed in the Liesl. While there he attempted to fire a bullet into his heart with a concealed pistol but only managed to wound himself.

Alma quickly forgot him and his letters to her and Manon conveniently disappeared, for there would be a trial now. Fortunately, Erich Cyhlar had remained loyal to the regime and to Dollfuss' successor, Kurt Schuschnigg. Given that the new chancellor was a close friend of Alma and her family—and, perhaps, knowing that Schuschnigg was in love with Anna Mahler—Cyhlar began to visit Manon as much as his work allowed. Whether he intended these visits to become the therapeutic courtship Alma projected is unknown. Being a bureaucrat and a creature of tact, he surely knew how to give her the right appearance. Furthermore, if seeming to be a potential suitor contributed to Manon's *Kur*, such a charity, such mercy would not go unnoticed or unrewarded by her mother and her friends in the government. Thus, Cyhlar would be the encouragement Manon needed to one day walk down the aisle rather than be rolled in a wheelchair. Although Anna Moll said that "no rooster would ever crow" for her granddaughter as she was, Cyhlar's presence proved Manon's earthy grandmother wrong. He only needed to steel himself from even more vulgar assertions and minds as to what kind of man he was and what he and his potential bride could or could not do behind closed doors.

Manon, too, had to consider what people thought about her and a man together. Thankfully, she still had Susi Kertész for a regular companion and, as the summer progressed, the promise of a new girlfriend whom she had only known as a distant correspondent over the years.

How Katherine Scherman, the daughter of Harry Scherman, founder of the Book-of-the-Month Club, learned of Manon began with her father's friend, Lincoln Schuster of Simon & Schuster. As Werfel's American publisher, Schuster had been a guest at Haus Mahler in the late 1920s. While he, Alma, and Werfel sat on the porch to talk and watch the deer graze on the wide lawn at dusk, he saw a girl who apparently had not been at dinner. She walked among the deer "herself as frail, graceful, and shy as a young deer" according to Alma's account.[43]

Not only did this strange, ethereal scene take Schuster by surprise, he saw the resemblance between Manon and Scherman's daughter. He saw it again when he called on Werfel and Manon opened the door to him. "Why, Kathy Scherman," Schuster blurted, "what are you doing here?" When she didn't respond, he assumed she didn't understand English rather than her being startled and shy. (Manon had the same English nanny as her sister Anna, who was fluent.)

43 The following passage is adapted from Mahler-Werfel, *And the Bridge Is Love*, pp. 219ff.

After Schuster shared these anecdotes with Scherman and his wife Bernadine, photographs were exchanged and the two girls began writing each other in French. None of the letters survive, but according to Alma they wrote about their cats, Manon's Siamese and Katherine's Persian. "They made an effort to tell each other what it was like to be a girl in Vienna and in New York, with the result that they came to know a good deal about each other [. . .] these two beautiful children [. . .] friends over three thousand miles of land and sea." Naturally, both families hoped that the girls might meet in person one day. The opportunity came in the summer of 1934, when the Scherman family arrived in Vienna after mountain climbing in upper Austria.

For the Scherman family, meeting the Mahler-Werfels had its rewards. *The Forty Days of Musa Dagh* had been translated into English in time for Christmas and Werfel would be pleased to learn of the Book-of-the-Month Club edition. His wife, as Gustav Mahler's widow, could reciprocate as well, for Katherine Scherman during this time wanted to be a cellist or concert pianist. Alma not only could advise the young woman but exercise enormous influence on her future should she continue her musical education. Lastly, here was the opportunity of having Katherine and Manon meet in person.

When the Schermans visited Villa Mahler, Alma gasped at Katherine's beauty and the uncanny resemblance to her daughter. "It was not merely a matter of looking alike," Alma wrote later, "this shy, soft-spoken American girl acted and reacted like Manon." She also saw that this healthy and walking double—a doppelganger in the real sense, of a mixed marriage between an Irish Catholic mother and Jewish father no less—should inspire Manon to get better. Upon learning that the Schermans intended to visit Hungary rather than return to New York, Alma insisted that they let Katherine stay with her so that their daughter might see Vienna, enjoy some chaperoned independence, and, without it being said, set an example for Manon.

"Along with Manon's beauty," Alma observed that Katherine had features of Manon's "reserve, her serious way with people, her withdrawals into art." Unlike Manon, however, Katherine had cut her nails and learned to play the piano in her youth. "She had great musical talent," Alma marveled as she watched Katherine play the piano in the room next to Manon's. "I saw tears in [Katherine's] eyes when she played the last chorus of the *Passion According to St. Matthew*," Alma wrote as the double now did things that Manon could not do, even before the polio. Alma compared her shock at seeing Katherine in her home to that of Ernst Lothar seeing Manon back in April, before she fell victim to polio. But rather than feel his pain, Alma took hope in the belief that Manon, too, would one day be "lovely and healthy and strong."

Alma virtually held the Scherman girl captive from late July into August. Thinking her too thin, Alma ordered the maid to start feeding her a glass of cream at seven in the morning, as well as some *pâte de foie gras* on white bread. "Katharine," Alma observed, amused and determined, "did not appreciate being wakened like this every day, but she bravely submitted to my fattening regime and always went back to sleep until breakfast time. As for me, I had the satisfaction of seeing her gain some much-needed weight during her stay." Alma, too, added alcohol to the young woman's proper Viennese diet. She made Katharine take a "morning schnapps." That the American girl had grown up under the strictures of Prohibition also amused Alma as did the impression that Katharine dared not refuse her drink out of politeness, shyness, or that one did not say no to the legendary Alma Mahler.

Alma and Werfel gave Katherine a party where she met some of Manon's friends. They also took Katharine sightseeing in the Prater, the Vienna Woods, the opera—and whenever they strolled through the city, it seemed to the young American woman that everyone knew Alma and treated her as if she were the "queen of the city."[44] Since she

44 Quoted in Hilmes, *Witwe im Wahn*, p. 264.

still seemed shy, Katherine's hosts also took her dancing at one of Vienna's charming "gypsy" cabarets, where Alma paid to have a professional dance partner and gigolo lead Katharine out onto the floor since Werfel could hardly do her "justice." And out of consideration for Katherine, Alma ensured that the handsome young man could speak English—a language barrier that had frustrated Manon, too, even though the girls had written each other in French. "Whether Katherine had any real contact with Manon during her stay I do not know," Alma wrote, revealing what had likely been a disastrous visit in the final assessment. "She did not speak German, and Manon was now usually too tired to talk much in a foreign language. Also, both of them were shy, and Manon's illness must have lain as a blight over their chats at her bedside. Perhaps Katherine was rather relieved when the return of her parents put an end to the visit."[45]

"I thank you a thousand times for the lovely bird book and the Japanese magazine," Manon wrote her father, who was touring the Dalmatian coast in August with her stepmother Ise. "I'm now getting much better. My back almost supports me freely. Things aren't so dull anymore, I'm already eating at the table and getting visitors. My friend, of whom I told you, right, is here with me for 4 weeks, isn't that sweet? Yesterday I had supper downstairs at the table for the first time."[46]

Seeing his daughter's natural handwriting again and hearing the news about her progress and Katherine Scherman's visit left Gropius both delighted and wistful. He had accepted an offer to work in England, which meant he could continue work in a hospitable country—and the realization that he might not be able to see Manon for a long time. "my sweet, you writing in your own hand made me incredibly happy; another new step on that tedious ladder of your climb

45 Mahler-Werfel, *And the Bridge Is Love*, p. 225.
46 Manon Gropius to Walter Gropius, August 10, 1934, BHA.

back. a few days ago i heard of a young man who, at 25, came down with the same disease as yours. after languishing for some time, he got rid of all of the doctors and, with incredible energy, assumed control over his own case. after a half year he could get around on two walking sticks and is now completely cured." Gropius wanted Manon to "revolt" against her disease like the young man, to "drive it out." More than ever, he spoke of her polio as possession. "i will continue to *rail* against your beelzebub," he promised, as though he were a priest, and asked for further details from her. "how are the veins behaving," he asked, "can those adorable legs [*haxen*] be treated?" He asked her if she could read unassisted and whether it overexerted her. Knowing the pleasure Manon took in studying frogs and snakes, Gropius promised to send her more picture books of "squirmy creatures [*eklige*]." He ended with a reminder that he would soon leave for England and how important it was for his career—and that he was learning English "with fire." "begin each day anew, my angel," he wrote of her own challenges, "so that you quickly overcome this mount everest."[47]

Gropius wrote Alma a few days later, thanking her for her devotion to their daughter—and with the implicit admission that he was helpless to take an active role and likely still seen as a pariah. "mutzi's letter has given me such boundless joy that I must tell you *how* happy I am that thanks to your exemplary care she has made such good progress," he wrote, acknowledging, "*how* overwhelmed you were when i was in vienna."[48] Such gratitude, while well intended, was wasted on Alma.

Father Hollnsteiner, whose position as the Mahler-Werfel family's spiritual advisor had risen during Manon's convalescence, knew Alma took a dim view of her own situation, especially when she lacked his charismatic presence. "Unfortunately for me," Alma responded to one of his inspirational letters, "things are taking their physical toll—and I

47 Walter Gropius to Manon Gropius, undated [mid-August 1934], ÖNB.
48 Walter Gropius to Alma Mahler-Werfel, undated [August 16, 1934], ÖNB.

am filled with anxiety too! Mutzi! But you will soon return."[49] She meant his "return" from an extended summer vacation, during which the priest had tried to offer his various jests for Manon in postcards—often with a stamp she might like for her collection. "Had need of your help to carry my suitcase because someone forgot to send the car to the station and I had to schlep my things," Father Hollnsteiner wrote from Bad Ems. "It would have been a good muscle exercise."[50] Weeks later, he wrote again from Vatican City. He had thought of her as he toured the Catacombs of Callistus and when he celebrated mass over the crypt of the virgin and martyr St. Cecilia. Her effigy, lying on its side with the face down must have reminded him of the bedridden Manon, even though, as the patroness of music, St. Cecilia is more often depicted with a violin or like instruments.

For a young woman whose father expected her to cast out a demon, whose stepfather saw her as beatified by her ordeal, and whose mother's priest friend kept her in his prayers, Manon Gropius found a way back to resuming where she had left off. In the early autumn of 1934, Susi Kertész enrolled in the Reinhardt-Seminar at the imperial theater in the Schönbrun Palace. Initially, Manon could only vicariously experience what Susi did—the demanding teachers, the curriculum that included theater directing, acting, and diction instruction as well as playwriting, literary history, gymnastics and dance, and set design. Since the early 1920s, the Reinhardt-Seminar had trained not only the best stage actors for the German-language theater (among them Susi's classmates Hortense Raky, Ilse Werner, and Annemarie Selinko), it also produced actors for the international stage and cinema and enjoyed an international reputation that reached Hollywood.

---

49 Alma Mahler-Werfel to Johannes Hollnsteiner, August 31, 1934. Quoted in Buchmayr, *Der Priester in Almas Salon,* p. 79.

50 Johannes Hollnsteiner to Manon Gropius, undated postcard (summer 1934), ÖNB.

According to Werfel, it was Susi's idea to bring an extra copy of her script to Villa Mahler so that Manon could help her memorize her lines. From her bed and wheelchair, she could now turn the pages with her weak but no longer totally paralyzed hands. This was the "spark from outside" to Werfel, who, perhaps a little disingenuously, saw his stepdaughter's old enthusiasm for the theater being revived at last. In the weeks that followed, Manon asked a family friend who came to visit her, Franz Horch, to give her lessons. Her choice was obvious.

Horch, at thirty-three, had long served as a repertory manager for Max Reinhardt in Berlin and Vienna and had also taught elocution and drama at the Reinhardt-Seminar. Horch was also now one of Paul Zsolnay's editors and chose the plays to be published. Horch could hardly refuse the request. A talented and sensitive man, he knew about Manon's aspirations and knew, too, that they had been frustrated. He also knew that it would be a hopeless task, as superhuman for her as it was for him. "[S]he understood death and submitted herself at his behest, a thing she guarded as her deepest secret," he wrote in the following year. "Thus, for not one moment, did she give him the satisfaction of being reluctant or rebellious. [. . .] Perhaps now and then she was deceived by her favorite pastime, to which she had been passionately committed and which she hoped to make her life's calling—acting, before an unreal expectation, on which the heart of the healthy girl had so happily been set . . . farewell performances for this playful person. Understanding this meaning from the first, she delighted in them for a little while."[51] Nevertheless, Horch saw his new student in the light of a young martyr, standing at the gates of life where life ends.

Manon could not walk and, in reality, she could not really sit up as she told her father. She had limited use of her hands and arms and

---

51 Franz Horch, "Der Tod und das Mädchen" [Death and the Maiden], *Bergland* 17(11)(1935), pp. 2–5, ULT.

breathed with only the musculature of her ribcage, which meant she could hardly project her voice from a real stage. Despite these limitations, Horch would work something of a miracle over the next months, a miracle made easier by Manon, who was no longer like the girl he saw at the Christmas parties and like gatherings from the previous year, when it seemed that all the light in a brightly lit ballroom seemed to come from her, when the young people seemed to circle about her and gentlemen kissed her hand and asked her to dance—that is, when she just seemed to be the somewhat too-sweet and spoiled child of her mother who seemed a little deviant herself. Now, however, even to the hardboiled cynic, she was a different person. He could detect "a hint of melancholy, which testified to her inner depth and manifold empathy" as well as a "vague awareness heavy with foreboding," which no longer made her this simply "playful" girl one saw at tea parties. There was what he called this "providential archness"—*Schalkhaftigkeit*—a word that means roguish, wanton, and waggish with "ironically penetrating remarks," which were never off the mark to Horch, but seemed right and fair, especially when it came to others around her. Perhaps, without saying so, he meant Alma and Werfel. Perhaps Manon confided in Horch, discussed her now confined life at Villa Mahler, while learning and speaking her lines. "Each day now, when her teacher showed up, she would be carried to some remote room," Werfel wrote of this time. "She didn't want anyone to know or talk about it. Those drama lessons that she took would remain secret. We didn't pry. We didn't worry about it. Still I see Manon before me, motionless, stretched out in her bed, as she spent hours learning parts with her bright red cheeks. When anyone entered, she hid that book."[52]

Horch also brought fellow actors to meet and work with Manon, Hermann Thimig, the Austrian actor (whose sister was Max Reinhardt's mistress), and the venerable Werner Krauss, the German cinema's "man

52 Werfel, "Manon," *Erzählungen aus zwei Welten*, p. 398.

of a thousand faces." The latter is still famous and famous for his role in the Expressionist film *The Cabinet of Doctor Caligari* (1919)—and infamous for another title late in his career, *Jud Süß* (1940)—he also returned to see Manon more than once. He, like Susi, took advantage of having such a beautiful captive and critical audience of one and practiced his lines with Manon. Krauss had been in Vienna for months, engaged by the Burgtheater for a Shakespeare cycle in which he played Richard III, Falstaff, and King Lear. Which of these roles he practiced with Manon is unknown, but he did confess to Alma that he had come to rely on her daughter's artistic instincts. "I'm desperate," he told Alma when she looked in on them one day. "I've read the soliloquy four times now, and Manon still isn't satisfied!"[53]

Krauss continued to come to Villa Mahler up until the early spring of 1935. He had accepted the title role in Herman Heinz Ortner's play *Beethoven*.[54] So as to elicit her thoughts about how he should play the composer, Krauss recited the scene in which Beethoven apprehends that he is going deaf and begins to curse his friend Dr. Malfatti as a quack. Then, as though to God, the composer reads verses that he had once set to music in praise of Him—the Gellert *Lieder* (Op. 48) "The heavens declare the eternal glory!" Krauss as Beethoven reads. "Their echo spreads forth His name." Then, to Manon, he shouted in blasphemy and misery—"Cursed be Your name—my life is over!"

Upon hearing this, Manon described Krauss' performance as "theater thunder," that is, bombast. Mystified, the actor asked her why, for he thought the lines had been rendered perfectly. Manon, however, shook her head. She was now very familiar with the play and surely read the parts for the scenes with Countess Giulietta Guicciardi, Beethoven's teenage student at the time he realized he was going deaf

53 Mahler-Werfel, *And the Bridge Is Love*, pp. 223–4.

54 The following account is informed by Rietenauer, *Alma, meine Liebe*, pp. 181–3.

and the woman he called his "Immortal Beloved." "Would you be insulted," she asked Krauss, "if I read it to you the way I feel it?"

With her teacher Franz Horch present, too, Krauss readily agreed to such a learning moment from the young woman. Thereupon, Manon took the actor's hand in both of hers and began to empathize with Beethoven himself: "Imagine—as a gifted musician faces the greatest dilemma of his life. He knows that soon he will be totally deaf. He is terribly afraid that he will no longer be able to hear his own music. Will he then be able to still compose? He literally bursts out: 'Why me now? Why did God give me talent only to take it right back?' At the moment of his greatest despair he hears his own music as the answer to his indictment!"

The others in the room were quiet as Manon now read from the script, not only, perhaps, for the profoundness of the effect she wanted to achieve, but that she could just as much have said the same to God about herself and her talent. Her Beethoven would sound like this: "Oh—I know that your song woke me from the grave to a new life!—That you hold my exhausted ears—in your heartbeat, you put mankind's entire hymn in my hands!—From my pain you build the altar . . ." Then Manon cried rapturously, "I praise your voice!—Your echo—Lord—in your world! I know man is nothing—and all, all—only you are."

Krauss did not play Beethoven. Soon after this visit to Villa Mahler, he was injured in a car accident and was forced to yield not only this role to Ewald Balser, but the one of coming to Villa Mahler. Convinced by Franz Horch to visit Manon as well, Balser continued to practice the Beethoven role with Manon and its final rebellious—epiphanic form found its way into the play's premiere in late April 1935, the one instance of Manon's imprint on the stage.

Four days before his daughter turned eighteen, Gropius closed his office in Berlin and put his furniture and papers in storage. He wrote Manon about his plans for the coming weeks. He would soon leave Berlin for Rome and a theater symposium hosted by Italy's ministry of cultural affairs. There he would lecture on his *Total Theater* concept. Knowing Werfel, too, had been invited, Gropius imagined that he might also see Alma. After Rome, he and Ise would then leave for England. Although his temporary visa allowed them to live abroad until the end of April 1935, Gropius did not anticipate returning to Germany anytime soon given his carefully chosen words to Manon. "before i disappear in a cloud of steam, i must file past you again," he wrote, alluding to her many visitors. "we sit in a dreadful disarray of packing, everything must be cleared out because the apartment has been rented to the daughter of lieberman.[55] [. . .] hopefully i'll see mommy or werfel [. . .] if you can give them a vacation!" Gropius asked Manon to write him and gave her the address of the architect Maxwell Fry, his English host. Thinking, perhaps, that Manon would find it amusing to think of her father in London, he wrote how curious he was about how he would "survive in this inartistic country with unsalted vegetables, bony women and an eternally freezing draft!? surely not very stimulating, but after all it is the one european country in which to find something like a 'boom,' especially in new housing." Gropius promised he would telephone her to see how her limbs were "behaving themselves" and, as he came to a close, he remembered a moment from the summer, while still traveling along the Croatian Riviera. He had a revelation—in all likelihood about himself—and was worth sharing with her. "say hello to mommy and werfel," Gropius wrote, "and draw yourself close to the state of mind and health of this philosophical newborn in whom I forged a friendship on the island of korčula."[56]

55 Käthe Liebermann Riezler, wife of the diplomat and philosopher Kurt Riezler and daughter of impressionist painter Max Liebermann.
56 Walter Gropius to Manon Gropius, October 1, 1934, ÖNB.

As wise and as fatherly as Gropius tried to be here, he had also said nothing of Manon's impending birthday. From Rome he called Villa Mahler to find out why Werfel and Alma had not come and learned to his horror not only had he missed his daughter's birthday once again, she had a cold that was steadily worsening. "i am utterly shattered having forgotten your birthday now of all times," Gropius wrote Manon on October 12. "i [. . .] find it unforgivable! [. . .] for you my angel i wish *imploringly* that you recover *quickly* from this horridness once and for all!" Gropius, however, trusted that she understood his faux pas in terms of his own vicissitudes and work. "we lead a busy life here at the congress," he continued, for what he did had to matter to Manon. "the proceedings get quite stormy and it would amuse you as they step into the arena, onto the 'box spiritual' as it was called today.[57] this evening a big gala performance of the figlia di jorio[58] in the presence of the duce! [. . .] tomorrow i will try to find something pretty to send you and make up for my appalling absentmindedness."[59]

Gropius found time to shop in Milan before hurrying back to the train station. He bought Manon a 400-year-old jade ring pendant. Knowing its lore and therapeutic value, he promised her that it would ward off the Evil Eye and that its contact with her body would bring health. She needed such a talisman, for her cold had become a lung infection. Modern antibiotics were still months away from becoming commercially available and bronchitis and pneumonia for a polio victim entailed a far worse ordeal than they did for a healthy person. Thus, Dr. Bien requested her friend and colleague come see Manon—Dr. Robert Klopstock, the lung specialist and thoracic surgeon—and the husband of Werfel's Hungarian translator. Klopstock's reputation was known

57 Gropius had encountered contentious resistance to his ideas in the form of the English actor-stage designer Edward Gordon Craig.

58 The tragic, pastoral opera *La figlia di Jorio* [The Daughter of Jorio] by Alberto Franchetti, with a libretto by Gabriele D'Annunzio.

59 Walter Gropius to Manon Gropius, October 12, 1934, ÖNB.

throughout Europe—but even then he was famous for being Kafka's personal physician and "last friend," for he had cared for Kafka before the writer's tuberculosis had entered its final stages in the early 1920s. When Kafka died at the Wienerwald sanatorium in June 1924, he did so in the arms of Dr. Klopstock who had given him the final dose of morphine to kill the pain in Kafka's upper lungs.

This event surely must have come up between Dr. Klopstock and Werfel when the doctor came to Villa Mahler to treat Manon during November and December—ten years after Kafka's death. Werfel had long been touched by how Kafka had praised his poetry—which had so many detractors among even close friends—in one of his letters to Klopstock. And Werfel felt humbled, too, and in a letter written to Klopstock after Manon got better, he saw himself as nothing but a "mere poet" compared to Kafka, that "messenger from the king," meaning the Jewish God.[60]

The elevated conversation and correspondence that came with the "honor" of tending to the daughter of Alma Mahler and Franz Werfel did not belie its cost. Physicians still sent their bills and the recipients paid them. Nevertheless, at least one of Manon's doctors rendered his services gratis as though money would be a vulgar form of compensation, as testified by Dr. Knöpfelmacher's thank-you note for what must have been a wonderful gift—a valuable landscape painted by Alma's father—which she had given the physician for Christmas.

Alma's other gift for services rendered was her daughter's hand in marriage. When Erich Cyhlar proposed to Manon or when Alma gave her approval to the engagement is uncertain, but it likely occurred

60 Franz Werfel to Robert Klopstock, December 2, 1934. Quoted in Hugo Wetscherik, ed., *Kafkas letzer Freund: Der Nachlaß Robert Klopstock* [Kafka's Last Friend: The Robert Klopstock Papers] (1899–1972) (Vienna: Inlibris, 2003), pp. 109–10.

before Christmas, a year after the young couple met, when such a formal announcement was appropos. For Manon, who was now presentable in her wheelchair and relatively healthy, it meant relearning how to walk in the coming new year of 1935. For Alma's circle, an engagement meant that her daughter was still desirable, chief among them was Father Hollnsteiner, whose New Years' greeting confided a dream to her in which he was Manon's priestly chaperone at a party in Venice where she was "bright and alive" and "flirted not a little!—Poor Cylarsch!"[61]

Ultimately, too, a man in her life would dispel any doubt about Manon's normal inclinations and aspersions that discounted her shyness. Johannes Trentini, however, saw something different in how she was one-on-one with boys her own age. Like his father for her mother, so the younger Trentini felt something for Manon. But he came to the realization that Manon had little interest in the opposite sex before her mother intervened. More often than not, she sent away the young men who came calling on her, something rare in the "society of that period."[62] Trentini came to believe in hindsight that Manon had been repelled, put off, or left frigid (*abschreckt*) by her mother's conduct. But he also carefully words how she was only *regarded* (*betrachtet*) as this virgin and angelic being, which leaves open what kind of virgin she was and was not.

Beside Alma's memoir, the only confirmation that Manon was engaged to be married is Canetti's *Play of the Eyes*, where a chapter is devoted to her. "For almost a year," he begins, "Manon had been presented in a wheelchair, attractively dressed, her face carefully made up, a costly rug over her knees, her waxen face alive with false hope. Real hope, she had none." What follows suggests that Canetti had attended a party at which Manon had been present or had access to an

61 Johannes Hollnsteiner to Manon Gropius, undated [December 24, 1934], ÖNB.

62 Quoted in Hilmes, *Witwe im Wahn*, p. 274.

acid description of one from a more reliable witness, namely, Anna Mahler, for his must be seen like other sources used here, as that of an impressionist rather than witness. "Her voice was unimpaired," Canetti observed or imagines, "it dated back to the days of innocence, when she tripped about on the feet of a doe and was regarded by visitors as the opposite of her mother. Now the contrast, which had always seemed incredible, was even greater. The mother, who went on living in her usual way, thought better of herself because of her beloved child's misfortune. The daughter, though paralyzed, was still capable of saying yes; she was engaged to be married."[63]

The "waxen" appearance resulted from the heavy makeup that Manon wore in public, which allegedly made her feel like a "devoted clown" for her mother's guests, the "circusgoers."[64] Had Canetti known of her desire to be an actress, her self-awareness as a performer would have redoubled his bitter reading of the future nuptials between Manon Gropius and Erich Cyhlar. "The choice fell on a young secretary of the Patriotic Front, a protégé of the professor of moral theology who directed the conscience of the regal lady of the house," Canetti writes, connecting Cyhlar with Father Hollnsteiner. "The young man, who had no compunctions about getting engaged to a woman who had only a short while to live, moved freely about the house when he called on his fiancée. By the side of her wheelchair he became acquainted with all the celebrities who came for the same purpose. With his ingratiating grin, his well-mannered bows and tremulous voice, he became a much-discussed figure: the promising young man, whom no one had ever heard of before, who sacrificed himself, his looks, his increasingly valuable time, to give the angel the illusion of a possible recovery. Being betrothed gave her reason to hope that she would marry." Canneti is also writing social commentary about a society in decay, on the verge

63 Canetti here and in the following passages is quoted from "The Funeral of an Angel," *The Play of the Eyes*, pp. 198ff.

64 Quoted in Rietenauer, *Alma, meine Liebe*, p. 179.

of falling in with Nazi Germany, and the fascist bureaucrats who made themselves useful in that outcome. How close he comes to seeing this one bureaucrat make himself so useful to Alma is illustrative of his powers as a *creative* writer. "It made quite an impression when the dinner-jacketed young man kissed his fiancée's hand," Canetti goes on in his unrelenting way. "As often as Viennese men say *Küss die Hand*—which rolls so easily off the tongue—[Cyhlar] actually did it. When he straightened up with the pleasant feeling that he had been *seen* doing it, that in this house nothing was done in vain, credit was given for everything, especially for depositing a kiss on this hand, when for a moment he prolonged his bewitching bow to his paralytic fiancée, he was *standing* for both of them. There were some who shared the mother's belief in a miracle and said: 'She will recover. The joy her fiancé gives her will make her well.'"

Canetti thought himself not alone in his anger and disgust, of cherishing "very different hopes" for the disgraceful spectacle that Alma directed. "They, and I was one of them, wished for just one thing: that mother and fiancé should be struck by lightning, which would not kill but paralyze them, and that the sick girl would jump up from her wheelchair in a panic and be *cured.* From then on her mother would be wheeled about in her stead, just as attractively dressed, just as carefully made up, with the same high-priced rug over her knees; the fiancé, standing but on roller skates would be pulled toward her on a chain and would try unsuccessfully to bow and kiss the old woman's hand. Of course, the girl would put all her purity and kindness into trying to make her mother a present of her recovery and resume her former condition in her stead, but would be prevented by the perpetually unsuccessful bowing and hand kissing. Thus the three of them would be frozen into a waxworks group, which could be set in motion now and then, providing for all time a picture of the state of affairs on Hohe Warte."

Thousands of miles away in China, Julius Tandler kept his promise to think of Manon when it was three in the afternoon in Vienna. He also kept up his virtually one-sided correspondence with her during the latter half of 1934, encouraging her to draw and write him letters. Mostly he had to imagine her across the vast distance and the disparities of time "via Siberia"—which he printed on his envelopes and postcards as the most direct route his mail should take. In this way Manon became yet another kind of liminal being before she was truly a revenant.

Tandler pieced together from Dr. Bien and Anna Mahler—and Manon herself—a picture of a young woman working hard on her recovery. He called her sheets of drawing and writing paper "practice fields" and asked her to send samples. "I have this ambition to be a landowner of [such] fields," he wrote, even though he was—ever the Social Democrat—"still for land distribution."[65] His letters are full of these ironic touches as well as his flirting and chaste innuendo. There is also much that suggests what Manon Gropius understood vis-à-vis Tandler. A curious phrase runs through his correspondence with her, a very literal watchword with which he signs off as being "on the wall." It is an allusion to the German nursery rhyme "Auf der Mauer, Auf der Lauer" (On the Wall, On the Watch") and Tandler's way of saying he would keep watch over her, like being a "fly on the wall." But it also means being a peeping Tom, too, and identifying himself with the little bug (*Wanze*) in the song and being mildly self-deprecating on the one hand and touching on his being Jewish and a socialist—the human vermin of Nazi propaganda.

Tandler wanted a long letter from Manon and when one finally reached him in Shanghai in September, he was elated and enjoyed how she had signed her letter as his "Niece." To elicit more letters, Tandler

65 Julius Tandler to Manon Gropius, August 5, 1934 [posted from Tokyo, August 16], ÖNB.

wrote about his journey into the interior of Hunan, of being nearly swept away by the famous tidal bore on the Qiantang River, of traveling in a rickshaw and being carried in a sedan chair, and of his medical clinic in Changsha. For her birthday, Tandler sent Manon two glass figurines for her collection and, in another letter, asked Manon to have Anna photograph her—and he barely disguised that he was in love with her, that he imagined her coming to China one day to stay with him. Nevertheless, Tandler knew he would have to eventually return to Vienna and expected Manon by that time to be waltzing with him, quoting a Viennese dancehall tune:

> *Bis i kumm bis i kumm—da wird es fein werden, da gehn ma drahn!*
> (*Till I come till I come—it'll be nice then, we'll spin round then!*)[66]

"No sitting in the garden in Breitenstein," he ordered Manon, "like comrades in arms, we want to be exchanging memories from 1934 shoulder to shoulder."[67]

Tandler confessed to worrying about Manon—and whether his letters even reached her. "Hopefully," he wrote, "this [letter] doesn't end up at the Elisabeth Promenade but rather at Manon Gropius' [house], where it's much, much nicer than at Elisabeth's, where my promenading is permanently impossible"—Tandler's wit simultaneously alluding to the Liesl prison, Villa Mahler, his arrest, and Manon's comparison to the sainted Empress Elisabeth.[68] But more often Tandler simply worried whether his concern would seem "stale" to her, being that they were "a world apart." "The invincibility of space & time intensifies one's concern," he wrote at the end of December when he learned that she was well again, "[but it] is defeated in the end by undaunted optimism. So I hope and wish that you laughingly lay

---

66 Julius Tandler to Manon Gropius, September 17, 1934, ÖNB.
67 Julius Tandler to Manon Gropius, October 4, 1934, ÖNB.
68 Julius Tandler to Manon Gropius, October 24, 1934, ÖNB.

these expressions of concernment aside and their baselessness be promptly acknowledged."[69]

In a charming New Year's greeting, which a fellow doctor drew in the manner of a Chinese ink painting, Tandler is depicted in his familiar broad-brimmed hat and walking a road that led from Changsha to Vienna, just over the next hill—but the city was no longer in Austria. "I am on the way to bring my wishes personally," Tandler wrote, "Past temples & pagodas to Manonia. In the distance the Vienna Woods hail and St. Stephan's Cathedral beckons. The path stretches but it will be walked"—the invitation that she walk, too, implicit. Continuing, Tandler wrote of the violence and racism that were so evident in China, which made him think about the Manon he knew, the one who was not the virgin saint—but one he knew, being so sick, had probably become different. "How much brutality I have seen perpetrated and that in the name of God," Tandler wrote. "He can't be all-knowing or, if he is, he is powerless. But neither are we right. With not one whisper will I demean a religiously sensitive soul. Perhaps you are such a one. I don't really know if we have ever spoken about it. You are right as you are with all the shortcomings & virtues. Please don't change for the better. I don't like the very good, they are not really real."[70]

Tandler signed his letter "Manoniac"—meaning his nationality and obsession with her and her recovery.

In White Face

"You have not written in such a long time," Manon began a letter to another remote person in her life—her father. He had not written her about his life in England and she wanted to give him some good news

69 Julius Tandler to Manon Gropius, November 12, 1934, ÖNB.
70 Julius Tandler to Manon Gropius, November 26, 1934, ÖNB.

for the coming Christmas holiday. "I am getting much better, as you can see, I am even writing in ink." She also exaggerated. "I do much better standing and sitting and I can move my upper body like a grownup," she wrote, without mentioning the means of support needed to hold her in place—her cranking bed, the nurses, the cushions placed to either side of her, and, perhaps, a strap to hold her upright in her wheelchair, for she was virtually helpless without these aids. "What all are you doing in England?" she asked, revealing, too, that she read the newspapers. "Were you at the wedding of the Duke of Kent? Do you have a place to live? How are the houses actually furnished there? Please write me soon and tell me everything. Have a wonderful English Xmas."[71] Alma's postscript informed Gropius that the rare books he had sent Manon as presents had just arrived and that she did not know about them yet. "What do you think of her handwriting?" her mother proudly asked.

Perhaps only days apart, Gropius wrote a letter that should not have crossed hers (which suggests that some of the letters she dictated or wrote during her illness were not always posted). He lamented not hearing from his daughter and once again begged her to be her own exorcist. "i hope your inner frustration is rising against this usurper inside you so that your energy will cast him out of your limbs as quickly as possible once and for all. don't make me beg so often for news, it makes me come off as nothing more than a mercifully tolerated papa!? i hope you have a wonderful christmas, free from every medical bother and with an unquenchable appetite for food for thought as well as the body. last week i sent you an old zoology book with charming english copper engravings that hopefully will amuse you [. . .]." Gropius then told her about his work for the British architectural firm Isokon and the offers that came from Istanbul, where he had been invited to reestablish the Bauhaus, and America to serve as a consultation to the

71 Manon Gropius to Walter Gropius, undated [late December 1934], ÖNB.

"roosevelt plan"—meaning the New Deal. Hearing that Alma and Werfel might be coming to New York, he assumed Manon would make the trip as well and asked how far along she was in her own "plans for america?"[72]

Even if *The Eternal Road* had opened as planned in early 1935, Manon would not have been able to travel. For most of the winter, Manon had a low-grade fever. She still had breathing problems. Every drink of water, every cup of tea or broth, and what solid food she could swallow entailed the physical and emotional trial of passing waste—which required two people to carry her to the W.C. or a bedpan and being cleaned up afterward like a baby that had soiled itself. And there had been nothing to show for all her physical therapy and various treatments, not even an infinitesimal twitch from a big toe. Dr. Pötzl began to consider a more aggressive line of attack, one in keeping with Austria's contributions to modern medicine.

Even before Dr. Tandler had purchased the country's first uranium for medical purposes, Austria had become a leader in radiation therapy and the leap from using X-rays to view the skeleton to bombarding malignant tumors and other abnormalities had been rapid. One of Pötzl's colleagues had been a leader in this, the neurologist Dr. Otto Marburg. In 1930, he published *Die Röntgenbehandlung der Nervenkrankheiten*—Roentgen Treatment of Nerve Disorders. The clinical trials and literature that followed revealed that gamma radiation not only healed nerves damaged by polio lesions, but also might stimulate regrowth. The possibilities of such a virtual miracle had already been observed on polio victims in a children's hospital in Freiburg in 1932. There some patients had shown a marked improvement when roentgen therapy had been tried with other forms of diathermy.[73]

72 Walter Gropius to Manon Gropius, December 22, 1934, ÖNB.

73 C. Noeggerath, M. Schneider, and A. Viethen, "Beobachtungen bei einer Röntgenbehandlung der epidemischen Kinderlähmung," [Observations of a roent-

Diathermy and X-ray therapy, however, also entailed certain risks not only to the patient but the physician's reputation, as one noted polio researcher noted, being one of the "most productive sources of litigation."[74] If such therapies are not performed carefully and with a protective ointment, they can result in skin burns. Deep-tissue diathermy with X-rays could cauterize healthy tissues and so risk the patient's life. And, if and when Manon received stronger dosages, these would have to be administered with equipment found at a clinic, namely, the nearby Rudolfinerhaus.

The great Yiddish writer Sholem Asch remembered Manon Gropius from his memorable visit to Haus Mahler in August 1929, which included accompanying her and her family in two cars on what Alma called a "Wild West" day trip to the Neusiedler See. He knew about Manon's illness from Werfel—one of Asch's correspondents—and had her on his mind on the first day of 1935. "Dearest Mutzi," he wrote, "Please permit me to call you by this name. [. . .] I have long wanted to write you and express my respect and admiration for the courage and patient endurance [. . .] by which God has tested you. I have heard [. . .] so much beauty and dignity about you that I have become firmly convinced that the sorrow that God has willed is for your value so that you shall be ennobled and refined out of illness. [. . .] This is what I wanted to say as my first thought for the New Year and I ask you to forgive me for the way I say it."[75]

For a young woman, however, who had been stricken with a cruel disease when she was beginning to be her own person (the so-called bad girl phase, to use an infelicitous term), such well-intended sentiments

gen treatment for epidemic infantile paralysis] *European Journal of Pediatrics* 53(1–2) (July 1932): 233–52.

74 Lloyd Paul Stryker, *Courts and Doctors* (New York: Macmillan 1932), p. 113. Stryker's book is a classic work in the field of malpractice.

75 Sholem Asch to Manon Gropius, January 1, 1935, ÖNB.

went with the expectation that she *act* the part. Manon surely played the serene sufferer to the saint-obsessed Werfel. To Gropius, Manon was not just a beautiful mind over matter, but beauty and mind pitted against the demon of paralysis to Gropius. To Father Hollnsteiner, she was a virgin ever facing the martyrdom of her perilous health.

Dr. Tandler had another expectation in keeping with what he knew of young people and the development of their personalities. He asked that Manon not to be *good* because he must have known she did not want to be that good, that way. During his first journey to China, Tandler had sent Alma and Manon a photograph of himself seated inside a railway coach, posed intimately with his arm draped over his pretty, smiling Chinese companion in Western dress—a young woman no older than Manon. A year earlier, such an image from a much older married man, with a wolfish twinkle in his eye, entertained its recipients with speculation. Now he had to be careful what he imparted in obsessing over Manon's personality and health. "The thought rose in me that my letters might not be welcome," he wrote in January, perhaps thinking of who might read them first, who would just see the wolfish man in the railway coach. "And I'm not much good at being the intrusive monologist. That major tremor of character [*Charakterbeben*], which we now undergo, calls for discretion and utmost reserve. You can compromise someone so easily. You know what I mean and don't take what's been said as wrong. [. . .] When I get back and if we still think and feel so much in common as before, then I will tell you about what I have learned. Restraint, though, dictated by general uncertainty compels me to write again after getting an answer from you first."[76]

Tandler, while he was surely homesick for the land of Manonia, was in no hurry to return to Austria. There was "sufficient reading in a Vienna newspaper" to cure him of what he told her, meaning weeks-old copies of the *Reichspost*—the newspaper of record "for Christian

76 Julius Tandler to Manon Gropius, undated [January 1935], ÖNB.

folk"—that celebrated the government surviving a "year of crises." The liberal *Neue Freie Presse*, which had the best international reportage, could not hide the fact that Austria had no real import in world politics, not even as the once robust experiment in social democracy. And the once reliable organ of the Social Democrats, *Das Kleine Blatt*, restricted itself to reporting the first real snowfall in Vienna, a total eclipse of the moon, horrific motor accidents, murders, crimes of passions, the Lindbergh Baby Trial, and the recent Saar plebiscite. The Treaty of Versailles had allowed the people of that German occupation zone to vote whether to remain a League of Nations protectorate under French administration or be reunified with Nazi Germany. Many Austrians saw themselves one day being given the same choice, to vote in overwhelming numbers for the Reich.

Illustrated pieces about exotic places, people, and animals, too, were especially newsworthy in the winter months, stories of Inuit people hunting walruses, rare botanical specimens the Schönbrunn's Palmhaus blooming in February, and, perhaps, much to the delight of Manon, insects that mimicked leaves, sticks, and even thorns. Alma, however, found an exotic person while reading the classified and personals advertisements. Among the country girls looking to be general domestics (*Mädchen für Alles*), requests for help finding missing persons (a lawyer looking for his runaway daughter), an old castle for rent, and jars of honey for sale, an advertisement had been placed for a piano teacher. The prospective student was an Ethiopian boy.[77] Curious and sympathetic, Alma inquired about this apparent prodigy and possible refugee, for a "crisis" had recently developed on the border of Ethiopia and Italian Somaliland, with Mussolini threatening war and Emperor Haile Selassie appealing to the League of Nations.

---

77 The following passage is informed by Mahler-Werfel, *Mein Leben*, pp. 247ff.; *And the Bridge Is Love*, pp. 225ff; and Bairu Tafla, *Ethiopia and Austria: A History of Their Relations* (Vienna: Otto Harrassowitz Verlag, 1994), pp. 138ff.

The advertisement stated that the music lessons would have to be gratis. This condition appealed to Alma's sense of *noblesse oblige*. She also had her daughter's welfare in mind as well as charity, for tutoring and boarding this "*Negerlein*" (little Negro) at Villa Mahler might provide her daughter with a live-in companion just as useful as the Rietenauer child had been. What Alma left unsaid about such *quid pro quo* is what he could have also been intended for and trained to do after his piano lessons—fetch things for the bedridden Manon, to be her arms and legs. If he were strong enough, he might also push her wheelchair. When Manon readily agreed to such a possible house guest—which surely seemed a charming experiment, suggesting Monostatos from *The Magic Flute* and like the little turbaned servant boys one saw on stage, Alma made an appointment to meet the boy and his guardians.

Following their directions, Alma drove herself to a working-class neighborhood in the Hietzing district of Vienna, on a "noisy" and "not-nice" street. After climbing a darkened stairwell to the top floor, she rang the doorbell. Greeting her at the door was a young girl, Erika Weinzinger, the daughter of the couple who had placed the advertisement. Her parents and older sister were not home, but Alma pieced together their story and how they came to have this child, who had run off to hide behind a chair.

The father, Erich Weinzinger, was a linguist, an expert in ancient Abyssinian languages, who had studied Amharic, Oromiffa, and Guragie at the Ecole des Langues Orientales in Paris. A lawyer, journalist, and entrepreneur as well, he had been living in Ethiopia since before the First World War and saw himself in a land that had been asleep since the thirteenth century and now needed to enter the modern era. Thus, Weinzinger served in various capacities to achieve that end, from being the Austrian consul to publishing the country's first academic journal, founding a college, and befriending and mentoring privileged young men such as Tafari Makonnen—the future Haile Selassie. Unfortunately, after Makonnen had been crowned in 1928, Weinzinger made the mistake of scolding the new emperor and making enemies in the court and government. Out of favor and "virtually penniless," he was forced to return to Austria with his family in 1932. And that family included the orphan boy, who Weinzinger had named "Georg." Erika told Alma that she and her sister had originally found the boy, naked and emaciated, being carried by an old woman begging outside a church in Addis Ababa. Wanting to do something for the baby, who looked close to death, Erika convinced her parents to buy him from his caretaker. When they brought him home, the Weinzingers could not help but marvel at how his weightless body felt. When they bathed him the first time, he seemed to float like paper on the surface of the warm water.

The boy's story reminded Alma of when she and Werfel had encountered a beggar woman in a gloomy park across the street from the Cairo Opera House. To their horror, they saw the corpse of a beautiful dead girl lying in her lap. At least something had been done for Georg—and more—for at last the girl coaxed him from his hiding place and presented him to Alma. What struck her first was his perfectly white teeth set off by a "big, woundlike mouth" and the way the whites of his eyes shimmered in the gloomy apartment with a "phosphorescent glow."

Feeling confident that she could do something for the boy—and if he could bring some cheer for Manon—Alma invited Georg and his foster family for lunch the next day at Villa Mahler. Only the father came with Georg and arrangements were made for the boy to be left in Alma's care. But as soon as Herr Weinzinger left, the child began to race around uncontrollably through the great house, tearing into closets and drawers to see what was inside. When he was brought to Manon's room, he could only run and jump around her bed, making her nervous and uncomfortable. Then he bolted from her room to once more go through the unfamiliar house, hiding from Alma and her servants only to reappear out of nowhere. At last, Georg was chased into the kitchen where he was locked inside.

Realizing that keeping the boy was impossible, Alma summoned Erich Weinzinger to come back for his ward. But he refused, claiming that he could no longer afford to keep him. Thus, Georg remained at Villa Mahler. "Every one of his physical reactions was abnormal," Alma observed, concluding that the boy was brain damaged. She also discovered that playing the piano calmed him—as did his peculiar way of "dancing" or locomotion. Georg, whether in the house or out in the street, would at times take long, loping steps, throwing out his arms, and spinning. If Alma saw him as a possible savant who might tirelessly fetch books, pencils, paper, food, and the like for Manon, it would take far too much effort. In a matter of days, she found a Vienna missionary hospital to take Georg off her hands. There he remained until the Weinzingers could afford to take him back until they went abroad once more, leaving Georg in an orphanage in Palestine on their way to Persia.

Had Georg become a part of the Mahler-Werfel household, he and Manon would have made for an even stranger pair, for often she appeared in whiteface. This was likely not the pancake makeup that Canetti saw, but rather a protective masque of zinc oxide and linseed oil—the same ingredients in diaper rash cream—or Raderma ointment, a German-made product specifically for the kind of X-ray treatments Manon experienced at the Rudolfiner clinic. To Erich Rietenauer, as he watched her being carried into an ambulance, Manon looked like a mime or clown. He also noted that when she came home from the clinic, the white face had to be washed off with some effort.[78]

During the winter, Manon taught herself how to type and sent one of her first efforts, a letter, to Dr. Tandler. "I just hope," he replied in

78 See Rietenauer, *Alma, meine Liebe*, p. 184.

February, "that you'll use me in the future as the object of practice for your typing. You can hardly believe how perfect I am for this purpose and the time will go by for you between two massages."[79] He told of his work: translating his proposal for the management of health throughout China and for the reform of teaching medicine into English and Chinese. He promised that he would be in Vienna by mid-March and, if she worked hard on her health, she could go with him to China on his return in the fall. "But let's arrange that verbally," he cautioned.

Meanwhile in England, Walter Gropius had also learned to use a typewriter. Though he had not written or telephoned Manon since the holidays, he made up for it in a letter about his new life in the Hampstead section of London. There he and Ise had been given an apartment at Lawn Road Flats, virtually a Bauhaus Master's villa writ small. Provided by his employer, Jack Pritchard, the head of Isokon, this block-long sculptural edifice liberally drew on Gropius' ideas for its streamlined appearance and unbroken surfaces of white-dyed concrete.

Gropius asked Manon for the name of her doctor so he could request a "serious medical report" about her progress. He described a demonstration of the first public television phone, a technology which would make it possible for him to call her and see her at the same time. He also wrote of his difficulties with living in England—"a stranger star"—learning English, and understanding the typical Englishman, who seemed to talk without parting his lips—add to that a pipe in the mouth. Gropius, too, wondered how far along his daughter was in English. "can you read easily?" he asked. "can i send you something [. . .]? i am completely engrossed in jonathan swift here. as a child i only had an abridged children's edition of gulliver's travels, which is nothing like the original. a magnificent satire about the human race full of the wildest fantasies and situations, in short, a high point in world literature."

---

79 Julius Tandler to Manon Gropius, February 12, 1935, ÖNB.

As Gropius continued, like Tandler's candidness, his tone suggests the intelligence, empathy, and maturity that these men saw in her. For her father, it must have been like explaining himself to a muse of architecture—but without realizing, as he alluded to the Lilliputians, that Manon was as prostrate and unable to move as Gulliver was, tied down by hundreds of threadlike ropes. "as you know," Gropius wrote, referring to some long conversation he had or some reading he had expected her to read, "my interest has been focused over the past ten years on the phenomenon of changing scales in relation to our fixed human size. herein i perceive the central issue of architectural efficacy, which increases when the scale of a building or a room seems greater than it really is. this is also the thing that works in swiftian prose. he not only shrinks things in the material sense one moment, then makes them gigantic compared to us the next, but rather takes on, in the intellectual sense, a like point of view's displacement with which he finally deals human vanity a deadly blow. a precious book that you must one day read."

Gropius devoted the next paragraphs to the British royals and meeting the Prince of Wales, the future King Edward VIII (and Duke of Windsor in abdication), who held progressive ideas about urban renewal and "functions like a true revolutionary in the circle of english architects." Gropius boasted of being an honorary member of an English club "where i always have breakfast" and of meeting such rich and influential people as Bryan Guinness, the brewer, who had the Gropiuses come stay with him in a "country cottage" that was really a castle and "the paper (*for the loo*) was in fine venetian glass bowls on mirrored tables [. . .] we laughed ourselves sick over the incongruity of this princely excess and our economic low tide that hardly allowed us to pay for our train fare or to give the butler his tip."

As Gropius' letter came to an end, his reduced circumstances became all the more clear, for he included a drawing of his apartment's floor plan, the only one known to be in his hand. In the small dining room that was part of the kitchen, he remarked in the margin that his meals were now "typical english fare."[80]

During the last week of February 1935 and into March, newspapers around the world reported the curious suicides of Elizabeth and Jane Du Bois, the daughters of the American consul to Naples. Considered playgirls by everyone who knew them, they had recently learned that the RAF pilots—to whom they imagined themselves engaged—had been killed the week before when their flying boat slammed into a mountain near Messina. After grieving all night in a London hotel, the Du Bois sisters attended a church service at St. Martin-in-the-Fields on Trafalgar Square and gave out half-crowns to a queue of unemployed men to drink in memory of the dead. The next day they booked all six seats aboard a De Havilland Dragon bound for Paris and, fifteen minutes into the flight, embraced each other. With their combined strength, they forced open the passenger door and fell as one into an empty English cabbage field. The lone pilot did not realize they were gone until well over the Channel.

For anyone in Vienna who read the installments of this tale and knew Manon Gropius, did she not have more reasons—her useless legs, her show fiancé, the air of false hopes—than these frivolous American girls to take her life? However, she soldiered on with her treatment and acting lessons. She read her animal books and magazines and received her visitors through the winter and early spring. Young Rietenauer, saved from losing his place to Georg, saw her once more around this time. She had longed to hear the Burschi read to her again from Wilhelm Busch's funny poems and picture stories, such as *Max and Moritz* and *Fipps the Monkey*. Save for her X-ray treatments, Manon's world was restricted to Villa Mahler. She could not be taken to the Burgtheater or the movies, as her mother feared her picking up an

80 Walter Gropius to Manon Gropius, February 3, 1935. ÖNB.

illness from the crowd. *Tarzan and his Mate,* dubbed in German and playing at the Sascha-Palast, would surely have been entertaining for her—Cheetah, the many jungle animals, Johnny Weissmuller even riding a rhinoceros to the delight of his "*Kamaradin*" Jane as Maureen Sullivan was billed.

Alma made sure that her daughter's life was as normal and unhindered as possible, even though she herself felt increasingly trapped in her big house. There would be no Easter in Venice this year, which fell late in April, and only Werfel had been left free to travel over the past year. Diagnosed with pleurisy, Alma spent much time in bed and began to write in her diary again after setting it aside for nearly eleven months. "At last I can write again. A year has gone by [. . .] and we still schlep on with [Manon's] illness. I must provide more details about this when there's more distance," she continued, in what is partly redacted in transcript. "This house, this unlucky house, is all to blame [. . .] this entire house was stupid madness [. . .]."[81]

Through March, Alma endured the Rintelen trial, which she found "ghastly." Without realizing her phone had been tapped by the government, she had been compromised by him. On the night before the failed coup of July began, Rintelen had implored her to go drinking beer with him and his friends at one of Vienna's most famous pubs, the Griechenbeisel. There she would have been seen toasting him in public—hours before his Nazi collaborators shot Chancellor Dolfuss and let him bleed to death on a sofa. Fortunately for Alma, her testimony convinced the court that she had not been an accessory to Rintelen's crimes against the state. "I'm sure he's made a deal like everyone in Austria," she wrote in her diary. "I'm even more certain that he had nothing to do with the murder of Dollfuss in the least. In some horrible way he got mixed up in this mischief."[82]

81 Mahler-Werfel, "Diary of Alma Maria", March 9, 1935, pp. 291–2, MWP.
82 Mahler-Werfel, "Diary of Alma Maria", March 9, 1935, pp. 291–2, MWP.

Every day, during the course of the trial, the newspapers published the proceedings. Even though Alma's name was hardly mentioned, she sat with Manon and lamented having been dragged into this "terrible situation" Rintelen had caused. What relief Alma felt, however, was soon dissipated by her maddening fears for Manon—and the sight of her still "chained to the bed" made her suffer everything else a "thousand times" worse. "I long to be out of this house with every fiber away away away!"[83]

Franz Horch had been working with Manon toward a goal—a private performance she would give for family and select friends. Her repertoire included a famous speech from Schiller's romantic tragedy, *The Maid of Orleans*, of nearly a hundred lines that comprised the entire first scene of Act IV. Thomas Mann, who called the play a "word opera," saw Joan of Arc's monologue as an aria of Schiller's verse given its shifts of rhymed iambic and trochaic lines as well as blank verse and ending in trochaic strophes. It was a set piece in German theater and remarkably suitable for a young actress's' exam—one that Manon might have taken to complete the Reinhardt-Seminar. Those in the household respected her shyness and need for privacy and kept to the opposite side of Villa Mahler from where Manon had been carried by Horch and his assistants to practice her lines with her. For Alma and Werfel her recital would be a surprise. For her father, however, her acting lessons remained a secret—or unacknowledged. None of Gropius' letters mention her studies, as well as her desire to act, which is mystifying given that he had introduced Manon to his sister-in-law, Ellen Frank.

As Manon prepared in March and April, the German playwright and screenwriter Carl Zuckmayer came to see her. He had befriended Manon in 1933, after his works were banned by the Nazis and he went into self-imposed exile with his wife, Austrian actress Alice Herdan, and

83 Mahler-Werfel, "Diary of Alma Maria", March 9, 1935, pp. 291–2, MWP. The phrase "out of this house" is crossed out in original.

their two daughters. From his summer cottage in Henndorf near Salzburg, Zuckmayer often came to Vienna and Breitenstein and began to socialize more with Werfel and Alma. To his surprise, he learned that he shared Manon's passion for the novels and stories of Karl May, which extended to christening his eldest daughter Winnetou, a name he had to sometimes explain to the incredulous as an obscure Scottish saint.

After Manon's illness, Zuckmayer indulged her with much of the same Indian *Spiel* that he treated his little girls to on their forest walks around the Wallersee, pretending to be descended from an Indian through his grandfather, who, he claimed, had fought in the American Civil War and married a squaw. He called Manon's bedroom her "wigwam"—and she played along, pretending to speak "Utah" and "Tonkawa" together, gibberish no one else could understand. She named him Nanap Varrenton, Chief Old Thunder, from Karl May's *The Treasure of Silver Lake.* Zuckmayer called her Kunpui, or Chief Fireheart, from the same book. They even became blood brothers and to further cement their bond, Zuckmayer sent her gifts from his trove of artifacts, including one that he considered her animal sign given her favorite reptile. "The rattlesnake skin I send you enclosed," he wrote in a cover letter, "(as a totem sign) was shed by a North American rattlesnake before my very eyes. I took [the snake skin] out of its box myself. It hung for some years in my wigwam—unfortunately a paleface housemaid, while attempting to dust or brush it, split it in half. But both the scalp, like the snake's tail, are well preserved. Put them in your totem bag, whose rule (in Tonkawa) is never forget. Your older brother who thinks about you often."[84]

According to Alma, Zuckmayer said that he had fallen in love with Manon such that he wished only to live with her—"crippled or not."[85] Although this would seem to be hyperbole from a woman who needed to know her daughter was still desirable, Zuckmayer was captivated by

84 Carl Zuckmayer to Manon Gropius, November 27, 1934, WB.
85 Mahler-Werfel, *Mein Leben,* p. 246.

the bedridden young woman. When he traveled to England in late March to see the film director Michael Korda and Charles Laughton for his screenplay of *Rembrandt* (1936), he kept Manon in his thoughts. Knowing her love of animals, Zuckmayer wrote her a letter on Mayfair Hotel stationery, describing his visit to the London Zoo. "I saw live hummingbirds at the zoo yesterday similar to, but not as dusty, as that one of yours," he wrote, remembering one of her Lauscha figurines—"dusty" because true collectors could not leave it to servants to clean such precious glass objects. Zuckmayer marveled at the many "tiny, whirring iridescences with long beaks" and how their keepers fed them with small vials from which "they sip as if it were cognac." He also mentioned the zoo's famous Reptile House, where he saw "fantastic snakes," including the "legendary ones such as the mamba from South Africa and a dreaded white cobra, which would have really guarded an ancient temple."[86]

As the weather warmed, Manon appeared outdoors in her wheelchair, sunning herself in the gardens of villas Mahler and Moll. Werfel noticed a change in her as Easter approached. "The remarkable translucence in Manon's features [had] increased. She seemed totally fulfilled, perfectly happy, as though this future were not waiting for her, the future the merciless old doctor had seen for her, the future of a miserable cripple."[87]

Despite her more aggressive X-ray treatments during April, Manon found time to rehearse the other speeches she would perform. In addition to Schiller's St. Joan, she would recite a monologue from another famous cross-dressing role, that of Viola in the German translation of Shakespeare's *Twelfth Night* ("I left no ring with her. What means this lady?") Finally, Dr. Horch deemed her ready for her first rehearsal before an audience on Palm Sunday, which fell on April 14. In Werfel's telling of events, Manon called her mother and step-

86 Carl Zuckmayer to Manon Gropius, March 21, 1935, ÖNB.
87 Werfel, "Manon," *Erzählungen aus zwei Welten*, p. 397.

father into the room where she had long concealed her drama lessons from them.

"I would like to perform something for you today," Manon said smiling. "Her teacher seemed as excited as she was," Werfel recalled. "The frail shape of the girl sat as always in a deep wingchair. Her black hair, parted in the middle, fell over narrow shoulders. Her long hands rested in her lap. Across her knees, a beautiful coverlet lay so that no one could see her legs." Then she recited the monologue from Schiller's *Joan of Arc* and performed two of Viola's scenes from Shakespeare's *Twelfth Night*. "For a finale, she followed with a folk-dialect passage from some cheerful, sentimental piece," Werfel continued. "Because she was paralyzed and could move only a little, all the power of her performance was in her words, in her eyes, in the movement of her lips, in her smile, in a few spare gestures with her hands. It was through her confinement that that girl brought off such an inexpressibly matchless artistic achievement. Her dark voice soared, her eyes lit up and went out, her mouth opened pleadingly, her hands trembled . . . from the waist down everything was still. I don't think this hour was overestimated by my love and pain."[88]

On the following Monday, April 15, Manon repeated her performance for a "great actor" whom Werfel did not name, who told him how surprised and shocked he was by the talented young woman. "The gift, which had so charmingly announced itself in that childish presentation of *The Force of Fate*, which only seemed to fizzle out before our eyes, had at long last come full circle and gotten around the deadly postponement of her illness," Werfel wrote. "No, it was Manon herself. She was responsible for realizing her gift through her seriousness, her zeal, her energy, which her suffering gave her, which makes others such bitter and tormented souls. She had made something from what had been given to her, knowing deep down that it was pointless and in vain.

88 Werfel, "Manon," *Erzählungen aus zwei Welten*, p. 398.

It was as though some genuine mercy, which lies in our souls, which can never really perish without blooming, had taken place if but for one time, without a purpose, for just a half an hour. 'You worked a lot during this half year,' I said afterwards, just to say something. 'It was a very marvelous half year,' she said."[89] In the English version of his "Manon" necrology, Werfel continued from this point. "As contradictory as it sounded to me, this simple little sentence said in a dreamy voice, expressed the full truth. The last half-year of Manon's illness was truly her best time [. . .] as though it were but a question of time until she stood on the stage as Joan of Arc."[90]

Carl Zuckmayer missed the second performance. However, he surely learned of it when he arrived at Villa Mahler on Holy Thursday, April 18, to give Manon a wonderful gift: an aquarium with two live small snakes. According to Werfel, the reptiles were a pair of ring snakes (*Natrix natrix*) and emerald green in color, with the male having a crown on its jewel-like head. According to Rietenauer—who would not have been allowed in Manon's room for fear of her catching the flu—Zuckmayer's gifts were blindworms (*Anguis fragilis*), a legless lizard species. Naturally, Manon was elated and asked to hold them. Presumably, Zuckmayer assisted her in this wish and the intimacy with which she handled the animals frightened Werfel. "You look like Cleopatra before the end," he said at the sight of them lying on her breasts. "A good role," she responded.[91]

On Good Friday, Alma had visitors, among them Ludwig Karpath, the venerable music critic who had written glowing reviews of Gustav Mahler. Karpath had known Manon all her life and he saw her during his visit. Dutifully, she told him about her acting, her health, and her prognosis. Once more, with the same cheerful optimism, she said that

89 Werfel, "Manon," *Erzählungen aus zwei Welten*, p. 398.
90 Werfel, "Manon," *The Commonweal*, May 1, 1942, p. 34.
91 Werfel, "Manon," *Erzählungen aus zwei Welten*, p. 399.

she would soon be sitting on her own again and, perhaps, stand and one day walk. Even if Manon believed herself, such encounters had become routine and performed for her mother's sake. Alma saw her daughter's paralysis, her withered legs, and her deformed feet as a divine insult, which, perhaps, even paled in comparison to the crucifixion. "Manon's illness for her," according to Oliver Hilmes, "became not only a terrible misfortune, but also a demonstration of her chosenness. That her only 'Aryan' daughter of all people was punished by fate, she interpreted as proof of her special status." Manon's "passion" (*Leiden*) became benediction, a sacrament at Villa Mahler to be celebrated. And the invalid herself became "a monstrance to put on show."[92]

On Holy Saturday, April 20—as the radio broadcasts from Germany wished Chancellor Hitler a happy birthday—Manon felt the first wave of nausea and cramps for which there had been no discernable cause. They happened quickly and soon took their course.

92 Hilmes, *Witwe im Wahn*, p. 265.

TRANSFIGURATION

Being perfected in a short time, she fulfilled long years.[1]
—Father Johannes Hollnsteiner

Hollnsteiner was always a striver, for God and for power. The power was snatched from him—and only the everyday remained forever. And Mutzi, she was never punished. She had, during that year of suffering, tasted through an entire woman's life without the limping horse foot that life invariably brings with it. She remained spared from everything, and she remains in the heart of mankind a saint.[2]
—Alma Mahler-Werfel

"Dear Professor," began Father Hollnsteiner's letter of April 25, 1935, to Walter Gropius, the title a mark of respect for his former status as head of the Bauhaus. Having never met the architect, he explained that Alma was too distraught to write about his daughter's last days and hours. "Until the afternoon of Holy Saturday Mutzi's health was totally normal," he wrote. "Nevertheless, we must take into consideration that the symptoms of her paralysis had only regressed very, very slowly. To speed this up, the roentgen therapy, prescribed by the best neurologist in Austria and one of the best in the world, resulted at first in a slight

1 Johannes Hollnsteiner, Grabrede für Mutzi [Eulogy for Mutzi], April 24, 1935, ÖNB. From the Catholic service for the burial of children. The source is The Book of Wisdom 4, 13 in the Old Testament of the Catholic Vulgate.
2 Mahler-Werfel, Diary of Alma Maria, July 24, 1941, p. 355, MWP.

rise in temperature and headache." The priest meant Dr. Pötzl and implicit here are the minor after-effects of what surely had been the dosage of the most recent X-ray treatments. "Anyway," Hollnsteiner continued, "the attending physician did not see anything out of the ordinary in the vomiting that took place on Holy Saturday afternoon."[3]

An unnamed internist called to Villa Mahler could do nothing to calm Manon. He listened to her heartbeat through his stethoscope and reported that it sounded weaker than normal. Soon other doctors arrived, among them Dr. Pötzl. What they did is not reported in any detail by Hollnsteiner, save that Manon had been stabilized, probably with a morphine injection to make her comfortable and allow her to sleep. "Thoroughly hopeful," the priest wrote, Dr. Pötzl left Villa Mahler during the evening of Holy Saturday and promised Werfel: 'By tomorrow you'll be able to celebrate a joyful Easter.' However, the night did not go as well as expected."

On Sunday, April 21, Easter morning, Manon begged to see Father Hollnsteiner, who intended to spend Easter at a monastery. Learning of her request over the telephone, he drove at speeds averaging 100 KPH from Upper Austria to Vienna and saw Manon there at sometime after two in the afternoon. Her condition seemed "grave but not entirely hopeless." The last sacrament was not needed, just prayer.

At one point seven physicians had arrived at Villa Mahler and consulted with each other and labored over their young patient. Pötzl remained the most optimistic, telling the priest in private that he still had high hopes for Manon to turn around. "The consultation around 9:00 in the evening brought greater clarity," Hollnsteiner continued, repeating some of the German medical terms the doctors used to impart their authority. "It was a resurgence and a further progression of the original illness [*Urkankheit*] from some insignificant and, until

3 Johannes Hollnsteiner to Walter Gropius, April 25, BHA. The following passage is informed by this account and other sources.

now, unclear cause. There were certain symptoms of poisoning in the body [*Organismus*], which, in connection to the original disease, led to a paralysis of the stomach and intestines."

The organ failure that Hollnsteiner described is indicative of other causes just as likely as those directly attributable to polio or post-polio. In the terminology of the present, Manon's cause of death would best be described as toxic shock. Being bedridden for a year can have a gradual and deleterious effect on the intestines and urinary tract. A bout of stomach flu that, for a healthy person, might mean stomach cramps, vomiting, and diarrhea for a few days, would have been life threatening for Manon. Food poisoning would do the same. Her new pet snakes could have made her sick. Reptiles can host the Salmonella bacteria and handling them or being bitten can be fatal for children, the elderly, and those like Manon with weakened immunity.

Then there is the possibility of an iatrogenic illness. Her X-ray treatments may have damaged or burned her intestines. Indeed, her symptoms correlate with those of radiation enteritis. Thus, like the doctors in April who performed Manon's lumbar puncture and injected her with drugs, Dr. Pötzl, may have set aside his oath "to do no harm" in order to appease Alma. Here his character must be weighed, his bureaucratic expediency and enthusiasm, both colored, perhaps, by his prior membership in Austria's Nazi party until Dollfuss outlawed it. Then there is his future conduct, for Pötzl rejoined the Nazi party to continue with the advancement of his career. He became a willing accessory to the Nazi *Euthanasie-Projekt* at Vienna's notorious Steinhof asylum, where he authorized "mercy killings" of handicapped and mental patients.[4]

Did Dr. Pötzl provide the same mercy for Alma? According to Hollnsteiner, Pötzl and Manon's other physicians did what was proper to relieve Manon's symptoms, including pumping her stomach and

4 See Wolfgang Neugebauer, "Racial Hygiene in Vienna 1938," (James R. Moser trans.) Documentation Centre of Austrian Resistance (DÖW), http://www.doew.at/information/mitarbeiter/beitraege/rachyg.html.

giving her injections of saline solution, glucose, and insulin. The pharmacopeia here sounds innocent enough. But enough insulin can cause insulin shock, leading to coma and death. The "black bag" of a typical physician of the 1930s contained ampoules of common drugs that could easily induce a heart attack, such as strophanthus, camphor, caffeine, or morphine.

To Hollnsteiner, Manon responded "surprisingly well" to the medicines and the doctors began leaving Villa Mahler after ten in the evening. Again Pötzl took the priest aside in confidence and expressed his high hopes. Like the night before, one doctor stayed behind with two nurses and Alma, who kept watch at Manon's bedside, while Werfel and Hollnsteiner remained nearby through the night of Easter Sunday.

Manon's suffering on the next day appeared far more horrific than what the priest—known to be tactful and guarded—described to Gropius. "In cruelty," Werfel wrote, "this second death outdid the first that she had overcome," meaning all she had suffered during the previous Easter holiday, a coincidence that the poet and novelist could not ignore.[5] Alma, however, during the early hours of Easter Monday, allegedly spoke with Manon. This would seem unlikely given that Hollnsteiner had told Gropius that his daughter had lost the use of her vocal cords. However, this relieved the priest and Gropius too of having to convey or ask if there had been any last words. If such had been forthcoming, only Alma heard and related them.

"Let me die in peace," Manon whispered with a failing voice, according to Alma. "I'm not going to get well anymore." Then, at once brutally honest, accusatory, and forgiving, Manon continued, "And my acting, you only persuaded me into it out of pity ... you will get over this, the way you get over everything"—and then she corrected herself—"the way everyone gets over everything ..."[6]

---

5 Werfel, "Manon," p. 399.

6 Mahler-Werfel, *Mein Leben*, p. 249.

"She said it without any sentimentality, without regret—oh, she knew what was in store for her," Alma wrote one year later. The statement appears in her diary transcripts only and in a moment of morbid self-reflection, thinking how it was pointless to mourn someone who had died and that her daughter had slipped away to escape the world and its chain of disappointment. This, came, as so many other revelations that came to Alma, without realizing that Manon might have meant her and the whole charade of her recovery—that *acting*.[7]

On the morning of April 22, Easter Monday, Manon underwent an agonizing death that, according to Werfel, would cause even the most believing person to doubt whether God had any compassion at all. "Why did that little, innocent Manon, with her eighteen years, have to suffer more than anyone else?" he asked.[8] The ever-prosaic Hollnsteiner, however, made it a beautiful death for her father. But before he did, he gave his assurance that everyone at Villa Mahler had gone to extremes in helping Manon and that the telegram sent to Gropius had been sent in time and in good conscience, and that it had not conveyed the appalling oversight that it really did.

"Against all expectations," Hollnsteiner continued in his long letter, "her pivotal deterioration set in. At around 7 in the morning the attending physician in the house was called in for consultation. Everything, whatever medical art could be employed was expended and everything was tried from 7 to 11:30, whatever was medically possible. Because of this new alarming situation, you were notified immediately in the expectation that you would catch the first airplane to be at the sickbed. With that wire about your child being in danger of death, no authority would have required an entrance or exit visa from you. Just before 11:00 the doctors informed me that everything that could be done had been done and that now I might fulfill my priestly duties.

7 Mahler-Werfel, Diary of Alma Maria, September 26, 1935, p. 300, MWP.
8 Werfel, "Manon," *Erzählungen aus zwei Welten*, p. 399.

Mutzi's strength faded ever more. Quietly, without struggle, she passed on to another life at 3:40 P.M. Her eyes released, lifted upward into this other world, a gentle smile played around her lips, the one known to all of us who were with her so often. The cause of death was diagnosed as acute stomach and intestinal paralysis. In the official certificate it is, in fact, called 'acutissima.'"

Walter Gropius would not read Hollnsteiner's letter for several days, possibly weeks. He began his Easter Monday morning of April 22 with attending to his correspondence and the next CIAM meeting in Amsterdam. The latter business required a letter of invitation to the Dutch architect C. H. van der Leeuw. But Gropius did not finish it. Where he broke off continues in Ise's hand, informing van der Leeuw that her husband would be in Vienna the next day—and reveals how quickly Gropius responded to Alma's first telegram, where its capital letters spelled out that Manon was gravely ill *in a clinic*, that he needed to come at once.[9]

For months, Gropius trusted that everything was going well with his daughter. Life in England had been difficult for him. The language barrier had taken much time to overcome, and he still felt uncomfortable speaking in English. He was virtually an expatriate, even though he had not renounced his German citizenship. The change of scene, too, had its rewards. He enjoyed the attention the English gave him. He lived comfortably—and had acquired a taste for Bass Ale, Milk

9 There are no extant telegrams from Alma to quote in this account. That Gropius had been told by Alma that Manon was being cared for "in a clinic"—the rationale for Gropius' initial attempt to see Manon while there was some hope of her surviving until then—is inferred from Reginald Isaacs, where he writes, "The young Manon's last hours had obviously begun even before the setting in the clinic (*noch bevor die Umgebung in der Klinik*), [where] the nurses and attending physicians were able to understand how serious it was for her" (Isaacs, *Walter Gropius*, VOL. 2, p. 736). His source is likely Ise Gropius, who also reviewed and made editorial comments in manuscript.

Stout, and J. Haig Whiskey. He also trusted that Manon would understand his personal and professional situations—of getting his "feet on the ground" as he had just wrote van der Leeuw—and pardon his long absence.

Since Austria virtually shut down for the holiday, Gropius knew he could do little from England save to make travel plans for the next day. With the help of his English host, he obtained the necessary papers and a reservation to fly from London to Vienna—an eight-hour journey via Imperial Airways that left at 8:15 A.M. and arrived in Vienna at 4:30 P.M. But later in the day, he received another telegram from Villa Mahler, in which he learned Manon had died. Although devastated inside, Gropius changed his travel plans, for he now lacked the special dispensation of a direly sick relative. He and Ise would fly to Germany instead and arrange to enter Austria in time for the impending funeral.

In the minutes after Manon Gropius' death, when everyone left her room, Hollnsteiner fetched Erich Rietenauer to serve as his altar boy. Two candles were lit and, as both the boy and priest wept, Manon's body was consecrated while a prayer was said ending with "Lord, give her eternal rest." They had to hurry, for outside the room her sister Anna waited to make her sister's death mask.[10]

In the years between Gustav Mahler's death in 1911, such objects of veneration were already seen as a morbid anachronism (although it lingered longer than the Victorian practice of postmortem photographs of babies and children). For Alma and her generation, however, and especially in Central Europe, a death mask conveyed a person's rank and accomplishments. Manon had the status, surely, and her face contributed something like the latter, for despite the suffering Werfel recorded, the sedatives given to Manon left her with an expression that had to be preserved. Its unearthly beauty and serenity of her "death

---

10 Rietenauer, *Alma, meine Liebe*, p. 189.

smile" rivaled that of *L'Inconnue de la Seine*—the unknown woman of the Seine—the most famous death mask in Europe. Many copies existed and it had become a cult object between the wars, especially among German actresses, who sought to emulate the erotic appeal of the *Inconnue's* Mona Lisa-like expression.[11] Rainer Maria Rilke praised the *Inconnue's* beauty and its deceptive smile, "as though it knew," in his novel *The Notebooks of Malte Laurids Brigge.* Writers such as Reinhold Conrad Muschler, Claire Goll, Hertha Pauli, and Ödön von Horváth wrote works based on the life of the girl behind the death mask—and a young Vladimir Nabokov wrote one of his earliest poems for her.

Unlike that of the *Inconnue*, whose body was placed on a huge block of ice in a Paris morgue, Manon's smile would soon slacken into a "death grin" and her body would stiffen with rigor mortis. Since a mask had to be made immediately—and because finding a professional mask-maker was out of the question on Easter Monday—someone experienced had to be found in the family. Carl Moll, however, had sworn to never make another after casting Gustav Mahler's face.

The task fell on Anna. Being a sculptor, she knew how to mix plaster and make casts from a human body. Too, she had no reservations about handling a dead loved one from her experience with Arthur Schnitzler's daughter Lilli. Quickly, expeditiously but gently, she tilted her sister's head back about thirty-five degrees on the pillow to get the best impression. Then Manon's face was smeared with oil to prevent the first, thin layer of plaster from sticking to the hair of the brows and eyelashes, the loose skin of the lips and eyelids.

According to the traditional methods, pure scented oil, such as the kind Hollnsteiner had applied earlier, is used. But mineral oil can serve the same purpose of ensuring that the mask will not adhere to the skin. Next the plaster is laid carefully over the nose, mouth, eyes,

---

11 See A. Alvarez, *The Savage God: A Study of Suicide* (London: Weidenfeld & Nicolson, 1971), pp. 133ff.

and forehead—the way a facial is applied by a beautician. Then Anna would have cupped her sister's head and pressed her face into a flat dish containing a finer layer of plaster. After the first layer has begun drying, a second, coarser and thicker layer of plaster is added to make a durable hollow mold suitable for making several copies of the death mask from such materials as plaster of Paris, wax, and even bronze.

Once finished, Manon's face would likely have been cleaned of any plaster residue as well as that which had dripped under the headband that pulled back her hair. This last procedure, however, was not necessary for her body. She may have been left as she was, looking as white as a ghost, as though once more covered in the thick makeup she had to wear in life.

While the plaster mold dried, Anna surely would have examined it for any flaws as well as the astonishing details that could be seen inside the cast, such as the hairs of Manon's lashes, her lips, the nose she inherited from her father (still showing the softness of having been broken), the slightly raised right eyebrow that added a little irony to her features, and the string of pearls that had been clasped around the dead young woman's neck. The impression, this strange collaboration of the living sister and the dead, turned out well—well enough that Anna would later make casts of Alban Berg, Werfel, Arnold Schoenberg, and her mother among others.

Despite the great awe, love, reverence, and work on the part of her sister, Manon's mask suffered an ignominious fate. After Alma went into exile following the Nazi annexation of Austria in March 1938, it was found in a cardboard box inside Villa Mahler's garden shed.

Werfel was likely the one to deal with the legal formalities of Manon's death, if a scene from *Embezzled Heaven* owes to real experience. Like Alma, the mother of the dead boy in the novel is too distraught and so it falls upon Werfel's character, the permanent guest, to help the attending physician fill out the death certificate—a "slightly gruesome" interaction due to its "correct professional manner."[12]

Manon's death certificate—*Totenbeschau-Befund*—still bears the one-shilling tax stamp and lists some curious details in addition to the cause of death, which lacks the musical name, like the title of a Latin hymn, which Hollnsteiner used—"acute intestinal paresis, gastro-enteritis." It further reveals that men representing the undertaking firm of Payer, Schmutzer, & Co. had arrived a little after six o'clock in the evening. They brought with them a double-sealed zinc casket, in which Manon's body was placed. She would not be embalmed. Given Vienna's stringent health regulations, the casket would have to be quickly soldered shut, for the corpses of polio victims were still considered contagious. Despite this seeming indignity, for the vocation of the deceased, Manon is described as a "Student" and below that a clarification. She is listed as an "Architect's daughter"—a detail that might have given her father some grim satisfaction.[13]

By late Tuesday, April 23, Gropius had at last arrived in Berlin. Meanwhile, Manon's obituaries began to appear in Vienna's newspapers. Not only did they provide the time and location of her funeral, they also added poignant details. The *Neue Freie Presse* reported that "[Manon Gropius] had been on the road to recovery when an unexpected relapse appeared and snatched her away," and that she "through her grace and beauty, enjoys the sympathy of all."[14] The *Neue Wiener Journal* christened the architect's daughter with a hyphenated name indicative of her social and legal status, that she was a "writer's daughter" too: Manon Gropius-Werfel. The author of this notice wrote more

---

12 Werfel, *Embezzled Heaven*, p. 113.

13 Totenbeschau [Coroner's Report], Manon Gropius, April 22, 1935, Gerichtsregister [Court Register] 16 Cg/1936, WSA.

14 "Eine Tochter Alma Mahler-Werfel gestorben" [A daughter of Alma Mahler-Werfel dead], *Neue Freie Presse,* April 23, 1935, p. 2.

elegiacally and betrayed his personal knowledge of the deceased. "A young person's life has been extinguished," he began. "Manon Gropius was, despite her long and difficult illness, which she bore with exemplary spirit and cheer for one so young, the sun of the Mahler-Werfel home. Her room, a flower garden summer and winter, testified to the love and adoration that this young creature received. She was so beautiful in mind and body, she is gone from us as well. Nevertheless, the countless people who loved her will always remain bound to her."[15]

If the obituary writer meant the impressive number of mourners, many not "bound" to Manon in life, so to speak, in a real sense, they filled the presbytery of the parish church of St. Michael on the morning of Wednesday, April 24. As they signed the registry and filed past Manon's body, they would have been disappointed to see that she did not "lie in state" on the catafalque, surrounded by wreaths and bouquets. The closed coffin hardly impeded the imagination of one mourner. This person shared a verse with the family in which he (more so than *she*) imagined Manon to be an ageless innocent, creature, immune from the "cruel, wild world / With [its] thousand mortifications, torments, wounds" to disfigure her "sweet face [. . .] walking beautiful and young / To where she radiantly flowers forever."[16]

Elias Canetti devotes another entire chapter in *The Play of the Eyes* to this event, its star attraction, and her mourners.[17] "Here again," he began, "every last possibility [. . .] was exploited. All Vienna was there, or at least everyone eligible to be received on Hohe Warte. Others came who longed to be invited but never were; you couldn't keep anyone away from a funeral by force." Erich Cyhlar struck Canetti as the picture of debonair grief. "[R]eality knows no justice," Canetti wrote, "and it was

15 "Manon Gropius-Werfel gestorben" [Manon Gropius-Werfel dead], *Neues Wiener Journal,* April 24, 1935, p. 9.

16 "Let her sleep," undated [April–May 1935], ÖNB.

17 Canetti, "The Funeral of an Angel," in *The Play of the Eyes*, pp. 199ff.

the impeccably dinner-jacketed secretary who followed the funeral service leaning on a column in the Heiligenstadt Church. That was the end of his engagement to Manon Gropius; she died as had been foreseen and instead of a wedding he had to content himself with a funeral."

After the church service, a hearse took Manon's body to Grinzinger Friedhof, one of Vienna's most beautiful suburban cemeteries, where she would be buried in a plot Alma had intended for herself. In a taxicab, Canetti followed the long cortege, accompanied by his wife Veza, Fritz Wotruba, and his wife Marian. Both couples were simply curious, albeit the Wotrubas needed to win Alma's favor with their presence for a proposed Gustav Mahler memorial. Desperate to get a look at Alma, Canetti swore at the driver to hurry. "A long line of cars filed up the narrow road to the cemetery," he continued, "no matter how frantic the passengers of a car might be for a place of honor, passing was unthinkable. In unchanging order, the long file struggled up the hill."

Canetti and his party followed the procession to the grave, pressing themselves through the other mourners to get a full view of the Mahler-Werfel family, and the last rites, and within earshot of the priest's eulogy, with an altar boy holding a long crucifix beside him—the boy Rietenauer, afraid that the press of all the people at his back might push him into Manon's open grave. They had all turned out "for the angel," Canetti wrote, "who was beyond the reach of Hollnsteiner's unction." Incredibly, Canetti saw Alma as the very picture of a "grieving mother," weeping tears "of unusual size," which matched her "enormous pearls, priceless jewels." He gasped at how she of all people personified mother love so perversely. "True, the child, as Hollnsteiner eloquently pointed out, had borne her sufferings with superhuman patience," Canetti observed.

To him the funeral was little more than a celebration of "the sufferings of the mother, who had lived through her ordeal before the eyes of the whole world, which had been kept constantly informed. Meanwhile all sorts of things had been happening in the world, other mothers had been killed, their children had starved to death, but none had suffered what this woman had suffered, she had suffered for each and all, she had not faltered, even now at the graveside she stood firm, a voluptuous but aging penitent, a Magdalen rather than a Mary, equipped with swollen tears rather than contrition, magnificent specimens such as no painter had yet produced. With every word of her orating lover, they went on gushing until at length they festooned her fat cheeks like clusters of grapes. That was how she wanted to be seen, and that was how she was seen. And all those present were at pains to be seen by her. That's what they had come for, to give her grief the public recognition it deserved." To Canetti, Manon's funeral and Alma's presence would be "one of Vienna's last great days before it staggered to its doom," before its Nazi masters "turned it into a province."

As everyone wandered away from the grave now piled high with wreaths and flowers, which would have to stand in until the family paid for a monument, Canetti overheard some "charming sentences" from one passerby that seemed to capture the bathos of Manon's funeral. "I lost it at the cemetery," she said to her companion. "I cannot just ask the gravedigger: can you look for my lipstick."

The great and small details Canetti provides are incredible and convincing. There is, however, the possibility that he was not there, too, that everything he writes is second-hand reportage. Even so, if the above is a personal interpretation of events from hindsight, with as many adumbrations as facts and factoids, that he chose to write about Manon and her funeral as a signature event of a Vienna, an Austria, a small world about to end as valuable as anything an eyewitness can say. That he may not have been there, that he "overshot the mark," as Oliver Hilmes writes, is evinced by Canetti's target, Alma's presence. She did not attend her daughter's requiem mass and burial. She still had her abhorrence of funerals and remained in seclusion back at Villa Mahler, waiting for Sister Ida and Werfel to bring her the details "second hand," as she preferred to hear them.

Not only did Manon's mother not attend her funeral and burial. Her father was absent too. He needed only a day more to get a visa and appealed to Alma to delay the burial. However, Gropius received no reply until Hollnsteiner's letter of April 25, written the day after, found him. This may have been weeks later—after the Gropiuses had returned to London without ever setting foot in Austria.

"Given the cause of death, medical and health department requirements stipulated carrying out the burial as quickly possible," the priest wrote with his usual *Takt*—to which he added some bitter salt of his own or for Alma. Although Gropius' wishes were "taken very much into consideration," they could not be honored. The date and place of the funeral had been published in the newspapers. "Thus," the priest continued, "the importance and meaning of your coming to Vienna went unrealized. I know that Manon had always secretly counted on a reprise visit from you. She definitely looked forward to your visit after that theater conference in Rome, which Werfel and Frau Alma did not attend because of her [Manon's] life-threatening pneumonia. For her even a spontaneous visit meant such joy, even though your work must have prevented it. Your coming to the funeral would have given you such relief from longing for your child after visiting her was no longer possible for you."

Gropius had also asked that a proper family obituary be printed—the kind with the heavy black rule around it—which would have named her father. But this request too was ignored. According to Hollnsteiner, the Viennese newspapers had already informed everyone about Manon and "a private notice would have been pointless and people would have disregarded it." That said, the priest assured Gropius that his daughter's coffin and grave had been decked "with flowers and love for her final journey" and that "all" of Vienna had turned out as if for a state funeral save for the absence of the federal chancellor, who had personally called to "get information about the inconceivable truth."

Two days after Manon's funeral, Werfel ventured into her room and picked up her New Testament, with those watchwords on the flyleaf—"Walk worthy of the gospel of Christ." That she lost the ability to walk at all was an irony that Werfel left uncommented. He did, however, add to the half-title page, writing the answer to a question someone might ask. "This New Testament belonged to our beloved Mutzili," he wrote and dated "On the Friday after her death, on the most painful Friday of my life until now, F.W."

That pain, on the part of her stepfather and her mother, had to be reconciled with facing the condolences of others who knew Manon. Carl Zuckmayer spent part of his Sunday writing a long letter to Werfel. He had not been able to attend the funeral and had only learned the news over the weekend. "Seldom in my life has the death of a person come as close to me as this one," he began. "I knew her barely half a year—and saw her only a few times. But to me it's like something irretrievable has disappeared from my life." He added that the day before, Sunday, had been his youngest daughter's first communion and that there had been a festive mood and joy in the house. Even so, he ended the day in his room, tired, alone, and thinking about Muzi." He saw her now in terms of light. He did not ascribe to the fashionable ideas about death that atheists, theosophists, and the like did. "The older I get the less I understand why there are people who do not believe in the immortality of the soul! [. . .] I can see no plant, no flower growing this spring without thinking about Muzi and sending my thoughts to her. [. . .] I see this face and this lovely sorrowful form unlosable before me—and her arrival into this unseen state and ever-presence would almost seem to me an expression of secret beauty and perfection."[18]

Zuckmayer also tried to comfort Alma in the same way, writing an elegy— an "imperfect requiem" as he called it—in which he imagined the funeral that he could not attend, one where Manon's soul as a breeze, drifting like the clouds, that made the heads of the mourners bow like leaves. He imagined, too, Manon's body as a "root" that would rise up and walk from "the pall and smell of graves" in a matter of time, as though the world would come to an end faster and for her.[19]

Ludwig Karpath did not want to see Manon forgotten either—and by the public who would be denied having the chance to see her talent. Rather than write a concert review in the *Wiener Sonn- und Montags-Zeitung* on Monday, Karpath wrote a necrology in which Manon's death was the "final act of a tragedy."

Having known Alma since Gustav Mahler courted her, the old musicologist was the first to please her in print and rehabilitate the teenage nonentity whom Werfel saw before the polio year. Karpath, ironically, saw another kind of nonentity given trite phrases as "a simple, unaffected creature," "a young fir, with stunning beauty, talent, a modest demeanor," "this innocence and purity of perception." Inadvertently, Karpath has also denied Manon reality, which is the occupational hazard of thinking about her and a *raison d'être* for her. But, at least, in saying that she "walked like an angel among us," he remembered that her feet touched the ground.

Karpath knew of another angel, too, the one Manon could not be, would never be. He thought his readers would be impressed that she

18 Carl Zuckmayer to Franz Werfel, April 28, 1935 in Wagener, Hans (ed.), "Alice und Carl Zuckmayer—Alma und Franz Werfel: Briefwechsel [Correspondence],", *Zuckmayer-Jahrbuch*, VOL. 6 (Göttingen: Wallstein-Verlag, 2003), pp. 108–11. "Muzi" is a variant spelling that lacks the silent *t*.

19 Zuckmayer, "An Alma M," undated [*c*.late April 1935], MWP.

had been picked out by Max Reinhardt, that the director wanted to "engage Manon as an actress without any training in drama school." But that "the Werfels would not allow, even though they agreed that Manon was destined for the theater." Thus, did Karpath let on, without intending anything by it to those same "worldly" readers—at least to those who knew that Reinhardt was now in Hollywood making a motion picture—that Alma and Werfel were stupid if not cruel. Nevertheless, Karpath did not lack for pathos. "In bed or in an armchair," Karpath recalled, "Manon busied herself enthusiastically, unceasingly with studying her roles, learning them, happily holding on to the belief that in this life she would step out onstage." [20]

The Uncanny Beatification

Ludwig Karpath was not the only one to write at length about Manon in this way. In November, Franz Horch published "Der Tod und das Mädchen" (Death and the Maiden)—the title taken from the Schubert song—in an unusual venue far from Villa Mahler and Vienna, the illustrated "alpine" monthly *Bergland.* This journal was more often devoted to Tyrolean life, but here Horch had written a "*Paraphrase*" about the life and death of Manon Gropius, a "harrowing psychological portrait" (*erschütternden Seelenbild*). The essay seems to have been placed where it might go unnoticed by Manon's immediate survivors, notably Alma and Werfel, the latter going unmentioned, which suggests Horch's *appropriation* of Manon as "an idea," while her father is only mentioned in an endnote and misnamed "Otto Gropius."

Horch had given Manon a great deal of thought from those times when he "wandered home" from seeing her as "an image of humanity

---

20 Ludwig Karpath, "Manon Gropius: Ein Wort des Gedenkens" [Manon Gropius: A Word of Remembrance], *Wiener Sonn- und Montags-Zeitung,* April 29, 1935, p. 9, ANNO.

that doesn't leave someone."[21] Not unlike Werfel, he saw her like a young martyr, as a girl the ancient Greek sculptors would choose as the model for "the incarnation of a young goddess," an object of veneration, an "Olympian protectress," a "young princess," a poetic figure of virginity (*Mädchentum*) out of Rilke's poetry who spoke from a "sphere not of this earth," and so on. Yet, to Horch, Manon was still very human, more human than others close to her saw. She knew she was going to die, knew that she was a "marked woman and a figure of pity," and had superhumanly, despite the greatest pain and mortifying bodily discomfort and appearance, still played the part of herself. To her drama teacher, she was simply an extraordinary student if not a serious artist, this "barely eighteen-year-old girl [who] worked, especially in the last year of her life, as though she were cut from one of Kriehuber images," an allusion to Josef Kriehuber, the Austrian painter and lithographer noted for his portraits of Austria's cultural elite during the Romantic Era. To Horch, she was already transfigured in life, "the image of an angel making the case for words of comfort. It wanted to know nothing of powerlessness and despair"—those states her mother assumed for herself.

"We are all still crushed—I don't think we can ever recover from this blow," Alma wrote Gropius on June 19, nearly two months after their daughter's death. "You would have experienced a great joy—despite all the difficulties if you had just come more often!—I cabled you about Manon's life-threatening illness (a year ago) and you did not come [. . .]. This angel of quality—this utterly beautiful creature—this spirit—which woke in her—we will never have that happiness again, to be allowed to look after her! I thank you for as long as I live for the privilege of bringing her into the world even if her journey was cut so short. I sincerely beg you to write me."

---

21 All quotations are from Horch, "Der Tod und Das Mädchen" [Death and the Maiden].

Alma made this request for she by now apprehended that the Gropiuses had not only been insulted by the funeral arrangements but uninformed. "I know of no cable from Alma indicating that the hurried interment was a government regulation for cases of the dreaded polio," Ise wrote in 1974, in the margin of the manuscript of her husband's biography, for its author had to present Gropius as a human being and caring father despite seeing his paralyzed daughter but once during her illness, failing to attend her funeral, or visit her grave.[22] The photograph that illustrates Gropius during this period in his life made the choice of words crucial. It was taken at a garden cocktail party back in London for his fifty-third birthday, given less than a month later, on May 18. Gropius is depicted smoking, conversing, and seemingly unaffected by the death of his only child. He looks the part of a man who has already moved on with his life and work. "The news that the beloved daughter was no longer alive had crushed him, every hope he had for a happier future for his child was destroyed. The pain rooted deep and came back to life with all its original sharpness whenever he thought of Manon."[23]

"Anger and discord have come between our respect for one another," Alma continued. "Therefore you can't hold it against me that the laws are strictly enforced here—and I recite the many reasons myself—what must have stopped you—from coming immediately when we told you about this deadly illness—Mutzi lives on with us. Her room is untouched. Her pictures surround me—Anna has made a death mask—we all want her kept alive—for us and others."[24] Even so, Alma soon departed for a long vacation in Italy to get away from the atmosphere of death in Villa Mahler.

---

22 Ise Gropius to Reginald Isaacs, editorial comment, August 1974, in *Walter Gropius: The Man and his Work*, msp. II-B-80-Mar 77, RIP.

23 Isaacs, *Walter Gropius*, VOL. 2, p. 740.

24 Alma Mahler-Werfel to Walter Gropius, June 19, 1935, quoted in Isaacs, *Walter Gropius*, VOL. 2, pp. 740–1.

The untouched room, the photographs, and death mask were not enough for Werfel. He had gone with Alma to Italy in early July and while in Venice—and in the nearby countryside—imagined the setting for his next novel, in which he would remake Manon's childhood into the life of a Paduan saint, Miranda of Monselice. Such a book might assuage the grief of her mother, which had taken a morbid course. Later that summer, while on Semmering, he imagined, too, his stepdaughter's presence there, the way she haunted her room in Haus Mahler, a time capsule of possessions, toys, costumes, and the like. Upstairs in his loft, he began with a dedication to her, writing in bold letters, "Stepdaughter/Alma Manon," to which he added her lifespan as it might appear on her nonexistent gravestone, still marked by a mound of dead flowers and wreaths. "Death has snatched you from us," he wrote beneath it. "Since then we go through the house and through life like invalids, half-paralyzed. What a heartbreaking effort it is to unlock the door and enter the room in which you are no longer there."[25] Much as he began with his story of the orphans at the beginning of *The Forty Days of Musa Dagh*, Werfel wished to express his impetus for the story to follow, one that would be far more obviously personal. The working title was *Legenden—Legends*—which, when used to describe the events in a saint's life, are a matter of faith to a Catholic sensibility.

"We happily gather the legacy of your girlish, everyday life and immortalize even the most transitory objects that you loved, which survive you," he wrote of the reliquary Manon's room had become. "We immerse ourselves again and again into your likenesses, into the all too few photographs that we have of you. Greedily our eyes seize on any trace of your real grace so as to catch some glimmer of your real smile—

25 This and subsequent quotations are translated from the original manuscript of *Legdenden*, FWP; and Franz Werfel, "Legenden—Skizzen" [Legends—Sketches], in *Zwischen Oben und Unten: Prosa, Tagebücher, Aphorismen, Literarische Nachträge* [Between Above and Below: Prose, Diaries, Aphorisms, Literary Addenda] (Munich–Vienna: Langen Müller, 1975), pp. 760ff.

but you pull back from us in your replicas with that superior aversion that the dead have. I don't want to lose you. I do not want some soothing paleness to be spun about you, the kind mourning so often longs for, which covers up the figure of the deceased and with it, mercifully, the pain. I do not want you—oh Eternal One—to shrink faraway into your unchangeable place as my life's journey rushes on. I want to be with you and by you."

Werfel's declamatory voice almost proposed a metaphysical marriage as well as a mission to return the revenant Manon to the world above—knowing well the myth of Eurydice, whose reluctance he could quote from one of his own poems, "I cannot, friend, take hold of your hand."[26] Manon's shade, however, would be Werfel's collaborator, a ghostly actress in his fiction's theater. "And so I will now write this work and carefully attempt to recreate *some things about the secret lives of God's blessed creatures* only during these days of summer, these days of summer without you [. . .]. Perhaps you will, with these appearances I awaken in my room, enter and stand behind me. I will hear your voice. That clear pureness of your spirit acquired through pain, which over death, will speak inside me, into the most inner ear of my own spirit. May it not suffer lies that persuade against establishing the truth."

"Eternal One" was not the only divine appellation Werfel gave to Manon. Miranda of Monselice would have two more. In the first part of the novel, she would be a kind of female aspect of St. Francis (*Franz* in the German). Werfel, however, could not decide which was best, "The Patroness—or Intercessoress—of the Animals," he wrote on the manuscript. Then he changed it to "Snakes," more in keeping with Manon's regard and interests. The second part was titled "The Intercessoress of the Dead," a legend devoted to a real saint, Christina the Astonishing, who woke from death during her requiem mass and

26 Werfel, "Fragment der Eurydike" [Fragment of Eurydike], *Der Gerichtstag* [Judgment Day], p. 30.

flew up into the rafters of the church before the priest and horrified mourners—a tale that Werfel could further resurrect Manon.

The first chapter of *Legends* begins as a protest against the very problem of publishing such a novel, as though Werfel could already see his publisher rolling his eyes over such an impossible book to sell after *The Forty Days of Musa Dagh.* Werfel's legend of a golden life would be an antidote and antithesis to the "biographical spume" of the bestsellers of the time, the *Legenda tyrannis* that examined "Caesar, Napoleon, Attila, Tamerlane, and whoever else seems popular" to explain the motivations of Adolf Hitler in 1935, still deliberately *unworthy* of being named in Werfel's list of great conquerors. He saw himself as a kind of diver going under the storm-tossed modernity of these books to descend, to immerse himself and those readers who would follow him "into the depths of a holy life"—the story of Miranda of Monselice.

The images of the storm and some refuge from it, and the name Miranda itself, all point to *The Tempest.* But then Werfel turns to a long discussion of stylites or pillar saints—which may seem strange until one considers that Miranda-Manon lived her last year paralyzed on an upper story of Villa Mahler. "Whoever wakes from a blackout or anesthesia apprehends like lightning the inverted path that every pillar saint seeks to expose through their decades-long stillness," Werfel wrote. "A sick person also knows, to the nth degree, that the suffering organ of his body only provisionally belongs to him [. . .]. The body then is not the I. But what is it? The ascetic penetrates the closest layers and scales of existence to press toward being."

St. Miranda, for readers whose attention spans were still absorbed by "fighter squadrons and shortwave" as noted in one of Werfel's redacted sentences, would be a saint like no other—a nonentity, a cipher. "The life of Miranda is no saint's life. She is not visibly transfigured. No miracle attests to her being chosen. The lovely sound of her name, from the Latin for "worthy of admiration" and concocted by

Shakespeare for the daughter of a sorcerer, votes against the possibility of her being canonized. And yet she appears to us as one raised on Franciscan love to be an intermediary between the below and above." Miranda is worthy of veneration to Werfel because "it's as if she had never lived," because hers is a "concealed life!" Rather than against each other for the next world war, humankind should train its "thousand-gunned eyes" on her in the stars, where "the last quiet reigns, the concealed lives, deeds, and mysteries are kept, [. . .] the fate of the universe."

The second chapter begins with a long meditation on the geography and folklore of the Euganean Hills, which jut out "like some formal protest" on the plain of Padua. Werfel catalogues the volcanic geology, hot mud springs, rock lizards, snakes, and amphibians—creatures that came under the protection of Manon—even a poisonous spitting frog, which he likened to the mythological basilisk.

Werfel describes the steam grotto of Battaglia, "that famous miracle cave" where Romans not only went to be healed but to conjure up their dead. The botany of landscape is also given in detail, from the elm and oak groves to the "ghostly asphodels," the flowers of Proserpina. Petrarch spent part of his life in this landscape and he is buried in the town of Arqua, where Werfel introduces the girl Miranda, called a "holy virgin," who walks hand in hand with her chaperone, Verecundia—the Latin word for deference.

It is the 1600s, the Baroque Era, the time of Manon's Venetian costume dress. Miranda's family owns land and a villa near Monselice and a palace in Venice. Her father is Michiel Renier, the owner of vast forests, a wealthy merchant, and a ship owner whose primary client is the Turkish sultan. Messer Renier, however, is a Renaissance man dissipated by his encyclopedic interests and hoarding. "[H]e had been student of the liberal arts in Padua and for a time during his life maintained a correspondence and a personal relationship with a few brilliant names at the university there. But learned specialists sneered at his unregulated zeal. They saw in him a contemplative dilettante of aristocratic absentmindedness who had become torn here and there from the criss- and cross-referencing of his changing inclinations and curiosities [. . .] a hodgepodge of the valuable and the worthless in the vast rooms and park of the villa [. . .].”

In appearance, Miranda is her father's child, with his fine hands and natural patience. Like Manon, she has the look of an eavesdropper, one listening all the time, but in a way that was lovely, assured, even *ethereal.* Miranda's mother is Madonna Cornelia, clearly drawn from Alma. She is the daughter of artists who keeps a salon and is the authoress of a famous sonnet on the nature of Olympic divinity. “Madonna Cornelia was an impetuous, an even stormy being surrendering to her passion, always possessed by some urgent project or at least by some mood where she stood and walked as this central sun around which a system of admirers of either sex and every color revolved: cavaliers, artists, musicians, gallivants, spies and parasites. [. . .] Cornelia was the force that brought the Villa Renier to life. Her love for antiquity and her predilection for the unusual defined her, often going about broad daylight in a long Greek robe dragging after her. Like some Pallas Athena or Artemis she moved at the head of guests through the rooms and galleries of the house [. . .]. Her golden laughter, her bewitching voice filled the cold, echoing apartments with human warmth and feminine radiance. She left Monselice to reside in Venice during Carnival and other festivals.”

With her self-involved parents of contrasting personalities, Werfel portrays Miranda as a treasured but neglected child. “Madonna Cornelia was not an indifferent mother like other women who cultivate beauty, talent, wealth like some constant aura. As a mother she was, like she was with everything, stormy and impetuous. She was beside herself over the least of Miranda's illnesses. While mixing and laughing her way through a large gathering in Venice, she could suddenly be overtaken by racing fear and anxiety and dispatch a rider during the middle of the night to Monselice or suddenly decide to leave the ballroom and return home."

"Miranda," Werfel continued, borrowing from his years of watching Alma and Manon, "accepted this profusion of motherly love with wild gratitude and at the same time with mortified dread. She sensed in Cornelia a beauty and power to such a superhuman degree that she could never measure up to it in the least. When she was old enough to compare for herself, she would torture herself with the thought that nothing of her mother's brightness would be passed on to her."

Werfel intended *Legends* to include the history of St. Christina the Astonishing, the twelfth-century Belgian saint who "behaved in a terrifying manner" as it was said to avoid the stench of sinful people through levitation, hiding in bread ovens, and jumping into the frozen River Meuse. But he offered no clues for pairing the most anti-social saint with—what—the shyest? Werfel surely wanted in Miranda the dead Manon assuming a higher purpose, a sublimated role "far removed" from her conceited parents. "Miranda was full of this hidden constancy," Werfel wrote before abandoning the novel. "Her soul possessed this drive, a way to consistently go to the end. As she grew bigger, by reason of this inner virtue she struck many as cold and superior. But it is not yet the time for adolescence. She is just shy of her eleventh year."

Werfel left *Legends* unfinished. One night, a year later, before going to bed, he looked with this "uneasy feeling [. . .] of having before me a painful episode of doing nothing. I thought about the *Legends* that I had promised to write [. . .] of which two chapters exist, I flew through slapdash. This is a terrible admission for me to make, the incidents for that legend, as I understand them, have virtually disappeared from memory [when] there had been something pathological about the intent 'to immortalize' the loss and beloved figure of Mutzi so soon."[27] Then, too, Werfel may have realized that he was disclosing too much about his family life, of things thinly disguised, poorly digested, or things Alma would disapprove of. Also, such a personal book, no matter how he cast it, would not have had the desired polemical effect on his readership, especially given the dire situation of the German Jews, the Nuremberg Laws, and what he felt was necessary given his stature as one of Europe's leading Jewish authors. Nevertheless, on the first anniversary of Manon's death, Werfel swore not to waste Manon's life. His obsession with her even spilled out, with her name barely disguised, in a 1937 address to the League of Nations ("One evening during a time of great sorrow, when I felt that I could never cease mourning the lost of one dear to me, I chanced into the resplendent opera house of an Italian city. They were playing *Mignon* . . .").[28] The theme of this speech, "Of Man's True Happiness," revealed that art was not for the "killing of time," but for the "killing of death." For Manon's, Werfel was already working toward killing it in another novel.

In 1936–37, he created another character—or *role*— for her in *Höret die Stimme—Harken unto the Voice* (1937, tr. 1938)—a biblical-historical novel about the life of the prophet Jeremiah. Manon is the model for Zenua, a young, pagan Egyptian woman who is the short-lived Jewish bride of the prophet Jeremiah. The novel, which is virtually a straight adaptation from the Old Testament, begins in the present with their reincarnations and the *eternal recurrence*, *déjà vu*, and "picture-ether." That is, *akâsha,* Sanskrit for how light records everything that it falls upon, which Werfel borrowed from Theosophy and spiritualism.

27 Werfel, "Legenden—Skizzen," pp. 773–4.
28 Werfel, "Of Man's True Happiness" [*Von der reinsten Glücklseligkeit des Menschen*] in *Between Heaven and Earth* [*Zwischen oben und unten*] (Maxim Newmark trans.) (New York: Philosophical Library, 1944), p. 13.

Fixed in this picture-ether is the writer Clayton Reeves and his young wife, the late Leonora, who died of a strange disease while touring Egypt. The episode is derived from Manon's insistence on going to Venice in March 1934. "Why did Leonora suddenly have that morbid desire to travel?" Reeves asks himself. "She said that if she could not go she would get ill. [. . .] I who am usually so fond of travel, why did I at the time have such an evil foreboding that kept on warning me? Why did I fight down the warnings instead of resisting her desire? And when Leonora took a capricious fancy to live in that Arab house by the water, why did I not simply say no?"[29]

Reeves is Werfel's alter ego and this makes the prophet Jeremiah an alter ego, too. In this way, Werfel and his stepdaughter would perform on the stage of this novel *intime,* as lovers! Like Bagradian and Iskuhi in *The Forty Days of Musa Dagh*, the October–April relationship in *Harken unto the Voice* would be chaste, but not lack in passion for the general reader. Nor would the novel lack in the avenues of speculation that Werfel's family, friends, and *enemies* might read into it, including Germany's Nazi book critics and literati who could point out Werfel's obvious decadence. This was a strange, undercutting risk to take—like the one taken in *Musa Dagh* vis-à-vis its mission about uncovering the Armenian genocide and warning of the same dangers that faced Europe's Jews—a warning now reprised in *Harken unto the Voice.*

Evidently, Werfel could rely on the love interest between Zenua and Jeremiah being passed over in silence and was left mostly intact for the English translation. "The whole conception of Jeremiah is almost literally Werfel's conception of his own mission," wrote Adolf Klarmann, the foremost Werfel scholar and his literary executor, to

29 Werfel, *Harken unto the Voice* [*Höret die Stimme*], (Moray Firth trans.) (New York: Viking, 1938), p. 28. In the German text, the Reeves character is named Clayton *Jeeves*—which English readers associated with books and films featuring P. G. Wodehouse's Jeeves the butler.

Ben Huebsch of Viking Press. "Certain incidents occurring in the life of the prophet correspond strikingly to events in Werfel's own life. The death of Mrs. Werfel's daughter plays an extraordinary part in the book, down to the very details of her fatal illness."[30] That part is mostly set in the chapters that comprise Jeremiah's exile in Egypt with the royal family of his patron, the late King Josiah of Israel.

Manon's character is introduced by her Egyptian name, Ha-rekhni.[31] She is a high-born orphan and ward of the Kher-heb, the Master of Ceremonies of Death, who presents her to the widowed Queen Hamutal to serve as her lady in waiting. Ha-rekhni can understand spoken Hebrew. Although her father was an Egyptian official, her mother was Jewish—and thus Ha-rekhni is attracted to the religious lessons that Jeremiah conducts for the queen mother's youngest son and his Ethiopian companion (whose twitching body movements and "dancing" are modeled after Georg, the Weinzinger family's ward). Werfel, who had tutored Manon in her acting and in other subjects, portrays her in Ha-rekhni as a wise child, with a range of facial expressions, tossed long hair, and gestures that are, presumably, Manon's. Like a priestess, she is fluent in the polytheism of ancient Egypt, but wishes to add the Jewish God to her pantheon and make him supreme, in part because she sees the face of that god in Jeremiah. Willingly, Jeremiah cultivates her desire, despite what would have been blasphemous to a Jewish prophet—her syncretic nature and her virtual deification of her spiritual mentor. Wanting to reclaim this lost Jewish girl with a lost Jewish name, Jeremiah gives her a new one—Zenua—which means *chaste* in Hebrew.

Soon the pair fall in love. The Kher-heb gives his permission for their marriage, but with a dire warning about changing one's faith.

---

30 Adolf Klarmann to Ben Huebsch, March 2, 1938, MWP.

31 In the German text, her name is He-Nut-Dime. The hieroglyph, a serpent, means mistress (Hnwt) and joined or married (dmA/dmi).

Jeremiah, too, knows that he is violating his role as a prophet of God if he takes a wife. And Zenua suffers an ominous vision of being transformed into a rigid pillar, the pillar of Osiris—which is realized when she falls ill on the eve of the wedding. Her paralysis, suffering, and death are a composite of what Manon suffered in April 1934 and 1935—none of this is wasted, even the pain Manon felt on being touched.

Heartbroken, Jeremiah goes to the temple where Zenua's body has been taken by the Kher-heb for the funerary rites that will allow her soul, in accordance with the Egyptian Book of the Dead, to enter Amenti, the land of the dead. The Jewish prophet is willing to sin, to follow her into a pagan underworld, to go through the trials her reborn soul experiences. In this, he is hardly dissuaded by the sobering sight of Zenua's mummified body and its "mask of wax or yellowish plaster" laid over her face not unlike the cast Anna Mahler used to capture her dead sister's features. "The most dreadful thing" about Zenua's cartonnage portrait is "the long streaks of soft dark hair which flowed out from behind the mask." But Werfel drew more than just these surface details from real life. He also borrowed from an obsession with Manon Gropius that changes everything about his work and motivations.

Jeremiah's journey into Amenti is experienced lying in a small room and in a drug-induced—even psychedelic—hallucination under the guidance of the Kher-heb. The prophet is assailed by horrific visions and shape-shifting monsters of the Egyptian afterlife. The Amenti chapter in *Harken unto the Voice* is an incredible piece of writing that has seen some scholarship. According to one Werfel scholar, Werfel created a virtual representation of psychoanalysis, "complete with a couch!" And the Kher-heb "is an analyst after Werfel's own heart."[32] However, who is at the center of Werfel's heart here—Manon Gropius—goes unnoticed or *judiciously* uncommented, for it would alter (compromise?) what other critics have written about *Harken*

32 Michel Reffet, "Werfel and Psychoanalysis" in Lothar Herber (ed.), *Franz Werfel: An Austrian Writer Reassessed*, (Oxford: Berg, 1989), p. 117.

unto the Voice, most recently as the "cornerstone of his Jewish identity and at the same time a reaction to the anti-Semitism of his wife 'that may have been boundless.'"[33] This observation takes on a special poignancy if one considers that Werfel, by reimagining Manon as Zenua, had appropriated her. She is no longer Alma's Aryan daughter, but what the Nazis called a *Mischling*, a mixed-race creature. She is also redeemed, saved as a Jewish saint, for the Amenti chapter ends with Jeremiah seeing an angel of God lifting Zenua from the underworld and intoning "Behold, this is Zenua Nephesh Hagoim, the chaste soul of the nations, who will remain in the place reserved for her until the time shall come. . . ."[34]

The *Anschluss*, Nazi Germany's annexation of Austria in March–April 1938, set in motion drastic changes in the lives of everyone Manon had known in life. Many saw this eventuality coming and had already emigrated, among them Julius Tandler, who died in the Soviet Union in August 1936. For the over 185,000 Jews still living in Austria, the vast majority residing in Vienna, it meant a sudden shift from relative security and safety—albeit with increasing forms of discrimination—to persecution and certain arrest. The doctor who brought Manon into the world, Wilhelm Knöpfelmacher, rather than be forced to wash the patriotic Austrian graffiti from the sidewalks, took his own life with an overdose of morphine. (Another admirer of Manon, Arnold Berliner, would also take poison in 1942 rather than be sent to Theresienstadt.)

---

33 Wolfgang Treitler, "Shma Yisrael: The Prophet Jeremiah in *Höret die Stimme*," in Weiss, Hillel, Roman Katsman, and Ber Kotlerman (eds), *Around the Point: Studies in Jewish Literature and Culture in Multiple Languages* (Newcastle upon Tyne: Cambridge Scholars), p. 350.

34 In a later chapter, Jeremiah is cast into a sewer pit to die. As night falls, the stench of the cesspool is replaced by the smell of incense and Zenua's appears to him as a swallow (the hieroglyph and symbol of the soul in the Book of the Dead) to comfort him and warn him of the coming destruction of Jerusalem.

Erich Cyhlar had overcome his grief for his presumptive bride, evinced by the photograph of the smiling young man in the company of Adolph Loewi and his two daughters on a boat ride off the Lido in September 1936. As a member of Austria's former government and fascist party, which had long bitterly opposed the Nazis, he would be forced into exile in Buenos Aires, from where he sought Werfel's influence in getting a newspaper writing job in the German-language exile press.

Another admirer of Manon who left Austria after *Anschluss* was Franz Horch. He arrived in New York City and founded a literary agency that specialized in the work of such prominent exile writers as Thomas Mann and his brother Heinrich and Werfel among others. He also represented a number of American writers, ranging from Edna Ferber to, incredibly, the pulp fiction novelist Jim Thompson. Working with the latter author reveals how far removed from Manon's world Horch's new life was. Unfortunately, he died at the age of fifty in 1951, but the agency he founded would survive him into the 1990s.

Young Erich Rietenauer remained close to Manon's maternal grandmother, Anna Moll, until she died in November 1938, as her husband Carl Moll, daughter Maria, and son-in-law joined the Nazi Party. (All three committed suicide during the Soviet siege of Vienna in 1945.) The "Burschi," like many young Austrian males of his generation, was eventually drafted into the German Army in 1942. He served as a radio operator on the Italian front, survived the war—and remained haunted by Manon. When American "culture" arrived in occupied Vienna, it took the form of such films as Walt Disney's *Snow White and the Seven Dwarves* (1937). Seeing a tall Snow White plant a kiss on a dwarf's cheek, reminded Rietenauer of a like kiss from Manon that may have been wishful thinking.[35] Later in the postwar years,

35 Despite Rietenauer's penchant for getting names and other facts wrong—he calls Dopey, Bashful, Grumpy, whoever, "Klopfer," which is the German translation of Thumper in Disney's *Bambi*—again, even if some of what he writes is fiction,

Rietenauer was reunited with Sister Ida, who had remained in Vienna and continued to serve as Alma's servant and representative. Her motivation was not only loyalty, but in part to dictate a book she hoped to write about her mistress and her charge, Manon, with Rietenauer's help. His fifty notebooks, however, largely based on Sister Ida's recollections were lost upon her death in 1977, thrown out with the trash.

Father Hollnsteiner left the priesthood and married. Although he had to give up his teaching duties, he returned to his monastery, Stift St. Florian, and became the curator of its library's special collection. As Herr Hollnsteiner, the former priest would lead a quiet and uneventful life until the arrival of Adolf Hitler and his entourage in April 1943. Hollnsteiner personally conducted the Fuhrer, a "Bruckner monomaniac" and let him see and touch manuscripts from the library's extensive collection of Brucknerianа—which still lacked the Third Symphony, for Alma's maladroit attempts to sell it and her Hohe Warte mansion as a package deal to the Nazis fell through.

Susi Kertész would become an actress in Switzerland, marry, give birth to a son, and die with her husband in a railroad-crossing accident in 1946. But well before that tragedy, Susi joined Alma and Werfel in exile. For a time, she lived with them in the town of Sanary in the south of France from 1939 to 1940, where she filled some of the void left by the dead Manon and became Alma's surrogate daughter.

Life was perilous for all three. Susi and Werfel were Jews. Werfel was recuperating from a heart attack. Alma had stepped up as their protector, for she still carried her pistol. Fearing it might be confiscated, however, she and Susi buried the gun under a tree, only to succumb to the fear that the roots would push the incriminating firearm to the surface. So, in the early morning, wearing only their nightgowns, they exhumed the gun. And on another occasion, Werfel was nearly arrested

---

his seeing Manon as Snow White makes certain accidental allusions as Alban Berg's Violin Concerto makes the intended.

for being a German spy. He had been accused of sending signals with a flashlight used to retrieve a manuscript from the medieval watchtower where he worked on new novels indeed, those with new "roles" for Manon to play in his fiction.

These characters *amount* to a kind of séance—one far from the real séances Werfel knew back in Prague with Max Brod and Franz Kafka. It is the occult hiding in plain sight that is more revealing of Werfel's faith of vacillation between Judaism and Catholicism and more in keeping with *Mother Right* and the arcanum learned from Otto Gross. As noted earlier, Manon's life and death—and promise—are found in the first part of Werfel's 1938 novel *Embezzled Heaven*, not only as the minor character Doris, an aspiring singer, but also as her brother. Manon is also the inspiration for the half-Jewish piano prodigy Cella Bodenheim in the unfinished trilogy *Krankheit, die zum Leben führt* (An Illness That Leads to Life, 1938), of which there is only a long fragment of the first part (published in translation as *Cella, or the Survivors*), most of it devoted to the events of the *Anschluss* and the imprisonment of Cella's father. Werfel planned on Cella playing a more central role in the rest of the book, leading up to her appearance in Carnegie Hall. It would have been a high point in a life not unlike Manon's had she never been stricken with polio, had she fled Austria with Alma and Werfel in 1938—and enjoyed a career as an actress on the American stage or even the Hollywood screen.

Manon's character in Werfel's novella *Pale Blue Ink in a Lady's Hand* (*Eine blaßbläue Frauenschrift*, 1941; translated 2012) is Vera Wormser at three different points in her life: a teenager, a university student, and as a doctor. The hair and eyes are unmistakably taken from Manon, but her personality is less the ingénue and more the person Rietenauer describes, a self-possessed, even tomboyish girl despite her floral-print dresses and waist-length hair. As the highly intelligent daughter of a Jewish physician, Vera becomes the obsession of her brother's home tutor, a colorless young man burdened with the heroic name Leonidas and drawn from the same coterie as Erich Cyhlar. When Leonidas realizes what a mistake it would be to give her roses—she would only laugh at him—he throws the bouquet away in shame. Time passes and the tutor's life undergoes a transformation. While attending the University of Vienna, Leonidas' Jewish roommate shoots himself over the knowledge that Richard Wagner was an anti-Semite, but before he does, he wills his tuxedo to Leonidas. With this suit, and his two redeeming attributes, his good looks and skill as a dancer, Leonidas becomes a lady-killer in the years after the First World War. He eventually marries well and quickly rises in the Ministry of Education as a Section Chief. On a fact-finding mission to the University of Heidelberg, Leonidas is reunited with Vera, now a philosophy student. No longer the shy young tutor, he finds that he can achieve a kind of intellectual rapport with her and, in so doing, begins to seduce her. For several weeks he conducts an affair with her, hiding the fact that he is married and, when they part, he promises Vera that they will marry each other. Instead, Leonidas deserts her and returns to his wife and villa in Vienna.

Many years pass and it is now Leonidas' fiftieth birthday. Among his congratulatory cards is a letter in pale blue ink. It is a letter from Vera, a formal request that Leonidas assist a young Jewish man who can no longer continue his education in Nazi Germany. Leonidas thinks the boy is his son, for Vera had sent him another letter years before, one he did not read but now, given the circumstances, he sees must have been a request for child support. To Leonidas, not only had he deserted Vera, but had they conceived a child. The novella's denouement is a meeting between Leonidas and Vera in a hotel. Once more he brings roses, pale yellow ones, and learns much to his relief that the boy is not his son after all, that Vera is merely his guardian. This revelation also comes as a mild disappointment. Leonidas had wanted a son of his own, for he and his wife are childless. However, when he foolishly admits to having not read Vera's first letter, she at last tells him that, indeed, he had a son by her and that their little boy died during a meningitis epidemic. Then she leaves him and his roses behind in the hotel lounge. The guilt, the wrong is palpable and a further projection of Werfel's obsession with Manon.

In the spring of 1942, Werfel published a long essay, simply titled "Manon," in the Catholic magazine *Commonweal.* He intended it to explain the dedicatory page in his new novel, *The Song of Bernadette* (*Das Lied von Bernadette*). This necrology, from which this text draws various quotations and descriptions, especially in regard to Manon's desire to be an actress, does not suggest that Manon is Bernadette Soubirious or her vision. By making it plain who this "Manon" is, Werfel would seem to be drawing readers away from connecting her in any way to the novel. For some readers, however, even without knowing the backstory of the abortive *Legends*, there are clues. The simplest one to begin with is Bernadette's performance before the grotto, when she is accused of pretending, that is, of being a little actress. Then there is the apparition in the grotto, which Werfel describes as a former pagan shrine, where he knew (as suggested earlier) that the ancient people of the region communed with their dead loved ones in the Underworld. In this way, Werfel establishes the premise that the Lady in White—for that is how Bernadette describes her—is not the Blessed Virgin Mary but someone else. And who? The apparition *performs* in the novel, dressed in her elaborate costume of shimmering robes and golden roses between her toes, up in the grotto, which is her theater. For the author-as-reader, the ultimate pleasure, or rather consolation, may have been his, for *The Song of Bernadette* can be read as Werfel almost openly communing with Manon's spirit. Then there is the subtext of the real, the beatified saint for the canny reader to call up. Bernadette's body in its glass case in the town of Nevers is the young woman who will never decompose, whose wax-coated face surely impressed Werfel with the comforting thought that Manon might be so untouched under the earth in a faraway cemetery in Nazi Austria. Since this required exhumation thousands of miles away, something Werfel never suggested and which Alma would never permit, he did live to see something close to an Incorruptible. And Werfel did not have to make the leap from the uncanny séances of his imagination and necrology to something broaching on necrophilia. He and Alma would get to see another lasting and modern means for incorruptibility—film stock—when they were invited to the studios of 20th Century Fox to meet and advise a young woman with a strong resemblance to Manon, Jennifer Jones, in her role as Bernadette, which won her an Academy Award in 1944.

Manon makes her final appearance in Werfel's posthumously published novel, *Star of the Unborn* (Stern der Ungeborenen, 1946) a parody of a traveler's tale in the spirit of Jonathan Swift's *Gulliver's Travels* and set in the year 101,943, the Year of the Virgin—and in the era of the Astromentals. The Astromentals (which in German sounds vaguely and ironically like "Austrians") are a race of perfected humans who live for centuries. Werfel comes from behind the curtain and plays himself in the novel, denoted by his initials F.W. He also alludes to the *séanceness* of his fiction, too, for he enters the story after his imaginary death in 1943 by means of an advanced form of spiritualism conducted by an Astromental family. Still dressed in the tuxedo he knew Alma would have him wear in his coffin, he is a surprise guest for their daughter, the Astromental beauty and virgin bride Io-La, on the eve of her wedding. At twenty-six, she is the age Manon would have been during most of 1943.

Io-La—who goes by her petname Lala—is responsible for preventing F.W. from going directly to Purgatory. Desiring to meet a man from the past, F.W. is escorted into her bridal chamber, where Lala lays on a bed surrounded by flowers—as Manon laid in her last year. On seeing her, F.W. provides yet another clue for the model, a hint of recognition. "Io-La, the Bride, wore a close-fitting, ebony-black one that imitated the waves and curls of youthful hair in stylized form," F.W. observes. "The color of her face was pale and white. [. . .] Lala's lovely eyes were blue [. . .] But the most significant factor for me was not the girl's beauty [. . .] but rather the fact that Lala's lovely face seemed less strange to me than all other human faces, in fact almost familiar."[36]

Lala, too, is as much impressed by F.W. She fingers his silk swallowtail suit and addresses him by a virile honorific of Greek origin that means both "spear expert" and "violent urge." Desirous of the good fortune Lala believes will come of F.W.'s touch, her great-great-grandmother—or simply "GR3"—exposes Lala's breasts for F.W. " 'Put your hand on my heart, Seigneur,' said Lala with regal indifference. And the Ancestress pulled my hand down with a light but unyielding pressure, as though I were resisting—which I wasn't—and laid it carefully, almost tenderly, between the little bare breasts of the Bride. [. . .] 'Touching the heart was an ancient sacramental custom of certain Islamitic mendicant orders," I said idiotically in a didactic tone."[37]

F.W. examines Lala's hands as well. Not only is her long Astromental lifespan present in the lifeline of her palm, her fingers are unreal, "as smooth and unmarked as those of wax dummies." He also enjoys further physical contact when she chooses him to dance with her in a waltz with other brides. Their flirtation inspires Lala to seek out the Jungle, the last place on earth where humans still live and die and—importantly—have real lives and purpose. She enters F.W.'s bedroom and wakes him in the night. Her association with Manon and her Easter death is also given away by the symbolism of the object Lala holds in the palm of her left hand, a thing "like a large egg," a kind of

36 Franz Werfel, *Star of the Unborn* (Gustave O. Arlt trans.) (New York: Viking, 1946), pp. 153–4.
37 Werfel, *Star of the Unborn*, pp. 163–4.

"boudoir lamp" diffusing "a mild glow about its bearer."[38] Lala informs F.W. of her intention of running away, for her marriage has been spoiled by her fiancé, whose black garb marks him as a parody of an Austrian Fascist or Nazi as does his prized collection of ancient firearms, intended for a revolution against the pacifist order of the Astromentals. In attempting to dissuade her, F.W. is silenced by Lala and her association with Manon Gropius is furthered. "In answer the girl took the ebony black helmet from her head with a strangely resolute gesture and held it above her crown for the space of three breaths. To speak of an abundance of black silky hair would be crude. It was an aura, a halo, an intimation of dark hair that Lala showed me for two seconds. [. . .] I thought the clock had struck 1920 or 1930, I drew Lala into my arms; I kissed her and received her kiss."[39]

F.W. follows Lala to the Jungle, half in love and half as a guardian wanting to bring her to her own kind. But he accepts her emancipation. His last encounter with her in *Star of the Unborn* is Mountaintown, where Lala is a waitress in the Central Beer Parlor, a parody of Vienna's Café Zentral, where Werfel had been a habitué before he met Alma. She wears a strange golden peasant outfit and leather buskins—clearly a theatrical costume. A great peoples' army is headquartered in the town, armed with "psychic artillery," and preparing to retake the world back from the Astromentals. F.W. calls its general "Constantine," after the first Christian Roman emperor but modeled after a Soviet officer, a man of action. Constantine has taken Lala as his war bride and entrusts F.W. with a peace mission.

Lala guides the blindfolded F.W. out of the Jungle. Near the border, she removes his blindfold. They stand before a small baroque village church. She has something to show him, both in the church and about herself. It is a statue of the Virgin Mary wearing the stylized helmet

38 Werfel, *Star of the Unborn,* p. 433.

39 Werfel, *Star of the Unborn,* pp. 438–9.

and dove-gray mantle of Lala as an Astromental bride. Before the statue's downcast eyes, Lala shows F.W. her hands. "Overnight these waxen, rose-tinted palms had developed a few delicate lines and signs and runes which crossed the three main markings and began to fill the former void with touching new life. These few delicate lines woke compassion in my heart like fresh wounds. They were not the stigmata of a saint, they were the stigmata of a real human."[40]

To an Angel

Franz Werfel suffered a fatal heart attack at his writing desk in Beverly Hills in August 1945. One of the last things he laid his eyes on was a framed late photograph of Manon Gropius wearing a white beret. She was a young woman to him by that time, and if one follows the development of her characters in his novels, from Iskuhi, Miranda of Monselice, Zenua, Vera, Bernadette, and Lala, she had devolved into something like herself. Werfel had reconciled himself to her being a discrete person, and let her go—given her back a life—at least in fiction. She was no longer the saint and legend, priestess and virgin, or the "angel" Alban Berg made of her for her mother ten years earlier.

On July 7, 1935, which was Gustav Mahler's seventy-fifth birthday, Alma wrote in her diary that everything seemed full of the dead around her. She longed desperately for Manon. "I cannot continue to live without her," Alma wrote. "She was closest to my heart. Nearer than any person who I loved once. For I love her idea alone, the idea of Mutzi [. . .]. I think only of the manner of my death. I would like to go to Venice—lay down in her poor bed and turn on the gas cocks. Thus can I only go on—always and in others. Hollnsteiner seeks to calm me down . . . Franz wants me happy, but both fail to pull me

40 Werfel, *Star of the Unborn,* p. 472.

away from my fixation on death . . . I love this eternally sweet creature unto death."[41]

Alma saw "Mutzi night and day," as one who was "so present" to her. She found someone to blame, worthy of the insult she took personally. "How terrible God is—if he exists, how abhorrent. He destroyed my continuance in its purest form! For she was my best self [*Ich*], something mixed with a very fine essence from somewhere beyond. But this child, who knew my every thought, indeed, anticipated [them]— this child has been snatched from me. I stand hurting like a beggar." Alma could only take comfort in that Manon no longer suffered "the torments of hell that someone inflicted upon her. She is either a void [*Nichts*] or a blissful creature in her sinlessness."[42]

When Alban Berg learned of Manon's death, he came at once from his cottage "Waldhaus" on the Wörthersee in Carinthia. There is no evidence that he arrived in time for the funeral, but he undoubtedly learned of its every detail and impression from others. (It was during this time that he befriended Elias Canetti.) Since Berg and his wife Helene had long been friends of Alma, and had known Manon from infancy, he wanted to express his condolences to Alma personally. However, he respected her seclusion and recognized that even the mention of her daughter's name would bring pain. "My dearest Almschi," Berg wrote in the note that accompanied a bouquet of flowers, "I do not know when I shall see you again and whether—even in a wordless embrace—I shall ever be able to express what cannot be said. Nor shall I attempt to find words [. . .]. But—one day—even before this terrible year comes to an end, may you and Franz hear in a score dedicated to the memory of an angel what I am feeling at this moment but cannot express."[43]

---

41 Mahler-Werfel, "Diary of Alma Maria", July 7, 1935, p. 296, MWP.

42 Mahler-Werfel, "Diary of Alma Maria", July 30, 1935, p. 297.

43 Alban Berg to Alma Mahler-Werfel, undated [*c.*early May 1935], MWP.

Berg already had a work in mind and in progress—a commission from the American violinist Louis Krasner in February 1935. A young and serious exponent of New Music, Krasner had requested a "sort of songful, emotionally rich concerto," one that "might break down the concert world's opposition to the 12-tone style."[44] Since Krasner now lived in Switzerland and eagerly wanted his project to take priority, his money—$1,500 (over $28,000 today), which went a long way in interwar Austria—prompted Berg to put aside his unfinished opera *Lulu.* Grief made it imperative that he repurpose Krasner's concerto into a requiem for a young woman. The goal was to finish the concerto by August, in time for Alma's birthday.

Berg worked furiously on the concerto during the spring and summer of 1935, often from morning to night, working thirteen hours at a stretch at his piano or desk. He used a golden fountain pen Werfel had given him. In June, Krasner arrived at Waldhaus to play the first movement and to help collaborate on the second. By early July, Berg could report to his friend and former student, Theodor W. Adorno, that the concerto was nearly finished and assured him that work would resume again on the opera—for Adorno considered *Lulu* far more important and worthy of the composer's energy.[45]

Berg saw the first movement of the Violin Concerto, consisting of an andante (prelude) and allegretto (scherzo), as an aural portrait of a young woman in the fullness of life. While the sentimental effect is intended, incorporating the popular belief that a person in his or her last moments remembers a happier time in his or her lifetime—what Berg had done in depicting the murder of Marie in the opera *Wozzeck*—here the music's program further establishes the "innocence" and character of

---

44 Allan Kozinn, "Louis Krasner, Violinist and Teacher, Dies at 91," *New York Times,* May 5, 1995.

45 See Alban Berg to Theodor W. Adorno, July 4, 1935, in Lonitz, Henri (ed.), *Theodor W. Adorno and Alban Berg: Correspondence 1925–1935,* (Wieland Hoban trans.) (London: Polity, 2005), p. 225.

the dying girl. The concerto then leads toward a *danse macabre* and later includes—or rather *samples*, to use a term in keeping with a hauntology—a risqué Carinthian folksong, "Ein Vogel auf'm Zwetschgenbaum"—A Bird up in the Plum Tree. Though Berg's quotation is only a bit of melody, anyone who recognized it would have heard the words of the Protestant boy who, were it not for said bird, might have been found in "Mizzi's bed," oversleeping in flagrante delicto with a Catholic girl.

To this day musicologists are mystified by the inclusion of such a bawdy image in a piece of serious music in veneration of an innocent girl, known by her family and friends as Manon and seen by them as an angel in conduct, a virgin, and a beauty. "When everybody else wants a rich and pretty girl," goes the song, for the naughty Mizzi does not have these attributes, but she has at least one quality and it should not be wasted. "Where should the devil take the ugly one?" her lover asks. The now accepted theory, by Douglas Jarman, is that the folksong is autobiographically programmatic, an allusion to a housemaid with whom a teenage Berg had fathered his secret child, Albina. Berg, however, had already dealt with his guilt in *Wozzeck* with the aforementioned Marie and her illegitimate child. So, why once more and in such an oblique way in a work for and *about* Manon Gropius? What if Alma knew the rustic ditty? Would she have been embarrassed, insulted, or pleased and titillated despite her grief? She wrote in her diary and memoirs that her daughter had experienced everything of a full woman's life during her last year. To what extent?

The second movement of the Violin Concerto also consists of two parts—an *allegro* (*cadenza*) and an *adagio* (chorale variations)—and reimagines the young woman now in her death throes. One can hear in the orchestration a scream and even a cry for help.[46] The *adagio* depicts the young woman's "transfiguration" and quotes from J. S. Bach's

---

46 See, for example, Gottfried Scholz, "More on Secret Programs," *Encrypted Messages in Alban Berg's Music*, (Siglind Bruhn ed.) (New York: Garland, 1998), pp. 48ff.

devotional cantata *O Ewigkeit, du Donnerwort* (O Eternity, Thou Word of Thunder), a fixture in the repertoire of Protestant funeral music. Its text is the poem "Es ist genug! So nimm, Herr, meinen Geist" (It is enough! So take, Lord, my spirit). In Berg's concerto, the melody is both played by a solo violin and followed by a quartet of clarinets in imitation of a church organ. Musicologists believe Berg used it to honor the sestercentennial of Bach's birth and the dialectic between the fear of death with the hope of eternal life that is an overarching theme in the concerto. However, Berg's sampling of Bach might be there to achieve another effect. There was no prohibition—save for the Holy Mass—against using Protestant hymns in a Catholic church service. The cantata, in whole or in part, would not be out of place inside a Catholic church. Thus, if Berg wanted to evoke the incidental music one might hear played from the organ loft of any Christian church, the Bach cantata made for a good and *authentic* fit for what people (and possibly Berg himself) heard as they filed by Manon's bier.

Berg ended the concerto with a hint of consolation surely intended to please Alma, for he had incorporated the "Sunrise chord" that closes Mahler's *The Song of the Earth*. And she would be pleased. On August 31, Berg's student, Willi Reich, published a piece in *Neues Wiener Journal* announcing that the concerto had been completed as a gift in time for Alma's fifty-fourth birthday. He also discussed the new work and its connection to the life and death of Manon Gropius. Soon after, Alma expressed her gratitude in a telegram to Alban and Helene Berg. "With this enormous deed of love you have made me the only birthday present that could give me joy," she wired. "My yearning for you both is insupportable. Alban, I kiss your blessed hand, and Helene, your dear mouth."[47]

As was her custom, Alma would have served Berg's favorite dish of celery salad forever—he had immortalized the memory of her

47 Alma Mahler-Werfel to Alban Berg, *c.*late August 1935, ÖNB.

daughter, the failed piano student, with his music. However, the Violin Concerto became a kind of requiem for its composer. Not long after he received Alma's telegram, Berg suffered a painful wasp or bee sting at the base of his spine and, like Manon's, his injury proved to be just as catastrophic. Prone to abscesses and infections, Berg had a painful "carbuncle" lanced by a doctor. Rather than comply with a prescription for bedrest, he returned to sitting at his piano and finalizing the orchestration of the concerto. The infection spread throughout his body. In November, Berg was hospitalized at the Rudolfinerhaus, where Manon had received her X-ray treatments. He died on Christmas Eve, 1935. And, like Manon, his death mask was also cast by Anna Mahler.

The Violin Concerto was premiered at the fourteenth International Society for Contemporary Music Festival held in Barcelona in late April 1936. Krasner had enlisted Berg's longtime friend and fellow composer, Anton Webern, to conduct the new work. Webern was the logical choice. He had been an intimate friend of Berg since the early 1900s and had conducted Berg's music before. After three days of rehearsals, however, Webern suddenly refused to work with the orchestra of the concert venue, the Palau de la Música Catalana, took the score off the podium, stormed out of the concert hall, and locked himself in his hotel room. Krasner and Berg's widow tried to reason with Webern and, at last, he agreed to give the score. Fortuitously, another conductor, Hermann Scherchen, who was also familiar with Berg's music, was found to conduct the piece. Incredibly, Scherchen familiarized himself with the complexities of the Violin Concerto in less than a day and with only a half-hour rehearsal.

The world premiere took place as scheduled on April 19, one year to the day that Manon suffered her final crisis. The stunning performance by Krasner and the Catalan orchestra so impressed a young Benjamin

Britten that he called it "great" and "best of the festival."[48] But the Violin Concerto's world premiere was the last major cultural event in Spain. Three months later the country would be plunged into a bloody civil war that was the prelude to the Second World War. Thus, the concerto is not only associated with Manon's dying. The haunting piece, with its atmosphere of European nostalgia, also could be said to mark "a turning of historical time" and the passing of "Vienna's utopian moment," its "peril and breathtaking promise," which, with Manon, had vanished forever by then.[49]

Her Stone

In the first years after Manon's death, Alma Mahler keenly felt her daughter's absence. The pleasures taken in Christmas and Easter were missing without Manon. The places associated with Manon lost their attraction. Casa Mahler was rented out and then sold. But Alma's reasons were as much pecuniary as the void Manon had left there. Manon's absence should have haunted Haus and Villa Mahler no less. Alma still accused the latter as "unlucky" and "entirely guilty" for the death of her child. Writing in September 1935, she wished to rid herself of the mansion "from every fiber of myself"—an assertion that was disingenuous, that made the grief less felt.[50] Alma continued to host lavish parties over the next two and half years despite any curse and retained ownership of Villa Mahler through a world war and exile.

As had been her custom since Mahler's death, there would be no outward grief for Manon—it would be interior and economic. The most striking form it took was over Manon's final resting place. Although

48 See Anthony Pople, *Berg: Violin Concerto* (Cambridge: Cambridge University Press, 1991), p. 44.

49 Kevin C. Karnes, Wagner, the Arts, and Utopian Visions in Fin-de-Siècle Vienna (New York: Oxford, 2013), p. 186.

50 Mahler-Werfel, "Diary of Alma Maria," September 3, 1935, p. 29, MWP.

she boasted to Gropius that their daughter had been buried like a queen, "as she lived," the grave fell into neglect well before her mother's exile. For weeks it was only marked by a "tower of wreaths" 3 meters high according to Rietenauer.[51] Afterward it remained unmarked—like a pauper's grave—in Section 6, Row 6 of Grinzing Friedhof. To Alma, Manon was either not there, no longer on demand with a call and a clap of her hands, or simply a presence in her dreams—as all her lost children had become. "If I would still have Mutzi, she was my *Heimat*," Alma wrote in New York, when she and Werfel came for the premiere of *The Eternal Road* in 1936.[52]

Alma had no need for a burial place, a place to light a candle or lay a flower. She contented herself with premonitions. "I still feel her kiss on my mouth," she wrote of one intense dream, experienced on her fifty-eighth birthday in August 1937. Anna Mahler and Father Hollnsteiner played a part as did Manon—perhaps bedridden, perhaps not—but unaware that she was doomed. "I keep embracing her," Alma continued, seized with fits of crying, "and she doesn't know . . . why."[53]

Another reason to let Manon's grave remain unmarked was that her body was interred in her mother's plot. After Alma's death, her monument would incorporate her child's name and anything done for Manon while her mother still lived would be superfluous. Others, however, could not wait and may have seen this as yet another denial of Manon's individuality or physical existence. One person who understood how a mother could overshadow a daughter was Anna Mahler, who took the matter of Manon's stone to heart. She either contemplated carving a new stone or repurposing one from her studio. Of the latter was an early work, bearing the serial number H724, that was a lifesize standing female *memento mori* figure holding an hourglass.

51 See Rietenauer, *Alma, meine Liebe*, pp. 194ff.

52 Mahler-Werfel, "Diary of Alma Maria", February 5, 1936, p. 298, MWP.

53 Mahler-Werfel, "Diary of Alma Maria", August 31, 1937, p. 306, MWP.

The model was surely young, slender, and long-haired—suggesting Manon herself. Unfortunately, Anna, being half-Jewish, had to leave Austria for England in 1938, before anything could be erected at Manon's grave. (The hourglass figure itself was destroyed by Allied bombs during the Second World War.)

Even without a marker, there was a certain poignancy about Manon's grave—and Manon herself—if you knew where to look. Among those who knew was the actress, writer, and feminist Lina Loos (whose marriage to architect Adolph Loos ended in scandal in 1904). She had been coming to Grinzing Friedhof since the beginning of the Nazi period and after the suicide of her close friend, actor and cultural historian Egon Friedell.

Friedell knew Alma, Werfel, Zuckmayer—and Manon herself—and to this milieu Lina belonged. But to what extent she knew Manon in the latter's lifetime is unknown. Lina did have much empathy for the dead young woman and wrote Franz Theodor Csokor about visiting Manon's grave. He, in turn, shared with Alma in their correspondence. "There just came a sad beautiful letter from Lina," he wrote Alma from exile in Hungary in February 1939. "Two sentences, which are for you, follow: 'Write Alma that I sometimes go to Manon's grave, she seems so abandoned to me.'"[54] A year later, Csokor reported to Alma that Lina had once more returned to her vigils. "Lina is now completely alone," he wrote, reporting on the latest Jewish suicides in Vienna—a lesbian couple—in September 1939, in the first days after Hitler's invasion of Poland and the declarations of war by Great Britain and France. "Her dearest friend, Dr. Ilse Friedmann [a translator and relative of Friedell's] hanged herself with Grete Gerngross [an artist].

54 Theodor Csokor to Alma Mahler-Werfel, February 23, 1939, MWP.

Lina's going again to Manon's grave in Grinzing Cemetery, which she likes to do."[55]

Sister Ida, too, visited and tended to the grave of her former charge. She also served as Alma's eyes and ears and factotum once more during the latter's exile. Manon's cousin, Willi Legler, also served in the same capacity—and both kept an eye on Manon's grave. Eventually, during the early war years, and at her own expense, Sister Ida had a plain concrete border placed around the grave and erected a large wooden cross with a brass plaque engraved with Manon's name and lifespan. With Germany's defeat and the Soviet occupation of Vienna, the grave once more fell into neglect. And though Alma returned to Austria during the postwar years to settle her affairs and see the damage to and loss of her property, she did nothing about the state of Manon's grave and returned to her new life in the United States.

More years passed and rather than go through Alma again, Willi Legler, now a practicing architect, found a more sympathetic ear. In May 1955, he wrote Walter Gropius out of the blue, addressing the older man both respectfully as a colleague and as his "Onkel." By this time, Gropius had become an emeritus professor at Harvard and had his own practice on Harvard Square in Cambridge, Massachusetts. He lived in a house of his own design in the rural town of Lincoln. He and Ise had adopted her sister Hertha's daughter Ati as their own child in 1936 and brought her to the United States in 1937. In the Lincoln house, whose design had been influenced by Ati's desire for a spiral staircase, there was not one photograph of Manon. Her name was rarely if ever mentioned—not only because Gropius still grieved for his daughter, but to spare his new child any further family tragedy, since her mother's death had left her orphaned. He also gave Ati her own existential space, unhaunted by the dead first daughter.

---

55 Theodor Csokor to Alma Mahler-Werfel, undated [spring 1940], MWP.

Gropius read the sad tale of Manon's grave, how the wooden cross had eventually "marched away" as Willi Legler delicately put it, perhaps repurposed for someone else's ad hoc grave among the many who had died during the Russian siege of Vienna. Legler also stretched the truth, writing Gropius that his former wife, "Almschi," had been keeping up the grave. The dutiful nephew also mentioned that his cousin Anna had made a sculpture that had been lost during the war—hence there was nothing permanent at the grave. Legler then appealed to Gropius to intercede. "No one," he wrote, "is more qualified than you to design Mutzi's grave."

Legler enclosed a drawing of the plot. He suggested to Gropius that the grave would make for a surprise gift to Alma, as if Gropius still had some affection for her, as if it would be an inducement for him to take on the project. But Gropius had had very little contact with Alma since the war years. Over a decade had passed since Werfel had sent Gropius *The Song of Bernadette*, but had embarrassingly sent the architect the copy inscribed to Heinrich Mann by mistake. Gropius sent it back and when he did get his own copy, avoided any mention of the dedication to Manon.[56]

Undoubtedly, despite the Legler's strange tale, Gropius was moved to do something. To make up for having not seen Manon in her final months? For not attending her funeral? For putting her out of his mind

56 Walter Gropius to Franz Werfel, May 3, 1942, FWC. Gropius apparently read the novel but did not let on that he noticed the dedication or any parallels to Manon. "[W]ith joy and intense interest I read your great and moving story of Bernadette and the manifold raptures of human failing that her incorruptible soul has evoked," he wrote Werfel. "You have cast a new light on that important glacis of religious sensibility that remains our perpetual admonition between the realms of ecclesiastical power and scientific enlightenment!—I dearly thank you for sending me this beautiful book and for your lovely letter as well. Hopefully you both are feeling well in California and not missing old Europe very much. It takes long time before one gets accustomed to the different scale on this side of the Atlantic."

all these years? Or to give his child some precedence, some individuality before her mother was buried there herself, exercising her eminent domain? (If he knew that Alma intended to be buried with Manon one day—for that had not been volunteered by Alma's nephew—Gropius had no knowledge or put it out of his mind.)

Preserved among Gropius' papers at Harvard is a curious, uncatalogued document in a folder related to the first performance of Alban Berg's Violin Concerto. It is a detailed contract to install a stone of light gray granite in the shape of an isosceles triangle—one of the elementary geometric shapes as taught at the Bauhaus—with rounded corners, the pinnacle pointing toward the head of the grave. At the base of the pyramidal shape was engraved the name MANON GROPIUS and her dates above it. Whatever the shape symbolizes is in the eye of the beholder. An Egyptian pyramid? Some correlation of perfection? In design? Intent? The angles of divine, human, and nature angles from the Theosophy? Manon's three parents? The love triangle that separated Manon from her father? Or some vague allusion, hardly discernable, suggesting the Nsho-Chi's monument Old Shatterhand designed for her? In *Winnetou, the Red Gentleman*, a pyramid of stones stacked around the trunk of a tree in which her body sits.

Gropius instructed an Austrian firm to have the stone carved to his specifications and mounted on a low plinth, closer to the foot of the grave and virtually flush with the grave's concrete border. He asked that the cemetery gardeners dig up two old arborvitae as well as other overgrown shrubs and replace them with three new ones to contrast, that is, not be level (*nicht einzuebnen*) with the flat stone, itself in keeping with his *Flachbau* principles of design. (This contrast is preserved by Alma's monument, a plain upright slab of dark brown granite designed by Anna Mahler.) Lastly, Gropius retained the preexisting grave lantern that Sister Ida had also donated. The site was completed in 1956 at the cost of 17,640 Austrian schillings, that is, about $700 dollars or over $6,000 at this writing. To document that the work had been finished to his specifications, several photographs were sent to Gropius to document his work—original work he omitted from his official *oeuvre*. There is no indication that Gropius corresponded with anyone other than the firm that performed the services rendered. He may have wanted it to be a surprise for Alma, but rather as *fait accompli*.

Given her antipathy for graves, Alma, unsurprisingly, makes no mention of the grave in her memoirs, which first appeared in English in 1958. But it was not the lack of recognition that left Gropius appalled on reading the book, the one omission that may have served as his only consolation for the horror of each page on which his name and his daughter's appeared. "The love story that you connect with my name in the book was not ours," he wrote Alma. The most wounding insult was its violation of his grief. "The memory of Mutzi should have kept you from using the essential content of our experience and its literary exposure is bound to kill also in me the flowers of memory," he wrote. "The rest is silence."[57]

57 Walter Gropius to Alma Mahler-Werfel, August 17, 1958, quoted in Isaacs, *Walter Gropius*, VOL. 2, p. 1049.

Bibliography

ARCHIVES AND COLLECTIONS

ANNO: Austrian Newspapers Online, http://anno.onb.ac.at/anno. htm.

BHA: Bauhaus-Archiv Berlin / Museum für Gestaltung Bauhaus-Archiv [Bauhaus Archive / Museum for Design, Berlin]

DE: Deutschen Exilarchiv [German Exile Archive], Deutsche Nationalbibliothek [German National Library], Frankfurt am Main.

FWP: Franz Werfel Papers (Collection 512). UCLA Library Special Collections, Charles E. Young Research Library, University of California, Los Angeles

MWP: Mahler-Werfel Papers, Kislak Center for Special Collections, Rare Books and Manuscripts, University of Pennsylvania, Philadelphia

ÖNB: Österreichische Nationalbibliothek [Austrian National Library], Vienna, Handschriften und Nachlässe [Division of Handwritten Documents]

RIP: Reginald R. Isaacs papers, circa 1842-1991, bulk 1928–91. Archives of American Art, Smithsonian Institution

ULT: Universitäts-und Landesbibliothek Tirol, Innsbruck.

WB: Handschriften, Wienbiliothek im Rathaus [Manuscripts, Vienna City Library]

WGP: Walter Gropius Papers, 1925–1969 (MS Ger 208). Houghton Library, Harvard University.

WSA: Wieners Stadt Landes- und Staatsarchiv [Federal and State Archive], Vienna

BIBLIOGRAPHY

BOOKS

BUCHMAYR, Friedrich. *Der Priester in Almas Salon: Johannes Hollnsteiners Weg von der Elite des Ständestaats zum NS-Bibliothekar* [The Priest in Alma's Salon: Johannes Hollnsteiner's Path from the Elite of the Ständestaat to Nazi Librarian]. Vienna: Bibliothek der Provinz, 2003.

BRUHN, Siglind (ed.), *Encrypted Messages in Alban Berg's Music*. New York: Routledge, 1998.

CANETTI, Elias. *The Play of the Eyes* (Ralph Manheim trans.). New York: Farrar, Straus & Giroux, 1986.

HILMES, Oliver. *Witwe im Wahn: Das Leben der Alma Mahler-Werfel* [Widow in Delusion: The Life of Alma Mahler-Werfel]. Berlin: Siedler, 2004.

HORCH, Franz. "Der Tod und das Mädchen" [Death and the Maid]. *Bergland* 17(11)(1935): 2–5.

ISAACS, Reginald. *Walter Gropius: Der Mensch und sein Werk* [Walter Gropius: The Man and His Work]. Berlin: Gebr. Mann Verlag, 1984.

JOSEPH, Albrecht, "Zu Besuch bei Alma Mahler-Werfel" [Visiting Alma Mahler-Werfel] in Weidle, Barbara, and Ursula Seeber (eds), *Anna Mahler. Ich bin in mir selbst zu Hause* [Anna Mahler: I Am at Home in Myself]. Bonn: Weidle and Seeber, 2004, pp. 84–6.

JUNGK, Peter Stephen. *Franz Werfel. Eine Lebensgeschichte* [Franz Werfel: A Biography]. Frankfurt am Main: Fischer, 1987.

——. *Franz Werfel: A Life in Prague, Vienna, and* Hollywood (Anselm Hollo trans.). New York: Grove Weidenfeld, 1990.

KRENEK, Ernst. *In Atem der Zeit:* Erinnerungen *an Die Moderne* [In a Breath of Time: Memories of the Modern Age]. Hamburg: Hoffmann und Campe Verlag, 1998.

LOTHAR, Ernst. *Das Wunder des Überlebens. Erinnerungen und Ergebnisse* [The Miracle of Survival: Reminiscences and Results]. Vienna: Paul Zsolnay, 1961.

——. *Kinder, erste Erlebnisse* [Children, First Experiences]. Vienna: Paul Zsolany, 1932.

——. *Kleine Freundin: Roman einer Zwolfjährigen* [Little Friend: A Novel of a Twelve-Year-Old Girl]. Vienna: Zsolnay, 1931.

MAHLER-WERFEL, Alma. *And the Bridge Is Love*. New York: Harcourt, Brace, 1958.

——, Alma. *Mein Leben* [My Life]. Frankfurt am Main: Fischer, 1963.

MONSON, Karen. *Alma Mahler: Muse to Genius.* New York: HarperCollins, 1984.

PAUL, John R. *A History of Poliomyelitis.* New Haven: Yale University Press, 1971.

PHILLIPS, Max. *The Artist's Wife*. New York: Holt, 2001.

POPLE, Anthony. *Berg: Violin Concerto.* Cambridge: Cambridge University Press, 1991.

RIETENAUER, Erich. *Alma, meine Liebe* [Alma, My Love]. Vienna: Amalthea, 2008.

SHELL, Marc. *Polio and Its Aftermath: The Paralysis of Culture.* Cambridge: Harvard University Press, 2005.

STEIGER, Martina (ed.). "*Immer wieder werden mich thätige Geister verlocken.*" *Alma Mahler-Werfels Briefe an Alban Berg und seine Frau* ["Again and again am I tempted by dynamic intellects": Alma Mahler-Werfel's Letters to Alban Berg and his Wife]. Vienna: Seifert, 2008.

WALTER, Bruno. *Thema und Variationen: Erinnerungen und Gedanken* [Theme and Variations: Memories and Thoughts]. Stockholm: Bermann-Fischer, 1947.

WEIDINGER, Alfred. *Kokoschka and Alma Mahler* (Fiona Elliott trans.). Munich: Prestel, 1996.

WEIDLE, Barbara, and Ursula Seeber (eds). *Anna Mahler. Ich bin in mir selbst zu Hause* [Anna Mahler: I Am at Home in Myself. Bonn: Weidle and Seeber, 2004.

WERFEL, Franz. *Der Gerichtstag* [Judgment Day]. Leipzig: Kurt Wolff, 1919.

——. *Embezzled Heaven*. New York: Viking, 1940.

——. *Gedichte aus den Jahren* [Poems from the Years] *1908–1945*. Frankfurt am Main: Fischer, 1946.

——. *Harken unto the Voice* (Moray Firth trans.). New York: Viking, 1938.

——. "Legenden—Skizzen" [Legends—Sketches] in *Zwischen Oben und Unten: Prosa, Tagebücher, Aphorismen, Literarische Nachträge* [Between

Above and Below: Prose, Diaries, Aphorisms, Literary Addenda]. Munich–Vienna: Langen Müller, 1975, pp. 705–42.

——. "Manon." *The Commonweal.* May 1, 1942, pp. 31–4.

——. "Manon" in *Erzählungen aus zwei Welten* [Tales from Two Worlds], VOL. 3. Frankfurt am Main: S. Fischer, 1954.

—— "Of Man's True Happiness" in *Between Heaven and Earth* (Maxim Newmark trans.). New York: Philosophical Library, 1944, pp. 13–20.

——. *Spiegelmensch* [Mirror Man]. Munich: Kur Wolff, 1920.

——. *Star of the Unborn* (Gustave O. Arlt trans.). New York: Viking, 1946.

——. *The Forty Days of Musa Dagh* (Geoffrey Dunlop and James Reidel trans). Boston: David R. Godine, 2012[1934].

Index of Names

Adorno, Theodor W., 280
Altenberg, Peter, 27, 30
Altschul, Lutz, 63
Anbelang, Emmy, 50
Anton, Margarete, 63
Apostel, Hans Erich, 115
Arminus, 166
Asch, Sholem, 100, 224
Aslan, Raoul, 151–3
Ast, Eduard, 118–20
Ast, Eduard II, 120
Ast, Grete. *See also* Bernatzik, Margarethe
Ast, Marie, 120
Attila the Hun, 261
Aycock, William L., 185

Baby Peggy (Diana Cary), 66
Bach, Johann Sebastian, 48, 282
Balser, Ewald, 212
Baranowsky, Alexander, 63
Bartók, Béla, 83
Bayer, Herbert, 80n26, 87, 122, 127
Bayer, Irene, 122
Beardsley, Aubrey, 28
Beethoven, Ludwig van, 1, 211–2
Belloto, Carlo (servant), 173
Belloto, Pina (servant), 173
Bemelmans, Ludwig, 66
Benemann, Maria, 53–4
Benjamin, Walter, *vii–viii*
Berber, Anita, 63
Berg, Alban, *vii*, *ix–xi*, 10, 38, 68, *112*, 115, 116n5, 181, 201n41, 248, 278–83, 289
Berg, Albina, 281
Berg, Helene, *x*, 38–9, 115, 116n5, 279, 282–3
Bergen, Anna. *See* Moll, Anna
Berger, Julius Victor, 6
Bergson, Henri, 21
Berliner, Arnold, 146–7, 269
Bernatzik, Hugo, 120n11
Bernatzik, Margarethe Ast, 120n11
Besant, Annie, 7, 15
Bien, Gertrud, 117, 162, 195, 197–8, 214, 219
Blavatsky, Helen, 6
Blei, Franz, 28–32, 36, 41
Blei, Sibylla, 28
Bonaparte, Napoleon, 261
Borgia, Lucrezia, 13, 156
Born, Max, 146
Brecht, Bertolt, 63
Breuer, Marcel, 84, 86, 106
Britten, Benjamin, 283–4
Broch, Hermann, 28
Brod, Max, 29, 272
Bruckner, Anton, 156, 271
Brunner-Orne, Martha, 200–1, 201n41

Buber, Martin, 29
Burchard, Ine, 128
Burchard, Joachim, 68, 128
Burchard, Manon Gropius, 10, 85
Burckhard, Max, 2
Busch, Wilhelm, 232

Caesar, Julius, 261
Calderón de la Barca, Pedro, 51, 168
Canetti, Elias, *x–xi*, *xvi*, 154–7, 216–8, 250–2, 279
Canetti, Veza, 251
Cavin, Antoinette, 173, 185
St. Cecilia, 208
Chantermesse, André, 8
Chaplin, Charlie, 122, 132
Charpentier, Marc-Antoine, 32
St. Christina the Astonishing, 260, 264
Chvostek, Franz, 9
Claudel, Paul, 28
Cleopatra VII, Queen of Egypt, 238
Cooper, James Fennimore, 84
Craig, Edward Gordon, 214n57
Csokor, Franz Theodor, 286
Cyhlar, Erich Sepp, 174–5, 202–3, 215–8, 250, 270

Da Vinci, Leonard, 13
D'Annunzio, Gabriele, 214n58
Darwin, Charles, 11
de Chirico, Giorgio, 73
Debschitz, Irene von, 128
Dell, Christian, 140
Derrida, Jacques, *viii*
Disney, Walt, 270–1
Dollfuss, Engelbert, 134, 138, 160, 166, 169–70, 191, 194, 197–8, 202, 233, 242
Drexel, Karl, 134
Du Bois, Elizabeth, 232
Du Bois, Jane, 232
Düring, Ernst von, 4
Duse, Eleonora, 101

Edward, Prince of Wales, 231
Einstein, Alfred, 58n1, 146, 185
Eisner, Stella, 100
Elisabeth, Empress of Austria, 172, 220
Elmhirst, Dorothy, 161
Elmhirst, Leonard, 161
Eurydice, 260
Euripides, 29

Ferber, Edna, 270
Ferdinand I, Emperor of Austria, 22
Förster-Nietzsche, Elisabeth, 51n62
Fraenkel, Joseph, 8, 11
Franchetti, Alberto, 214n58
St. Francis of Assisi, 158, 260
Frank, Anne, *viii*
Frank, Ellen, *107*, 127–8, 234
Frank, Hermann, 69
Frank, Hertha, 69, 128, 287
Frank, Ilse. *See* Gropius, Ise
Franz Ferdinand, Archduke of Austria, 12

Franz Josef I, Emperor of Austria, 1, 22, 38, 172, 188
Freud, Sigmund, 5, 195
Friedell, Egon, 286–7
Friedmann, Hermann, 181–3, 186–7, 195
Friedmann, Ilse, 287
Fry, Maxwell, 213
Fülöp-Miller, René, 128

Gebauer, Agnes Ida, 51–5, 58, 60, 63–4, 73, 97, 130–3, 141, 145, 148, 163–4, 180–1, 253, 271, 287, 290
Gellert, Christian Fürchtegott, 211
George, Duke of Kent, 222
Gerngross, Grete, 287
Gessner, Adrienne, 177
Giedon, Siegfried, 76
Glaser, Maria, 136
Goebbels, Joseph, 138
Goethe, Johann Wolfgang von, 48, 59
Goll, Claire, 247
Gropius, Alma Mahler. *See* Mahler-Werfel, Alma
Gropius, Ati Johansen (stepsister), *xii–xiii*, 287
Gropius, Alma Manon, *ii*, *vii–xiii*, 1, 3, 18, 24–7, 31, 33, 35, 37–49, 51–101, *102–10*, *112*, 113–7, 119–44, 146–54, 156–279, 281–90
Gropius, Ise (stepmother), 69–70, 73–4, 78, 78n23, 79–87, 91–4, 122, 127, 128, 141–2, 165, 178, 190, 206, 213, 230, 245, 245n9, 246, 258, 287
Gropius, Manon Scharnweber (paternal grandmother), 10, 17, 18, 20, 142–3
Gropius, Martin Johannes, 38, 40, 41–2, 44–5, 52, 191
Gropius, Walter, *viii*, *ix*, *x*, *xii*, 4–7, 9–26, 28, 31–5, 37, 40–50, 52–8, 62, 64, 68–87, 91–3, 96–7, 99, *102*, *105*, *107*, 116, 120, 122–5, 127–31, 136–7, 139–44, 149–50, 156–8, 160–2, 164–5, 189–90, 193–6, 199, 206–7, 212–4, 214n57, 222, 225, 230–1, 234, 240, 243–5, 245n9, 246, 249, 253–4, 256–8, 285, 287–90
Gross, Otto, 272
Guicciardi, Giulietta, 212
Guinness, Bryan, 231

Hanausek, Marie, 77
Hanussen, Erik Jan, 61
Hauptmann, Gerhard, 140n28
Herdan, Alice, 234
Herterich, Franz, 99
Hildebrandt, Lily, 48, 53, 54
Hilmes, Oliver, *ix*, 2, 7, 75, 113, 239, 252
Hitler, Adolf, 114, 141, 150, 166, 189, 239, 261, 271
Hoffmann, Josef, 118
Hofmannsthal, Hugo von, 51, 82, 168

Hollnsteiner, Johannes, 145–9, 166, 175, 207–8, 216–7, 225, 240–7, 249, 251, 253, 271, 285
Horch, Franz, 209–12, 234, 236, 256–7, 270
Hováth, Ödön von, 247
Huebsch, Ben, 267
Hvizd, Agnes, 35

Immisch, Marie, 101
Innitzer, Theodor, 145
Issacs, Reginald, 245n9
Itten, Hilde Anbelang, 50
Itten, Johannes, 30, 42–3, 48, 50, 64

Jaksch, Hans, 130, 131
Jaksch, Walter, 130
Jarman, Douglas, 281
Jones, Jennifer, 275
Joseph, Albrecht, 172
Jungk, Peter Stephan, 64

Kafka, Franz, 28–187, 215, 272
Kammerer, Paul, 11, 20–1, 125
Kandinsky, Wassily, 69
Karpath, Ludwig, 238, 255–6
Kemp, Barbara, 63
Kertész, Susi, *108*, 150–1, 163, 197, 203, 208–9, 211, 271–2
Kestranck, Clara, 77
Klarmann, Adolf, 266
Klee, Paul, *vii*, 45, 69
Klimt, Gustav, 2, 11, 27, 50, 173
Klopstock, Robert, 214–5
Knöpfelmacher, Wilhelm, 24, 42, 44, 194–5, 197, 215, 269
Kokoschka, Oskar, 11–5, 17, 33, 43–5, 58, 65–6, 71, 82, 96, 156
Kolig, Anton, 120n11
Korda, Michael, 236
Krasner, Louis, 201n41, 280, 283–4
Kraus, Karl, 14, 29, 62
Krauss, Werner, 210–2
Krenek, Ernst, *vii*, *x*, 68, 73, 155
Kriehuber, Josef, 257
Kronacher, Alwin, 63

Lasker-Schüler, Else, 29
Laughton, Charles, 236
Leadbeater, C. W., 7
Legler, Grete Schindler, 6, 27, 130
Legler, Wilhelm, 130
Legler, Willi, 130, 288
Lewis, Sinclair, 140
Liebknecht, Karl, 49
Lieser, Adolf, 11
Lieser, Justus, 11
Lieser, Lilly, 11, 17, 27
Lindbergh, Charles, 91
Liszt, Franz, 48
Loewi, Adolph, 175, 182, 187–8, 270
Loewi, Katherine, 175
Loewi, Kay, 175
Loewi, Marlene, 175
Loos, Adolph, 286
Loos, Lina, 286–7
Lothar Müller, Agathe, 75, 75n21, 76, 130, 150–1, 162–3, 177, 183, 191

Lothar, Ernst, 75, 75n21, 76, *110*, 122, 130, 150, 163, 172, 177, 177n11, 178, 186n18, 205
Lothar Müller, Hanni, 75–6
Luigi (servant), 182, 187–8
Luxemburg, Rosa, 49

Mahler, Anna, 3, 15, 27, 35–9, 42, 48, 53, 57, 61, 66–8, 73–4, 83, 88–9, *102*, *104*, 117, 126, 128, 145, 151, 154–6, 164, 174, 179, 182, 187, 196–7, 202–3, 216, 219–20, 246–8, 258, 268, 283, 285–6, 288, 290
Mahler, Gustav, *ix*, 1–12, 19–20, 22, 30, 57, 59, 66, 115, 119, 146, 155, 191, 204, 238, 246–7, 251, 255, 278, 282, 285
Mahler, Maria, 3, 9, 22, 185
Mahler-Werfel, Alma, *viii*, *ix*, *x*, 1–83, 85–90, 93–9, *102–3*, *108*, *110*, 113–28, 130–41, 144–8, 151, 154–8, 160, 163–4, 166–7, 169–82, 184, 188–96, 200–7, 210–1, 213–8, 222–9, 233–5, 238–40, 242–6, 248, 251–3, 255–9, 263–5, 269, 271–2, 275, 277–90
Makonnen, Tafari. *See* Selassie, Haile
Malfatti, Johann Baptist, 211
Malipiero, Gian Francesco, 177
Mann, Heinrich, 270, 288
Mann, Thomas, 48, 131, 140, 234, 270
Marburg, Otto, 223
May, Karl, 84–5, 135, 235
Mayreder, Rosa, 77
Mengelberg, Willem, 53
Metchnikoff, Élie, 8
Miklas, Wilhelm, 134
Moll, Anna Bergen Schindler, 2, 5–6, 64–5, *104*, 132, 141, 148, 151, 194, 203, 270
Moll, Carl, 6, 11, 12, 65, 130, 130n19, 132, 151, 166, 169, 247, 270
Moll, Maria, 65, 68, 270
Mona Lisa, 13
Mörike, Eduard, 147
Moser, Kolomon, 46
Müller, Engelbert, 134
Munch, Edvard, 26
Muschler, Reinhold Conrad, 247
Musil, Robert, 28, 155
Mussolini, Benito, 137, 226

Nabokov, Vladimir, 247
Nadé, Mademoiselle (governess), 164, 171, 173, 179, 180
Nietzsche, Friedrich, *viii*, 2, 6, 21, 51, 51n62

Ortner, Herman Heinz, 211
Osthaus, Karl Ernst, 33
Ozawa, Seiji, 201n41

Pallenberg, Max, 176
Pancera, Gabriele, 77
Passek, Frédy, 185
Pauli, Hertha, 247
Perlman, Itzhak, 201n41

Perutz, Leo, 106, 164
Petrarch, Francesco, 262
Pfitzner, Hans, 43
Phillips, Max, *viii*, 191
Piscator, Erwin, 128
Pötzl, Otto, 195–6, 200–1, 223, 241–3
Pritchard, Jack, 230

Raky, Hortense, 208
Redlich, Emmy, 36
Reich, Willi, 282
Reimers, Georg, 121
Reinhardt, Max, 51, 167, 167n64, 168–9, 176, 209–10, 256
Reininghaus, Carl, 26
Renard-Stonner, Adele, 77, 95, 115, 119
Renner, Karl, 125, 145, 170
Rietenauer, Erich, 131–3, 140, 145, 148, 151, 157–60, 162, 166–7, 167n64, 169, 173, 183–4, 193–4, 227, 229, 232, 238, 246, 251, 270–1, 271n35, 273, 285
Rilke, Rainer Maria, 4, 28, 201, 247, 257
Rintelen, Anton von, 137–9, 146, 166–7, 172, 174–5, 188, 192, 202, 233–4
Rodin, Auguste, 119
Roller, Alfred, 47
Rosé, Emma Mahler, 51
Rosé, Justine Mahler, 5
Rosé, Wolfgang, 115
Sabin, Albert, 185
Salten, Felix, 121
Schawinsky, Xanti, *x*, 87, 122, 128, 161
Scherchen, Hermann, 283
Scherman, Bernadine, 204
Scherman, Harry, 203–4
Scherman, Katherine, 203–6
Schiller, Friedrich, 48, 101n52, 234, 236–7
Schindler, Emil Jakob, 2, 6, 22, 193
Schindler, Ewald, 63
Schlemmer, Oskar, 86–7
Schnitzler, Arthur, 126, 247
Schnitzler, Lilli, 126, 247
Schober, Johann, 113
Schoenberg, Arnold, 10, 30, 42–3, 248
Schopenhauer, Arthur, 21
Schreker, Franz, 10
Schuschnigg, Kurt, 170, 179, 188, 191, 202
Schuster, Lincoln, 203
Selassie, Haile, 226, 228
Selinko, Annemarie, 208
Sexton, Ann, 200
Shakespeare, William, 211, 236–7, 262
Shields, Brooke, 66
Silesius, Angelus, 181
Sinclair, Upton, 155
Sommerfeld, Adolf, 91
Soubirious, Bernadette, 274
Spirk, Gertrude, 29, 34

Spitzer (servant), 130
Stifter, Adelbert, 92
Sullivan, Maureen, 233
Swift, Jonathan, 230, 275

Tagore, Rabindranath, 161
Tallyrand, Charles, 193
Talmey, Max, 58, 185
Tamerlane, 261
Tandler, Julius, 51–2, *108*, 117, 131, 133, 138, 145, 162, 166–7, 196–9, 219–21, 223, 225, 229, 231, 269
Täuber, Harry, 63
Tchaikovsky, Pytor Ilyich, 179
Thimig, Hermann, 210
Thompson, Dorothy, 140
Thompson, Jim, 270
Tietze-Conrat, Erica, 30, 77
Tietze, Hans, 30
Trentini, Albert von, 22, 174, 191
Trentini, Johannes, 174, 174n7, 216
Turner, Maud, 3, 7, 35, 37, 38, 44, 151

Urach, Albrecht von, 175

van der Leeuw, C. H., 245–6
Veidt, Conrad, 122
Velazquez, Diego, 67
Veneto, Bartolomeo, 13
Verdi, Giuseppe, 32, 67, 73, 98–9

Wagenfeld, Wilhelm, 164
Wagner-Jauregg, Julius, 195
Wagner, Richard, 6, 8, 12, 32, 48, 147, 189, 273
Walser, Robert, 28
Walter, Bruno, 157, 178
Webern, Anton, 283
Weill, Kurt, 167
Weinzinger, Erich, 227–8
Weinzinger, Erika, 227
Weinzinger, Georg, 228–9, 232, 267
Weissmuller, Johnny, 233
Werfel, Alma Mahler. *See* Mahler-Werfel, Alma
Werfel, Franz, *viii*, *x–xi*, 19, 28–34, 36–7, 40–3, 45–7, 51–2, 54, 56, 58, 58n2, 59–67, 71–4, 78, 83–4, 87–9, 91, 93–101, *102–3*, *110*, 114–7, 119, 123, 125–7, 130, 133–6, 141, 145–6, 153–6, 157–8, 162–4, 166–7, 167n64, 168–73, 175–80, 182–3, 187–8, 191–4, 197, 200, 202–6, 209–10, 213–5, 223–5, 228, 233–8, 241, 243–4, 246, 248, 253–7, 259–72, 274–5, 277–8, 280, 284–6, 288, 288n56
Werfel, Rudolf, 66
Werner, Ilse, 208
Wilson, Woodrow, 40
Wittgenstein, Ludwig, 98
Wolff, Kurt, 29, 58n2, 62
Wotruba, Fritz, 154, 251
Wotruba, Marian, 251

Zimmerman (clergyman), 25
Zsolnay, Alma, 128, 184
Zsolnay, Amanda "Andy," 117, 128
Zsolnay, Paul, 67, 117, 154, 174, 182, 209
Zuckerkandl, Berta, 14
Zuckerkandl, Emil, 14
Zuckmayer, Carl, 234–6, 238, 254–5, 286
Zweig, Stefan, 28